CONSTABLES AND TOBACCO PLANTERS IN ORANGE COUNTY, VIRGINIA, 1735-1769

LIZABETH WARD PAPAGEORGIOU

CLEARFIELD

Copyright © 2011
by Lizabeth Ward Papageorgiou
All Rights Reserved.

Printed for Clearfield Company by
Genealogical Publishing Company
Baltimore, Maryland
2011

ISBN 978-0-8063-5521-4

Made in the United States of America

*To Stathe, Melissa, Antonio, and the two doves on my balcony
and a special thanks to*
*David Grabarek at the Library of Virginia and Irini Solomonidi
and the staff of the Gennadius Library, Athens, Greece and my
editor, Eileen Perkins, for her patience and encouragement*

Also by Lizabeth Ward Papageorgiou

*The Colonial Churches of St. Thomas' Parish, Orange County, Virginia
With Notes on Sites in Orange, Greene, and Madison Counties*

CONTENTS

Preface	vii
Map 1. Mainland Virginia (and West Virginia) 1738	
Map 2. Orange County 1735–1769	
Map 3. Culpeper County 1750	
Map 4. Frederick County 1738	
Map 5. Augusta County 1738	
Introduction	1
Orange I	23
Orange II	32
Orange III	42
Orange IV	49
Orange V	56
Culpeper I	61
Culpeper II	67
Rappahannock	74
Madison I	75
Madison II	79
Frederick I–IX	83
Augusta I–XX	94
Appendix: Orange County, Virginia, Tithable Precincts, 1735–1757	113
Table 1. Tobacco Planter Lists: Concordance	125
Table 2. Tobacco Planter Lists: Statistics	127
Notes	137
Bibliography	159
Index	165

PREFACE

Over two decades ago, Barbara Vines Little transcribed and published seventy lists of tobacco planters who were living in today's Orange, Culpeper, Madison and Greene Counties between 1735 and 1769. Her work, *Orange County, Virginia, Tithables 1734–1782*, is an incalculable contribution to eighteenth century Orange County, Virginia, scholarship. Constables compiled these lists while inspecting the tobacco plantations in their precinct in the late summer–early fall. These rare colonial documents give us not only the names of over a thousand tobacco planters and the number of tithables—all males sixteen and older and all male and female slaves sixteen and older—in their household, but also tell us the general area where they lived.[1] These lists—as well as county court orders directing residents to lay or maintain roads in their neighborhood—are often more reliable than a deed or land patent for identifying the general place where a planter was actually living. A planter may not have necessarily lived on land he had purchased, and it was not uncommon for someone to live and work on land years before they patented their land (for example, see p. 155n. 224).

The idea for this monograph came about when I tried to use the court descriptions of the constable precincts to draw the boundary lines of the precincts where members of the Cave family owned tobacco plantations. I soon realized that in order to draw the boundaries of one precinct, it was necessary to identify the boundaries of the neighboring precincts. However, because the court only described these boundaries a few times and because the descriptions were often unclear, drawing these boundaries was like assembling a jigsaw puzzle. And this puzzle was so much fun—and frustrating—that I had to try to solve it.

Using Little's *Tithables* and this work, one can locate the precinct where a tobacco planter was living one or more years between 1735 and 1769. For example, to find the precinct where David Cave lived, check Little's index: David Cave appears on the tobacco planter list on page 9, then go to my table 1 where this 1737 tobacco planter list is identified as a list from the 1737 Orange II precinct. The boundaries of this precinct are drawn on Map 2 and described in the section, "Orange II."

All quotes from eighteenth century documents retain their often peculiar punctuation, abbreviations and orthography, including the long 's' which was written 'f' (Robin$f$on) and the last letter of an abbreviation which was placed in superscript (s^d = said). The different spellings of a person's name are written and indexed as they appear in each document.

Up until 1752, all Virginia documents used the Old Style dating of the Julian calendar with the beginning of the year on 25 March; thus, 1 January to 24 March 1732 (O.S.) was 1733. From 1752, the New Style dating of the Gregorian calendar was adopted. In this work, pre-1752 documents dated 1 January to 24 March note both the Old and New Style date (2 February 1732/33).

When the present borders of Orange, Culpeper, Madison, Rappahannock and Greene Counties (formed from Orange County between 1749 and 1838) and the present borders of Frederick County and Augusta County are referred to, the county appears in quotations; that is, Swift Run in "Greene" County.

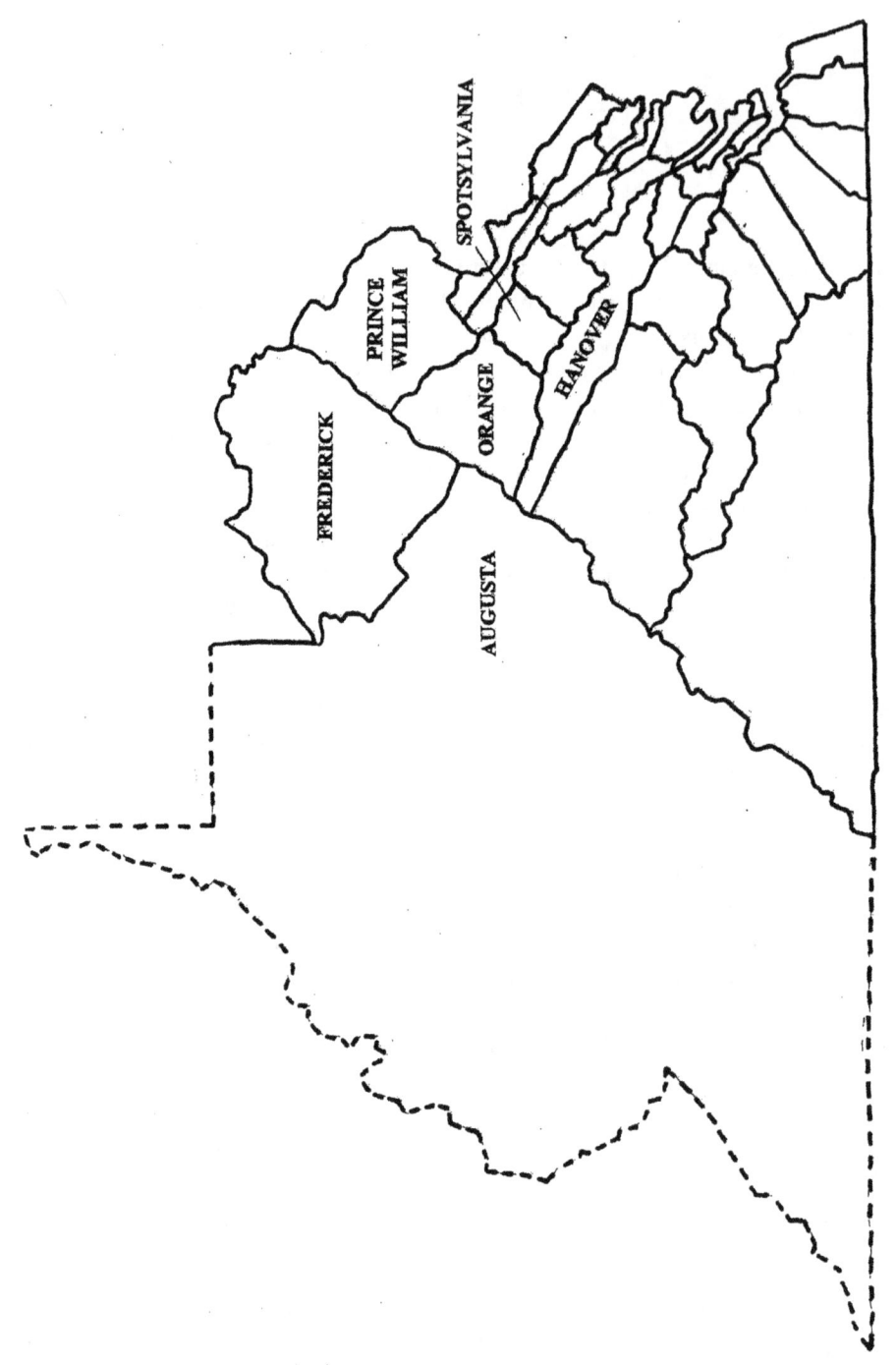

MAP 1 ~ MAINLAND VIRGINIA (AND WEST VIRGINIA) 1738
Orange, Augusta, Frederick and Neighboring Counties

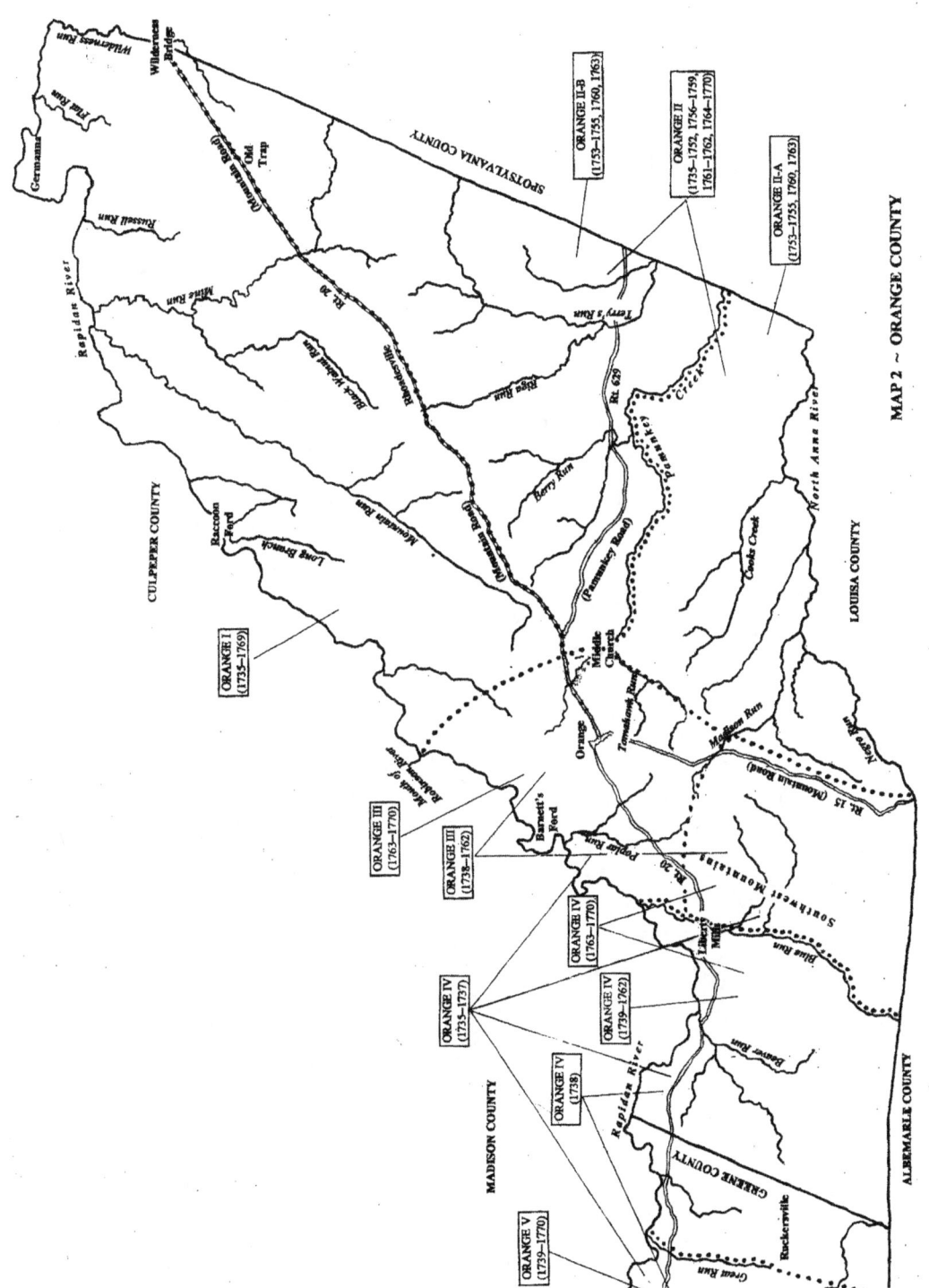

MAP 2 ~ ORANGE COUNTY

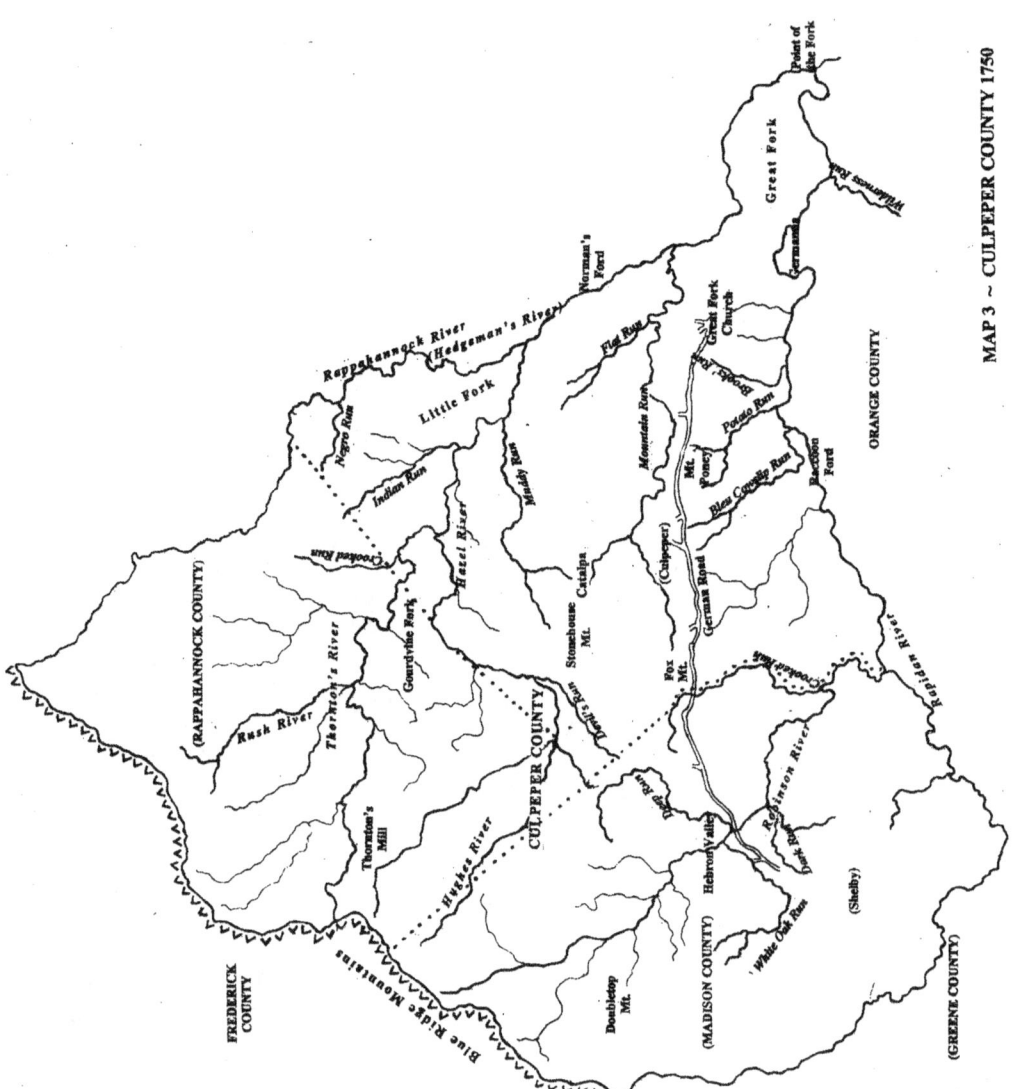

MAP 3 ~ CULPEPER COUNTY 1750

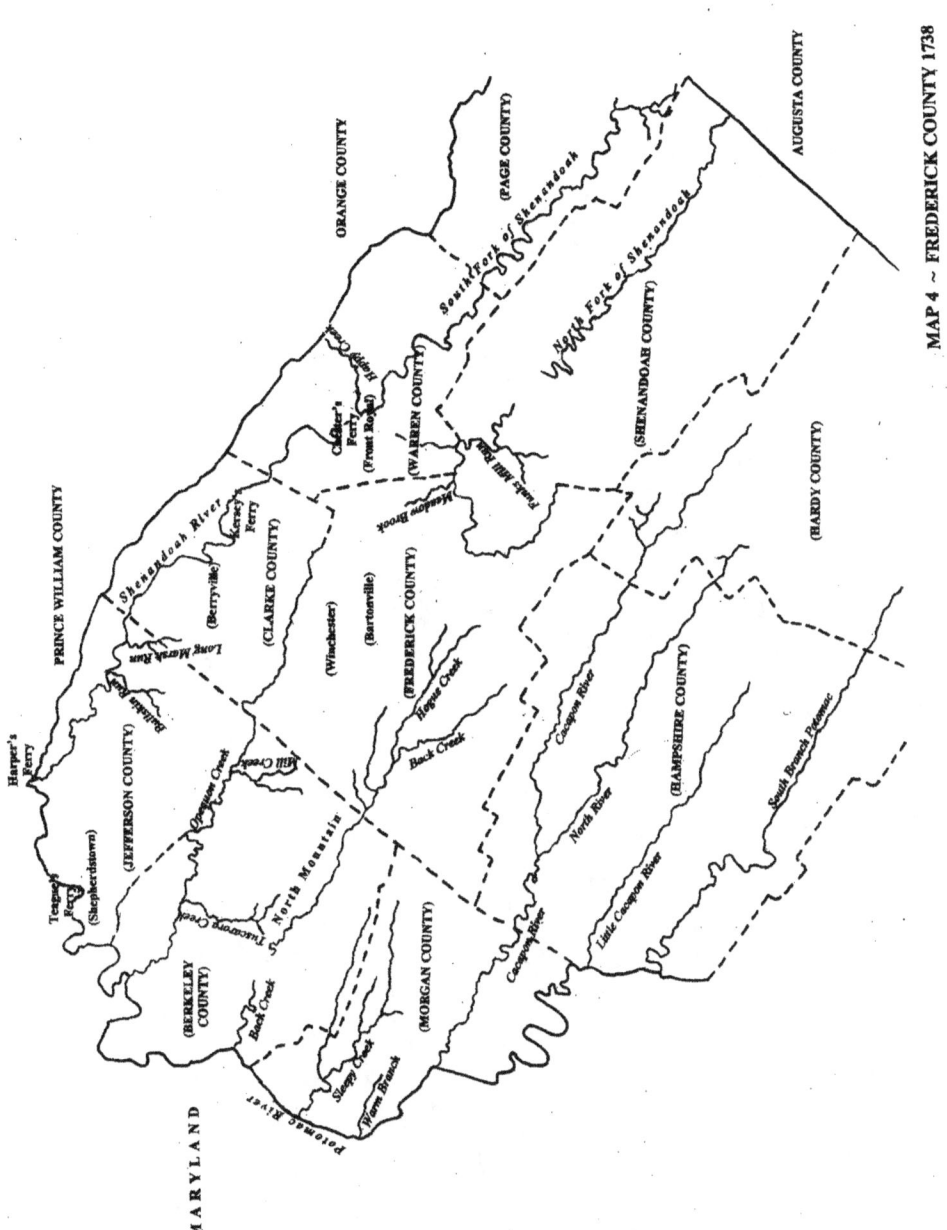

MAP 4 ~ FREDERICK COUNTY 1738

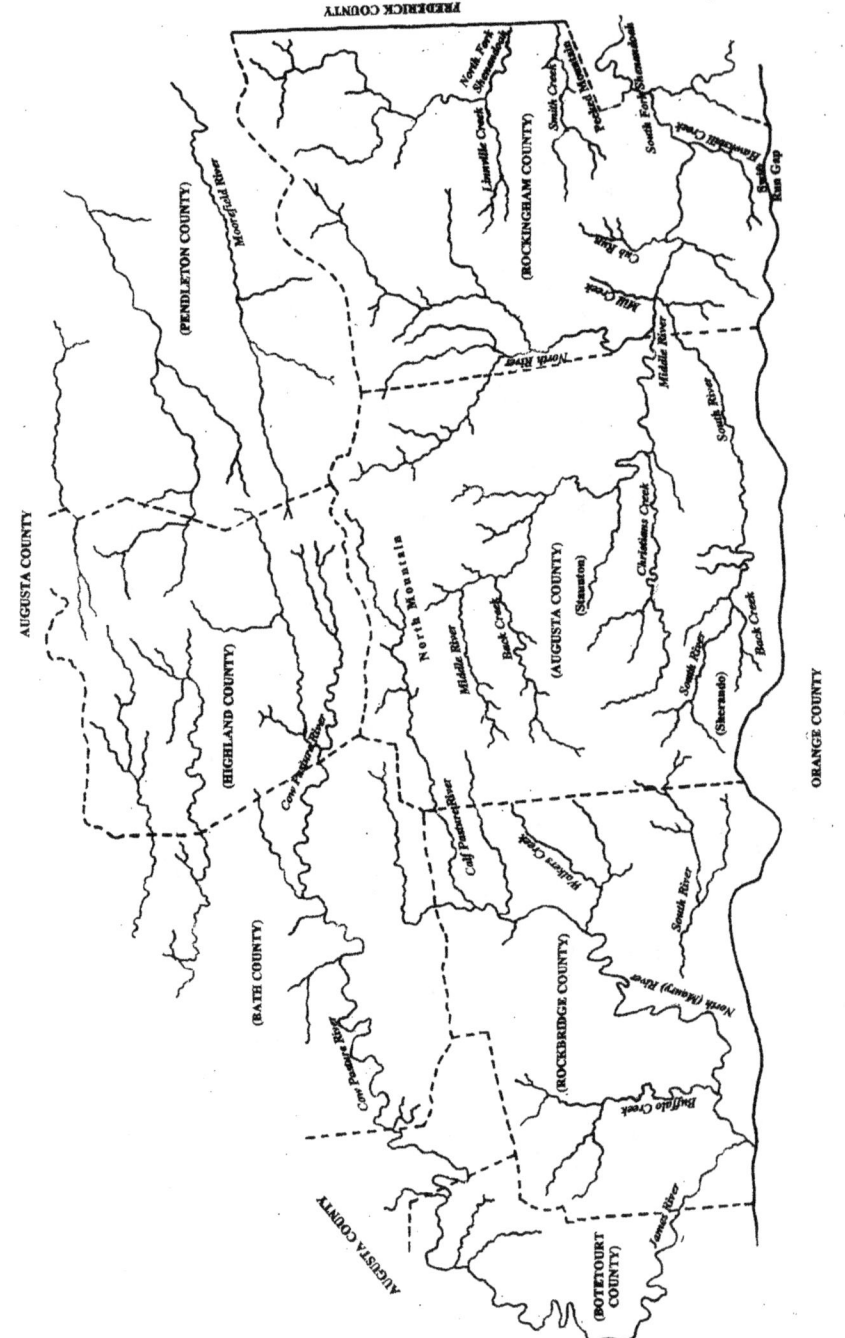

MAP 5 ~ AUGUSTA COUNTY 1738

INTRODUCTION

Students of colonial Orange County, Virginia, enjoy the rare fortune of having seventy lists with the names of over a thousand tobacco planters who were living in the county between 1735 and 1769. County constables compiled these lists every year when they inspected the tobacco plantations in their precincts to ensure planters were observing the Virginia Assembly's prohibitions against cultivating debased tobacco. During the thirty-five years between 1735 and 1769, the Orange County court appointed over two hundred constables to more than forty precincts where they performed a variety of duties in addition to inspecting tobacco plantations. For the purpose of this monograph, I have designated these constable precincts Orange I–V, Culpeper I and II, Rappahannock, Madison I and II, Frederick I–IX and Augusta I–XX. The boundaries of these precincts and the constables appointed to them are treated in the next section; but first, it is interesting to see what contemporary documents reveal about these lists and the constables who compiled them and what the lists tell us about eighteenth century Orange County.

Tobacco In Colonial Virginia

John Rolfe, an Englishman living in Jamestown and husband of Pocahontas, was reputedly the first to cultivate tobacco in Virginia for the English market in 1614, with seeds he brought from the West Indies. By this time, tobacco, a native plant of the Americas, was already known to the rest of the world. Christopher Columbus mentioned seeing tobacco leaves in San Salvador in 1492. By 1531, Europeans were cultivating tobacco in Santa Domingo for a European market. Tobacco was at first used as a medicine for everything from headaches to dysentery, but when people started to smoke it for pleasure—in taverns and brothels because it was considered harmful and immoral—tobacco became a lucrative commodity. In 1586, one Englishman reported seeing some Virginia colonist in Plymouth smoking tobacco from pipes, "These men . . . were the first that I know of that brought into England that Indian plant which they call Tabacca and Nicotia, or Tobacco."[2] By the 1620s, a mere decade after John Rolfe shipped the first Virginia tobacco to England, tobacco became Virginia's chief export. It was virtually the coin of the realm and it had an impact on every facet of life in the colony. However, Virginia was not the only tobacco-growing colony; Virginia planters had to compete with Maryland and North Carolina planters for the best price from Britain, the only country the colonists were permitted to sell their tobacco to.[3]

Tobacco Cultivation ❧ The cultivation of tobacco is a year-round occupation. In colonial Virginia, tobacco was planted soon after Christmas in about a quarter acre of enriched seedbeds and then covered with branches to protect the seedlings from frost. Reckoning loss of the seedlings to disease, frost or pests, as many as ten times the number of seedlings needed were planted in widely separated beds. Around late April, when the planter judged the seedlings properly developed, the delicate step of transplanting the seedlings to the fields began. Because the soil had to be soaked so the seedlings could be removed without harming their roots, transplanting often took place in the rain. Transplanting could stretch into late May or early June. During the summer months, as the tobacco grew and ripened, each plant was carefully tended and weeded. "One former slave retained into old age vivid memories of her failure [in picking worms off tobacco plants] and the punishment for her negligence: 'Old Masser . . . picked up a handful of worms . . . an' stuffed 'em inter my mouth.' This achieved the desired effect of having the girl, aged five or six at the time, exercise greater care in inspecting the tobacco plants."[4] After the plant produced eight to twelve leaves, the top of the plant was cut off (topped) to prevent it from flowering and diverting nutrients from the leaves. After topping, the planter watched for the appearance of secondary shoots at the base of the stalk (suckers), which were cut off (succored) so all nutrients were forced into the primary leaves.

In September, the tobacco leaves were ready to be cut. With other crops, this harvesting marked the end of the season, but the tobacco planter still had to perform the arduous and tricky task of curing the tobacco leaves. If this was not done correctly, the crop was lost. Each tobacco plant was cut off at the stalk and hung to dry in special curing barns until the leaves were pliable enough to pack: not so moist as to rot, not so dry as to be brittle and disintegrate when handled. When the leaves were judged ready to pack, they were stemmed by removing the large fibers from the web of the leaf. This required a lot of time, and slaves commonly worked through the night over single leaves. Finally, the leaves were laid in compressed layers in large, specially constructed, five-foot long barrels called casks or hogsheads, which could weigh as much as a thousand pounds when fully packed. (In one Orange County debt case, a plaintiff demanded payment of "three hogsheads of good Merchantable tobacco eight hundred neat each hogshead," and in another case, a plaintiff asked for "nine hundred & twenty two pounds of [illegible] tobacco in one hogshead.") A rope was passed through the center of the hogshead, harnessed to draft animals and rolled along specially laid "rowling roads" to tobacco warehouses (called rolling houses up to around 1720). The Orange County court orders are full of petitions for the laying and maintenance of these wide rolling roads and the construction of sturdy, wide bridges to support the weight of these hogsheads. The tobacco warehouses were on major waterways with deep-water ports, which could accommodate the oceangoing ships carrying the tobacco to Britain. If the planter was fortunate enough to live close to a deep waterway, the hogshead could be transported all or part of the way by water. (Several rolling roads to the Rapidan River are mentioned in the Orange County court orders.) However, it was not unusual for a planter to roll a hogshead over a hundred miles to the nearest warehouse, which, at two miles an hour, would have taken many days. In the mid-eighteenth century, the closest warehouses for planters living in Orange County were the Fredericksburg and Royston Warehouses in Spotsylvania County, Conway's Warehouse on the Rappahannock in Caroline County and Crutchfield Warehouse near the fork of the South Anna and North Anna in Hanover County.[5] Planters in Frederick County may have transported their hogsheads on the Potomac River to one of the warehouses near Alexandria. While there are many orders about rolling roads and tobacco warehouses in the Spotsylvania County and Orange County court order books, neither of these subjects are mentioned in the Frederick County or Augusta County order books.[6]

Once at the warehouse, the hogshead was inspected to ensure it contained "good, sound, well-conditioned [tobacco], and [was] free from trash, sand, and dirt." After inspection, the planter was given a receipt for the total pounds of tobacco accepted by the inspector, and these tobacco or crop notes were used as cash by the planter. By this time, in late December or early January, when the planter returned home from the warehouse, the cycle of tobacco production had begun again.[7]

TOBACCO AS CURRENCY ❧ Up to the Revolutionary War, virtually everything in Virginia could be paid in tobacco: public officials' fees, salaries of everyone from ministers to day laborers, parish and county levies, material goods and much else. In 1752, the Orange County court ordered William Smith, Jr. to pay his debt, in part, with his crop note, the note issued by the tobacco warehouse for Smith's hogshead of 937 pounds of tobacco. Defendants or plaintiffs paid witnesses they summoned to give evidence in their court cases a set amount of tobacco for each day spent in court, plus a set amount for each mile to and from court if the witness did not live near the courthouse. (In 1762, a witness received 25 pounds of tobacco per day spent in court.) Only a few things, like property transfers, security bonds, quit rents and duties, were paid in cash. Some things, like alcoholic beverages sold in ordinaries (taverns) and debts and fines, could be paid in cash or tobacco with the rate of exchange regulated by the Virginia Assembly. David Bruce was fined "ten Shillings Curr^t Money or one hundred pounds of tobacco" for missing church for two months, and a defendant in an Orange County civil suit was ordered to pay "three Pounds ten Shillings and Eight pence . . . in tobacco at 12/c p^r cent which amounts to five hundred & Eighty Eight pounds of tobacco."[8]

LAWS REGULATING TOBACCO ❧ The Virginia legislature wrote innumerable laws to ensure that the quality "of our indeed onely commoditie of tobaccoe" received a good price in England.[9] From 1621 to the Revolutionary War, regulations were written, repealed and rewritten about every aspect of tobacco: when it was planted; how many plants each household could plant; how it was cultivated; when it was cut; when, in what, and how it was packed; when it was to be delivered to a warehouse; and a multitude of laws about the warehouses, their tobacco inspectors and the transportation of the tobacco to Britain. These laws and the fines for non-compliance governed everyone from planters, overseers, slaves, local officials—justices, sheriffs, constables—and warehouse inspectors to the captains and crews of the ships carrying the tobacco to England.

The Virginia Assembly was especially intent on prohibiting "the tending and curing tobacco slips and suckers, for the making of seconds, [which] is greatly prejudicial to the people of this colony, by debasing the quality and depreciating the value thereof." Slips were cuttings from a full-grown tobacco stalk, and suckers were the secondary shoots removed from the base of the stalk after topping. Slips and suckers could be rooted to grow "seconds," a plant of inferior quality. In 1632, the legislature enacted the first law prohibiting the growing of seconds, placing responsibility for enforcement on the planter and setting fines for non-compliance. In 1640, facing the fall in the price of tobacco due to the overproduction and low quality of Virginia tobacco, the Virginia Assembly restricted (stinted) the amount of tobacco to be planted for the next two years and "appointed men of experience and integrity for the careful viewing of each man's crop of Tobo." These viewers were to go to each plantation and burn all substandard tobacco and half of the good tobacco and mark the remaining tobacco as inspected and approved with a seal. These viewers were the first tobacco inspectors. In 1656, another law was enacted which offered informers a reward for reporting planters tending seconds and slips. However, the ineffectiveness of these regulations against seconds is revealed in yet another act in 1720: "Whereas, the tending and making of seconds, is greatly prejudicial to the staple of tobacco, and the laws made for preventing thereof, have been evaded, & the penalties therein given against persons who shall be convicted of tending seconds, are found insufficient to restrain persons from such undue practices," the legislature increased the fine for tending seconds, promised informers a financial reward, and ordered sheriffs of each county to read this law in the courthouse every June and July.[10]

Then, on 21 May 1730, at a time when the price of tobacco had fallen so low that planters were struggling to survive, Sir William Gooch, the Lieutenant Governor of Virginia, convinced the Virginia Assembly to pass the Tobacco Inspection Acts "for the better and more effectual improving the Staple of Tobacco."[11] These laws addressed every aspect of tobacco from planting to shipping to Britain and included new legislation against tending seconds:

> That every constable within this colony, shall yearly, between the last day of July, and the tenth day of August, and between the twentieth day of August and the tenth day of September, and at such other times as any constable shall think proper, repair to all the several fields and places whereon tobacco shall be planted or tended, within their respective precincts, and diligently view the same, in order to discover whether any slips or suckers shall be turned out or tended, from the stalks from which any tobacco-plant hath been before cut or taken, above the height of nine inches from the ground. And if any constable shall find or discover any such slips or suckers growing upon any plantation within his precinct, and the owner or overseer of such plantation being thereunto required, shall refuse or fail to cut up and destroy such slips and suckers, such constable is hereby impowered and required to cut up and destroy, or cause the same to be cut up and destroied. And if any owner or overseer shall refuse to shew to such constable all such fields and places on his or her plantation or plantations, where tobacco hath been planted or tended in any year, every owner or overseer so refusing, shall forfeit and pay five hundred pounds tobacco, for every person emploied in making tobacco on his or her plantation or plantations that year.
>
> And for encouraging the constables to perform their duties herein, Be it further enacted, That there shall be levied on every tithable person in each county, one pound of tobacco; to be distributed to the respective constables, in proportion to the number of tithables in their respective precincts: . . . and for every hundred tobacco stalks which shall have any sucker or slip growing thereon, of the height of nine inches from the ground, which any constable shall cut up and destroy, there shall be paid to such constable, by the owner of such tobacco-stalks, or his or her overseer, twenty pounds of tobacco, and so proportionably for a lesser quantity: To be recovered, with costs, before any justice of the peace of the county wherein the said tobacco stalks shall be so cut up and destroyed.
>
> And be it further enacted, by the authority aforesaid, That the court of every county within this colony, upon the information of any constable, to them made, against any person or persons, for the breach of this act . . . made against the tending of slips or seconds, shall order and direct the attorney appointed to prosecute in such court for his majesty, to bring suit against such person or persons, for the respective forfeitures by them incurred, by the breach of any of the said acts.[12]

In 1736, the legislature amended the Tobacco Inspection Acts by ordering constables to report anyone in his precinct tending slips or seconds to his county court, instead of destroying the slips or seconds himself. More acts followed which imposed fines on plantation owners or overseers who "shall weed, top, hill, sucker, house, cure, strip, or pack any seconds, suckers, or slips of tobacco."[13] Then, on 7 November 1769, the legislature repealed that section of the Tobacco Inspection Acts which directed constables to view tobacco fields for slips or suckers:

And whereas the penalties inflicted on persons who shall tend seconds for tobacco, are judged sufficient to restrain that practice, and the tobacco levied for the constables, as a reward for their viewing tobacco fields, in order to discover whether slips or suckers are turned out or tended, is an unnecessary burthen upon the county: Be it therefore . . . enacted, [that the acts of 21 May 1730] against tending seconds, . . . as directs the several constables to view all tobacco fields within their respective precincts, to discover whether suckers or slips of tobacco are turned out or tended, and which directs the justices of the county courts to levy for the constables one pound of tobacco per titheable, for such their services, be, and the same are hereby repealed.[14]

Opposition to the Tobacco Inspection Acts—chiefly to the power of inspectors at the warehouses—was widespread and, in some counties, violent. Three petitions presented to the Orange County court in 1736, 1738 and 1740 probably addressed these laws: "Charles Dewitt in behalf of himself and others the Subscribers presented a paper as their proposition for repealing the Tobacco Law which is ordered to be certified at the next Assembly."[15]

When the Tobacco Inspection Act was passed in 1730, Orange County—not formed until 1734—was still part of Spotsylvania County. The first mention of a constable viewing tobacco in the Spotsylvania County order books was on 5 September 1732, when Thomas Pulliam replaced Abraham Abney as constable between the Rivers Ta and Northanna and was "sworn to view the severall fields of tobacco within his precincts for preventing the tending of Seconds Slips & Suckers &c. as the Law directs." The annual Spotsylvania County levy credited seven constables for viewing tobacco in 1732, five constables in 1733 and eight constables in 1734. The first mention of constables viewing tobacco in neighboring Goochland County was in 1731, when two constables informed the justices of planters tending seconds, and three constables were credited in the county levy "for inspecting seconds."[16]

An interesting precursor to tobacco-viewing, passed by the Virginia legislature in the mid-seventeenth century, "ordered that all constables within their severall lymitts and precincts shall take a veiw of every man's corne upon the ground" to ensure "there be two acres of corne planted for every worker in the ground." Laws to ensure the colony was self-sufficient in corn for consumption and for livestock fodder were passed at the first session of the Virginia Assembly, in 1619, because planters were forsaking the cultivation of corn in favor of the very profitable tobacco crop. The legislature also prohibited the colonists from trading with Indians for corn—a prohibition intended to weaken the economic status of Indians.[17]

THE CONSTABLE

Although much has been written about virtually every facet of tobacco in colonial Virginia, the literature—with only a few exceptions—is strangely silent about the role of the constable in this story.[18] The constable, as an officer of the law, dates back to the end of the twelfth century in England. The earliest evidence of this public official in Virginia is said to be 1637 or 1645; the constable is first mentioned in the laws of the Virginia Assembly in 1643.[19]

QUALIFICATIONS FOR THE OFFICE OF CONSTABLE ❧ Several Virginia statutes described the office of constable as "inferior" and constables as "commonly persons in low circumstances." Constables gave no security as a condition of office, unlike all other appointed county officers like, for example,

Francis Smith, who was appointed deputy sheriff of Orange County in 1757 and "acknowledged [himself] indebted to James Madison, Gent., Sheriff, in the sum of one thousand pounds current money to be levied of [his] goods and chattels lands and tenements . . . on condition that if [he] keep harmless . . . from all or any damages . . . of anything done by Francis in his Office as Deputy Sheriff."[20] But even if constables were considered the lowest ranking public officers in the colony—at least between 1730 and 1769 when constables viewed tobacco fields and recorded the names of the planters they visited—they had to be "persons of intelligence with regard to the tobacco planted on the lands," and they had to be literate. However, the spelling on some tobacco planter lists shows marginal literacy; for example, it is amazing how many ways Orange County constables spelled the word precinct: precint, presint, presink, prespe, percinct, persinct, persink, percint, perint, pircinct, pirsink, pircint, porsinct, pursink, purcink and prosink.[21] Like all county officers, constables had to be Protestant. (Although almost all residents—and constables—of Orange County were Anglican, some were not: Orange IV constables John and probably William Cleveland were Quakers; and, at least two Madison II constables, Zacharias Blankenbaker and Richard Burdyne, were Lutheran.)[22] A constable also had to be free enough from the time-consuming, year-round work of tobacco cultivation or the obligations of a lawyer, physician or mill owner, in order to walk the tobacco fields in the late summer–early fall and perform all the other demanding duties of his office. However, apparently a constable—at least, in Orange County—did not have to be above reproach. In 1739, a grand jury returned a bill against two future constables, John Goodall and Honorias Powell, and one serving constable, Thomas Callaway, for "with Sword & Staves and knives on John Newport . . . made an Afsault and him did Menace beat Wound & evil entreat & other Injuries to him then & there offered ag^t ye peace." And, in 1743, the court "Ordered that the Sheriff take Honorias Powell [a serving constable] from the barr & put him in the flocks for an hour for appearing drunk in court."[23]

A number of Orange County constables were sons of tobacco planters, which allowed them time away from the fields; others had such small land holdings that they may have gladly accepted the position because of the lure of the fees they could earn. Judging by the number of tithables in the households of Orange County and Goochland County constables, Mary Gwaltney Vaz concluded that they were not very wealthy.[24] Most of the Orange County constables had one to three tithables in their household (a few had as many as seven) at the time they served, which was less than the average number of tithables in the households of other planters in the county (see table 2 for the average number of tithables in each Orange County precinct between 1735 and 1770). Whether or not constables were "commonly persons in low circumstances" at the time they served, a number of Orange County constables went on to become burgesses, county justices, vestrymen, and militia officers.[25]

THE APPOINTMENT OF CONSTABLES ❧ The procedure for appointing constables was well established by the time Orange County was formed in 1734. County court justices divided the county into precincts and appointed a resident of each precinct to serve as constable for one year. (In the first years of Orange County, some sitting constables suggested their replacements: "On the petition of Samuel Morris [Frederick IV (1735)] Isaac Pennington is appointed Constable in his room.") The court described the boundaries of these precincts when the first constables of a newly formed county were appointed, when a precinct had become overpopulated and was split, when the precinct boundaries were slightly altered or when the court simply rephrased the description of the same boundaries.[26] When the court changed the boundaries of one precinct, it resulted in new—but usually not described—boundaries of neighboring precincts. Most precinct boundaries are easily understood waterways, county lines and roads. But almost all the Orange County precincts had an indistinct boundary like a residence, which, open to the interpretation of the constable assigned to the precinct, occasionally resulted in some planters appearing one year on the tobacco planter list of one precinct, the next year on the list of the neighboring precinct, and sometimes on the lists of both precincts in the same year (see pp. 42, 49). However, the court did not describe or in any way identify the boundaries of a precinct each time a constable was appointed. In most cases, they ordered one constable to replace another or simply appointed a man constable without even saying whom he replaced or without describing his precinct. Therefore, to identify which precinct a constable was assigned, it is often necessary to trace constable-replacing-constable back to the original assignment or to find where a constable lived at the time of his appointment.

When the newly formed Orange County court sat for the first time on 21 January 1735, the justices ordered, "that the . . . Constables that were in those offices before the dividing of the County continue in the said Offices." Four constables appointed by the Spotsylvania County court before 1735, continued as constables of Orange County. Then, at the second meeting of the court, on 18 February, the court divided the county into seven precincts and appointed constables to each precinct.[27]

The Orange County court usually directed the constable appointee to present himself at court to be sworn into office and often recorded in a later order the oaths he took when he came to court. These court orders varied in their formulaic wording, but the procedure is clear. In most cases, the court ordered the sheriff to summon the appointee to appear at the next meeting of the court to be sworn constable. Even when the order did not specifically say the sheriff was to perform this duty, it was so understood. For example, Charles Robinson was "Summoned to appear to the next Court to be ſworn into the s^d Office" of constable of Augusta I on 28 May 1741; one month later, the court noted that "the Sheriff having returned on the order [to summon Robinson] not executed for want of time its ordered that he be ſummoned to appear at the next Court to be ſworn into ye s^d Office." Occasionally, the outgoing constable, instead of the sheriff, was ordered to summon his replacement to appear before a Justice of the Peace instead of at the courthouse to be sworn: "Ordered that George Boman be made a Constable [of Frederick I] in the room of Lewis Stevens and it is further ordered that the said Stevens Sumons ye s^d Boman before a Justice of the Peace for this County to be Sworn into the Said office accordingly." Such an order was usually directed to constables in Frederick and Augusta Counties.

Several orders make it clear that whether an appointee was sworn constable at the courthouse or nearer home by a justice, the appointee still had to appear at the courthouse to take the oaths of a constable. Zachary Gibbs, Orange III (1748), was ordered to "be sworn into his said Office before a Justice of this County and be summoned to take the other Oaths at next Court," and the court ordered the sheriff to summon Thomas Turk, Augusta IX (1742), and five other appointees "to appear on ye fifteenth of next Month at the house of Patrick Campbell [who lived in Beverely Manor in Augusta County] there to be ſworn into ye s^d Office by W^m Ruſsell James Patton John Lewis & John Buchannan Gents or any one of them & then to appear at next Court to take the oaths appointed by a late Act of Parliament."

Constables, like all public officials, were obliged to swear several oaths before assuming office. (Oaths taken by attorneys, a Presbyterian minister and by non-British Protestants who sought to be nationalized also appear in the Orange County order books.)[28] The wording of the oaths taken by constables—at least, in Orange County—changed over the years; but even though written many different ways and in long or short versions, they all demanded the same thing: loyalty to the British monarch and Anglican Church and vows to uphold the specific duties of their office. In 1735, 1736 and 1737, there is no record in the Orange County order books of any constable taking an oath before assuming office. In 1738, only one constable, John Tilly of Augusta II, was "Sworn Constable & Subscribed the test." On 22 March 1739, the court ordered the sheriff to "Summon all the Constables of this County to appear at y̆ next Court to take y̆ oaths enjoyned by the last Acts of Aſsembly to be taken by them."[29] Then, after 1739, the court orders record almost all constables swearing their oaths before assuming office. These oaths were described basically three ways: "the oaths prescribed by Acts of Parliament & the oaths prescribed by late act of Aſsembly Subscribed the Tests" or "Oaths appointed to be taken by Act of Parliament instead of the Oaths of Allegiance and Suppremacy and took and subscribed the Oath of Abjuration and subscribed the Test and . . . all the Oaths required to be taken as Constable" or "the Oaths to his Majesty's Person and Government and the Oath of Abjuration and subscribed the Test and took the Oath of a Constable and the Oath appointed by the Tobacco Laws." The first part of all of these oaths was an abbreviation of

> the Oaths appointed by act of parliament to be taken instead of the oaths of Allegiance and Suppremacy the oath appointed to be taken by an act of parliament made in the first Year of the Reign of his late Majesty king George the first [1714–1727] entitled an Act for the further Security of his Majesties person and Government and the Succession of the Crown in the Heirs of the Late princess Sophia being protestants and for extinguishing the hopes of the pretended prince of Wales and his open and Secret abettors.

The Abjuration Oath was instituted in 1702 by William III to abjure the claims of the Stuart Pretender and his heirs. Subscribing the Test—the Test Act of 1673—required office holders to take communion according to the rites of the Church of England and to swear disavowal of the Catholic doctrine of transubstantiation, the belief that the communion bread and wine, by consecration, became the body and blood of Christ. On 22 September 1737, William Williams, a Presbyterian minister living in Augusta County, swore allegiance to the Crown, subscribed the Test and "Subscribed a declaration of his approving of Such of the thirty nine Articles of Religion [the 1563 tenets of the Anglican Church] as is required."[30]

The "Oath of a Constable" does not appear in the Orange County order books, but one of the oaths required to be taken by constables is known: the 21 May 1730 "Oath appointed by the Tobacco Laws"

> I A. B. do swear, That I will diligently and carefully view the several fields and places whereon tobacco shall be planted or tended, within the precincts whereof I am constable; and will cut up and destroy, or cause to be cut up and destroied all stalks from which any tobacco-plant shall be cut or taken, and all slips or suckers growing from or out of the same which I shall find standing or growing in any of the fields or places aforesaid, above the height of nine inches from the ground: and that I will make information of all persons within my said precinct, whom I shall know to be guilty of the breach of any law of this colony made against the tending of slips or seconds, to the next court held for my county after the same shall come to my knowledge. So help me God.[31]

Four Orange County constables also swore an oath for the "Preservation of the Breed of Deer." This oath upheld a law passed by the Virginia Assembly in 1738, which instructed constables to confiscate the skins of red deer killed out-of-season and report the owner of these skins to the county justices. It is curious that only four constables were ordered to swear this oath in 1747 and 1753. Another oath, enacted in 1742, required constables, sheriffs, and under-sheriffs to swear to report anyone selling or shipping uninspected tobacco out of Virginia. Constables may have sworn other oaths as well to uphold their many different duties.[32]

For many constables, the ride to the courthouse to swear their oaths of office was a very long trip. Between 1735 and 1749, the Orange County court was located in three different places in today's Orange County. In 1735 and 1736, the courthouse was at the home of Henry Willis on Black Walnut Run; from 1737 to 1749, it was near Raccoon Ford on the Rapidan River; and after the formation of Culpeper County in 1749, the county court moved to its final location in what would become the Town of Orange. Thomas Kennerley, the 1738 constable of the Rappahannock precinct, would have had a long day's travel. He lived on the Rush River, a tributary of Thornton's River, some fifty miles on today's roads from Raccoon Ford. And appointees living in Frederick and Augusta Counties had an even longer trip. In 1746, Marquis Calmes, a witness in a trail held at the courthouse at Raccoon Ford, petitioned the court for the plaintiff to pay him "for coming Seventy Miles out of Frederick County."[33]

Most constables took their oaths from one to five months after they were appointed, but four constables took their oaths more than nine months after they were summoned: Zacharias Blankenbaker was appointed 28 August 1746, but he did not take his oaths until 23 July 1747.[34] John Williams took the oaths of a constable two times during his ten-year consecutive term. However, of the 270 constables who served between 1739 (when the Orange County court first recorded constables taking oaths) and 1769, there is a record of only 120 constables taking the oaths of office. Why is there no record of an oath being taken by more than half of these constables? Was it an oversight on the part of the court clerk, was it not deemed necessary to record, did the constable take his oaths someplace other than the court? Of the 120 constables who did take their oaths at court, one-fifth took their oaths on the same day they were summoned to appear at court. Were these men in court on other business on the day they were appointed?

In some cases, men performed constable duties before they were appointed or they were described as a constables but there is no record of their appointment. George Thurston, who was described as a constable of Frederick II when he transported two runaway slaves back to their owner in June 1738, was not appointed constable until a month later. In another case, the court appointed John Tilly constable of Augusta II, and in the same order directed him to take someone accused of assault into custody. There is no record of two men, who were described as constables in the Orange County levies, being appointed constables: "William Waters Constable" was paid for summoning two coroner's juries in 1745, and George Taylor, assignee of "Samuel Drake Constable" was paid for summoning a coroner's inquest in 1746. I found no information about a William Waters, but Samuel Drake lived near Robert Bickers on Berry's Run in the Orange II precinct in 1744. However, Drake could not have been the constable of Orange II in 1746—unless two constables were appointed to the precinct—since John Mallory was constable at the time.[35] And, in 1751, James Isbell was paid 35 pounds of tobacco for summoning a coroner's jury—a constable duty—but there is no record of his ever having been appointed constable.[36]

There was no set time of the year when constables were appointed; whereas, all justices who collected the lists of tithables—all males sixteen and older and all male and female slaves sixteen and older—were appointed every year on the same day, usually in May (see Appendix). Some constables who were appointed in late August or even September—during the months the legislature had directed constables to view the tobacco fields—still inspected the fields and returned their lists on time for the county levy. John Griffin, who was appointed constable of Orange IV on 22 September 1768—twelve days after the prescribed time for viewing tobacco fields—returned his 1768 list to the court, but the court did not record it until 1769.[37]

Constables were probably appointed throughout the year because it was not always easy to find someone willing or able to accept the position. For example, in March 1741, Abraham Yates was ordered to appear at court to be sworn in the place of Henry Robinson, constable of Frederick V; in May, "failing to appear," Yates was again summoned; in June, William Davis was ordered to appear at court to be sworn in the place of Robinson and warned "that if he fail to appear he be fined"; finally, in July, Gilbert Guilder was appointed to replace Robinson and was sworn the next month. Thirty appointees were summoned two or, in a few cases, three times. Almost all of these summonses were issued to men living in Frederick and Augusta Counties, and half of these were issued in the months before the Augusta County court assumed responsibility for appointing constables. A few times, the court repeated their summons because "the Sheriff having returned on the order not executed for want of time" or the sheriff told the court he was unable to deliver any summons because of the bad weather. In 1738, three constables were ordered to summon their replacements to be sworn into office and were further ordered "not to leave the s^d office till ye s^d [replacement] be Sworn into it."[38]

Forty men were appointed to serve as constables but did not heed the court's order to appear to be sworn. In most cases, no reason was given for their refusal. William Bell, Orange III (1740), refused the office because he had "lately been Constable." Bradley Kimbrow, Orange IV (1752), "was not qualified for that office" either because he was illiterate—he signed documents with an "X"—or because he lived in another precinct. John Tradan, Frederick IV (1740), "refused to Swear alledging that he was Roman Catholick" and as such, would not swear loyalty to the Protestant church or subscribe the Test. Gilbert Campbell, Augusta XIV (1741), "defired to be freed from being Constable Setting forth that he was Sick and ailing." The court dismissed his summons, and two years later he was again summoned but again did not serve. When John Gollorthun, Orange II-B (1753), was reappointed to a third term, the court replaced him because he had "removed himself out of the County." Another constable, John McQuin, appointed to Frederick I in 1740, "being aloofe [a loose] man is absconded & the precinct is left without a Constable." But the ultimate excuse was death. In February of 1736, James Kirk was appointed constable of Culpeper I. In November, a grand jury charged him for not viewing tobacco, a dereliction probably explained in February 1737 when William Taylor replaced the deceased James Kirk. Then, a few months later, Isaac Haddock replaced Taylor when Taylor died.

Most constables served only one year; however, Rowland Cornelius, Culpeper II (1749), served only one month. A number of constables served two years, and several served between three and seven years. John Williams, Orange I (1755–1764), and John Cleveland, Orange IV (1738–1747), served ten years. Occasionally, the court reappointed a constable a few years after he had served: John Henderson, the first constable appointed to Orange II in 1735, was reappointed in 1748 and in 1755, but did not serve.

The court usually recorded the end of a constable's term by simply appointing his replacement, but sometimes the court would add that the constable "be discharged from that Office." Several constables were discharged not once, but twice: John Carr, Augusta XIII (1745), was discharged in February, then again in August when his replacement was summoned a third time. A few times, when a replacement declined the office, the acting constable continued in office—usually a few months, but in one case for three years—until a replacement could be found. Honorias Powell, Orange V, was first discharged in July of 1745, but did not leave office until July of 1748. Eleven constables—most having served a year or less—petitioned the court to be discharged.

DUTIES OF THE CONSTABLE ~ The varied duties executed by constables reflect the changing demands on the Virginia colony: from the realization of the colony's dependence on tobacco for economic survival in the seventeenth century to the strain on parish finances in the face of destitute parishioners and vagabonds in the eighteenth century. The legislature regulated the duties and set the amount of tobacco paid a constable for performing his duties; constables also occasionally executed or assisted in the execution of a sheriff's duties.[39] County justices, the county clerk, coroner, sheriff and parish churchwardens could order a constable to perform a task. Tasks ordered by justices were recorded in the court orders, but those ordered by the county clerk, coroner or sheriff were verbal, and evidence—if any—of these duties was only occasionally recorded in the annual county levy or, in a few cases, noted by the constable on his tobacco planter list. Tasks ordered by churchwardens may have been recorded in the parish vestry books, but there are no such orders in the vestry books of the parishes responsible for the parishioners of Orange County—St. George, St. Mark and St. Thomas—between 1721 and 1769.[40] Mary Gwaltney Vaz divided the duties performed by constables into two groups: order duties, such as keeping the peace and serving warrants, and property duties, like viewing tobacco.[41] The following duties, collected from Hening's *Statutes at Large*, could have been performed by constables in Orange County between 1735 and 1769.

Constables were often the first to be notified of a robbery or murder in their precinct, and it was the constable's duty to enlist as many men in his precinct as needed to pursue and capture the accused. Constables also assisted sheriffs or under-sheriffs with arrests, guarding prisoners and putting prisoners in the stocks, for which they were paid 10 pounds of tobacco. In 1747, the Orange County court "Ordered that the Sherif & Constables of this County have Power to Prefs & ask So many Men as will be Sufficient for taking and Apprehending Tom a Negro man slave belonging to Michael [illegible] and [four other male Negro slaves] that they take the said slaves & have them here on Saturday next to answer the Conspiracy with which they stand Charged." In 1738, John Tilly, who lived in the Augusta II precinct, informed the court that "William Fraser hath dangerously wounded one Samuel Rofe," and the court "ordered that the said Tilly who is hereby appointed Constable take the said Frazer into Custody and deliver him unto the Sheriff." In September 1751, Margaret Bruce was accused of stealing a glass tumbler and some yarn from the home of Timothy Crosthwait. The county paid the constable of Orange I, Alexander McDaniel, 7 pounds of tobacco "For Searching Margaret Bruce by an Order." Although the items were found in her custody (by Constable McDaniel?), she denied the charge and was tried and found guilty of petty larceny by a grand jury, and "[t]hereupon the Court hath ordered the Sheriff take her from the Bar and lead her to the Whipping Post and there give her fifteen lashes on her bare back well laid on and that she be discharged." And in 1758, after a slave was found guilty of theft, the court ordered the sheriff to burn his hand and give him thirty-nine "lashes on his bare back well laid on and that the Sheriff deliver him to the Constable to be conveyed to his Master."[42] Although the Virginia Assembly specified that guarding prisoners was a constable's duty, few of the men credited for this duty in the annual Orange County levy were constables.[43]

A number of duties involved escorting runaways and undesirables out of the county or parish. Constables returned escaped prisoners to jail, runaway seamen to their ships and deserters to their commanding officers. In 1741, the Orange County court "Ordered that the Kings Attorney prosecute Leonard Ziegler for refusing to obey and a/sist Timothy Terrill a Constable [of Madison II] in conveying a prisoner that had broken out of Goal & was retaken by the said Constable."[44] Constables also returned runaway servants and slaves to their owners. There are a number of petitions in the Orange County order books, like that of David Zachary, who "produced a certificate . . . for taking up a runaway Woman Servant . . . about ten miles from her said Masters house." This certificate, issued by a justice, confirmed the identity of the runaway and the conditions surrounding her capture and entitled Zachary to 200 pounds of tobacco (paid by the county and reimbursed by the owner of the runaway). The justice then consigned the runaway to a constable, who was ordered to whip—no more than thirty-nine lashes—the runaway and return her to her owner; the owner of the runaway was required to pay the constable 10 pounds of tobacco for the whipping. If the runaway's owner lived outside the constable's precinct, the constable passed the runaway on to the constable of the next precinct, and so on until the runaway was returned to his or her owner. In 1738, the Orange County court ordered the sheriff to summon Abraham Wiseman to appear at court "to answer ye Compl^t of George Thurston Constable [of Frederick II] for refusing to a/sist him to carry two Runaway Negroes to their Master." In 1751, "John Grigsby informed the Court that pursuant to Certificate from a Justice he carried a runaway to William McDonough, Constable [of Orange III], who refused to take the runaway into his custody. Its therefore ordered the Sheriff summon said McDonough to appear at next Court to answer the Complaint." Constables also suppressed and whipped unlawful assemblies of slaves or slaves who possessed any "weapon, whatsoever, offensive or defensive."[45]

Another order duty performed by the constable concerned the militia. In colonial Virginia, every free male aged 16 to 60 was obliged to report for militia musters. In the 1750s, troops or companies mustered every three months and general musters occurred twice a year. If a militiaman failed to attend these musters, the constable of their precinct was paid to deliver that person to the county court for punishment.[46]

Constables were paid 5 pounds of tobacco for summoning a witness and 50 pounds of tobacco for summoning a jury or a coroner's jury and the necessary witnesses to court. Alexander McDaniel, constable of Orange I, was paid 50 pounds of tobacco for "summonsing a Jury upon Andrew Mannens P Servt fellow Natt" in 1753. Of the eight records of Orange County constables who summoned a coroner's jury of inquest, only one was paid 50 pounds of tobacco, the others were paid 35 pounds of tobacco: in 1766, Constable William Leek requested 35 pounds of tobacco for "Summoning a Coroner's Jury on Bettey Sellers Child," but Constable Alexander McDaniel was paid 50 pounds of tobacco "For Summoning an Inquest Jury at Arnolds House" in 1752.[47]

Sheriffs, under-sheriffs and constables were paid 10 pounds of tobacco for serving warrants issued by a justice "to enter any suspected houses, and break open all doors, either by day or by night to search" for illegally packed or uninspected tobacco and for goods, like spirits, for which no duty had been paid. In 1736, Constable Lewis Stephen, Frederick I, was ordered to mark gallons of rum brought into Virginia by Samuel Hews with the "broad arrow"—a mark of confiscation by the government—because Hews had failed to pay duties on the rum. Constables were also empowered to arrest cattle drivers who did not possess a manifest, to search and seize skins or furs from people travelling on the frontier and to confiscate skins of red deer killed out-of-season (in 1747 and 1753, four constables swore an oath to uphold this 1738 law for the "Preservation of the Breed of Deer"). In 1743, Joseph Edwards, constable of an unidentified precinct in Frederick County, "ſeized nine Deer Skins which were in ye hands & poſseſſion of John Pearcy who was found travelling with the ſame in order to carry them out of the Colony without paying any duty for ye same."[48]

In 1756, officers of the law were ordered to confiscate arms and horses over a certain value found in the homes of Catholics. This law was passed after the outbreak of the French and Indian War in 1754, a conflict between the French and British over control of territories in North America. In 1755, when British troops were crushed by the French at Fort Duquesne on Virginia's western frontier, and Virginians feared invasion, the Reverend Samuel Davies, of Hanover County, called Virginians to battle, lest "Indian savages and French Papists, infamous all the world over for Treachery and Tyranny, should rule Protestants and Britons with a Rod of iron." This centuries-old wariness and fear of Catholics crops up occasionally in the court's business. In 1743, a presentment was brought by the St. Mark's Parish churchwardens against Patrick Campbell "for Abuſing and ill Using Elizabeth Cragen . . . and that ye s^d Campbell hath neglected to bring her up in Christian protestant principles but has endeavoured to bring her up a Roman Catholick."[49]

Parishes were responsible for the care of the poor, and the annual vestry accounts usually included some record of this charity. In 1728, The St. George's vestry paid 1,000 pounds of tobacco "To Mary Day and Mary Day her Daughter for a maintenance the Ensuing year," and in 1747, the St. Mark's vestry paid Doctor Joseph Gibbs 500 pounds of tobacco "for Doing his utmost endeavor to cure the Weddow George." But by 1748, the cost of caring for more and more vagabonds passing through the parish—in addition to their own parishioners who had fallen on hard times—was a serious enough problem that the Virginia legislature required all travelers to carry certification proving they had paid their taxes and were not rootless. Acting on orders of the parish churchwardens, constables removed "any person, suspected to become chargeable to the parish" from the parish. The parish, which would have had to support the vagrant, paid the constable 2 pounds of tobacco for every mile he travelled to and from the parish border to escort the vagrant from the parish. In 1755, churchwardens were authorized to order constables to conduct beggars to the parish workhouse for the poor. Constables also apprehended "persons of insane and disordered minds" and collected fines from people who did "profanely sweare or curse or shall be drunk" or in other ways infringe on the moral code of the community. In 1740, Thomas Callaway, constable of Orange V, informed the court that he gave "notice to the Church wardens of St Marks Parish according to Law of a bastard Child born in [George Douglas'] house."[50]

Constables were also responsible for a number of duties involving property: serving attachments, weighing hemp, culling dogs, confirming a minimum acreage of corn was planted on each plantation and inspecting tobacco fields. Sheriffs, under-sheriffs and constables were paid 30 pounds of tobacco for serving attachments issued by the court against the estates of debtors. A number of these orders are prefaced, "the Attachment . . . directed to any Sheriff or Constable in Virginia." There are numerous records of sheriffs serving attachments in the Orange County order books, but comparatively few of constables performing this duty. Between 1739 and 1756, fourteen constables executed nineteen attachments, and during the same period, fourteen attachments were served by unnamed constables.[51] Most of the attachments executed by constables—presumably against people in their precinct—occurred between 1741 and 1743 far from the administrative heart of the county in the Culpeper, Madison, Frederick and Augusta precincts. All court records of the execution of an attachment relate the same events: the constable went to the debtor's residence, removed saleable property, held it until the court asked him to produce it or to turn it over to the sheriff, and the sheriff sold the property in order to settle the debt claimed by the plaintiff. One attachment, made by an unnamed constable against the estate of George Richards, who owed 800 pounds of tobacco, is interesting because it stands apart from the usual attachment of livestock, farm equipment and household goods:

> the Conſtable . . . Attached all of the Defts Estate in this County to wit one old Coat & Veſt one p^r Scarlet britches an old Virginia Cloath Veſt two old Caps three old bands two p^r of old Cotton hoſe one p^r brown Linnen britches one p^r Chequered d^o [i.e. britches] one p^r kneebuckles one Cap and one ſhirt one Joyners Rule and Compaſses one [illegible] one leather apron one old Wallet Saddle & bridles one horſe and one old p^r of Shoe . . . And its ordered that the Sheriff ſell the goods Attached by public Auction."[52]

Some of these attachment records, like that of Constable Thomas Rucker, Madison I (1741), were entered in the order books from a few months to as long as a year after the constable had been dismissed.

In 1730, the Virginia Assembly passed the first of many acts to encourage the growth and production of "good and merchantable hemp fit for exportation, [which] will be not only beneficial to the inhabitants of this colony, but also . . . advantageous to the navigation and commerce of Great-Britain." It is said that well over one hundred thousand pounds of hemp for rope and canvas was used to build the United State's oldest naval ship, the USS Constitution. Hemp was also used domestically for making linen and other cloths. Recognizing the importance of this export, the Virginia Assembly guaranteed farmers a bounty for their hemp. To qualify for the bounty, hemp-growers had to pay a justice of the peace or a constable five shillings per ton of hemp to weigh their hemp, and then the hemp-grower, like the overseer James Clark of Orange County, "produced into Court a Certificate under the hand of Wm Price Constable for the Weight of 3769 ^{pd} hemp and the s^d Clark made oath that the hemp therein mentioned was Duly Weighed and at that time was Winter rotted and made upon the Plantation of [Joseph] Jones in this County & that the Same was Dry Bright and Clean."[53] The soil of Orange County and the rest of the Piedmont was ideal for hemp. For some reason, the Orange County court recorded applications for this bounty only in 1767 and 1768: four of the seven certificates were signed by justices, and three were signed by William Price, constable of Orange I.[54]

Another property duty, which may or may not have been performed by constables in the mid-eighteenth century, was ensuring that every farmer grew a set acreage of corn (see p. 5). Although there is no mention in the Orange County court order books of constables performing this duty, presentments were brought against four men "for not tending Corn" in 1739 and 1747.[55] The last constable duty—save tobacco-viewing—concerned dogs. In 1755, the legislature ordered "constables at the time of their viewing tobacco fields, to examine into the number of dogs kept at the several negroe quarters in their precincts, and to kill and destroy every dog kept thereat, exceeding two. [Because] dogs frequently ramble from home and destroy great numbers of sheep, and some persons are so unneighbourly as to refuse their being killed." If Orange County constables performed this duty, there is no evidence of it.[56]

CONSTABLE REMUNERATION ❧ The Virginia Assembly set all fees to be paid constables and all other public officials for the performance of specific duties.[57] When a constable executed a duty normally performed by a sheriff, he was paid the same fee as a sheriff. Duties performed by a constable and the pounds of tobacco due him were recorded in the annual county levy. On a few tobacco planter lists, constables described tasks they had performed and how many pounds of tobacco they were owed, but it is strange that none of these duties reported by the constable were described in the county levy.[58] Constables also received fees from the vestry for tasks performed for the parish and from people who had directly benefited from a task, such as returning runaway slaves to their owners or certifying the weight of a farmer's hemp.

The low fees paid a constable—from 5 to 50 pounds of tobacco for order duties—reflected the low status of this public official. Constables were paid less than other public officials for work requiring a good deal of time in the saddle: riding from his home to court, to plantations to summon witnesses or a coroner's jury, escorting runaways out of his precinct or assisting the sheriff in serving warrants or executing attachments. Even the more considerable fees constables collected for travelling from one plantation to the next when viewing tobacco—1 pound of tobacco for every tithable living on the plantations he visited—was not so much considering the time and effort it took to perform this duty. Between 1735 and 1770, the Orange County court paid constables from 22 to 743 pounds of tobacco for viewing tobacco fields, an average of 252 pounds of tobacco (see table 2).[59] Mary Gwaltney Vaz figured a constable was in the field about twenty-eight days viewing tobacco: "an 11 day period at the beginning of August and a 22 day period at the end of August and beginning of September" minus Sundays. So, by Vaz's reckoning, a constable who was paid 252 pounds of tobacco, received 9 pounds of tobacco a day for inspecting tobacco plantations. This was considerably less than the 30 pounds of tobacco a day paid an estate appraiser who did not have to travel far because he usually lived near the estate being appraised. But did a constable inspect the tobacco fields for twenty-eight days as Vaz suggested or did he inspect the tobacco anytime during these twenty-eight days, "at such other times as any constable shall think proper"? If you were paid per tithable and not per day, any sensible worker would finish his work as soon as possible, and this would make the average daily wage for viewing tobacco more than Vaz suggested.[60] The exception to the low fees a constable received for duties requiring time and travel, was the fee he received for weighing hemp. In 1767 and 1768, William Price, constable of Orange I, issued certificates to three hemp-growers for weighing a total of 8,810 pounds of hemp. At five shillings per ton of hemp, Price was paid 22 ½ shillings. In 1736, ten shillings equaled 100 pounds of tobacco, so Price earned the equivalent of 225 pounds of tobacco. However, according to the Orange County court orders, William Price was the only constable paid for weighing hemp. Assuming most constables earned about 250 pounds of tobacco for viewing tobacco, plus about 200 pounds of tobacco for some other tasks, what would 450 pounds of tobacco buy? In the 1740s a pair of shoes cost 50 pounds of tobacco, a bushel of corn 125, a pound of sugar 8, a cow 500, and a horse 1,500 pounds of tobacco.[61]

But there were other compensations for serving as a constable. The legislature enacted laws "for their [constables'] encouragement to perform their duty" exempting them from public, county and parish levies and from militia duty while holding office. Several county levies record the reimbursement of levies paid by constables. In 1736, the court reimbursed three men 15 pounds of tobacco each for levies they had paid the previous year when they served as constables. In 1747, "John Cleaveland [was reimbursed 46 pounds of tobacco] for Levies for the years 1744, 1745 & 1746 he being Consble during that time." Constables, ordinary keepers, mill owners and surveyors of highways were exempt from serving on a grand jury because their work did not allow them the time needed for this civic duty. In addition, viewing tobacco provided a chance to visit neighbors and to see how they ran their plantations and to exchange news and gossip. For men with political ambitions, this was an opportunity to make friends and forge allies.[62]

On the other hand, many of the constable's duties—bringing militia shirkers to court, whipping runaway slaves and servants, serving attachments on debtors, "enter[ing] any suspected houses, and break[ing] open all doors, either by day or by night to search" for contraband and reporting people for unacceptable behavior—must not have endeared the constable to his neighbors. In fact, in 1735, the court ordered the sheriff to arrest Providence Williams "for his Contempt or abuse of John Petite Constable [of Frederick II] in executing his Office," and in 1744,

> Roger Topp Constable [of Culpeper I-A] having informed the Court that James Hopkins is a Person of Lewd Life and Converſation & a Common Disturber of his Majesties Peace & that s^d Hopkins did aſsault & abuse him when in y^e [illegible] of his Office & from the [illegible] threats of the s^d Hopkins & other Enormities declared he is afraid to execute the Precepts committed to him, It is therefor Ordered by the Court that the s^d Hopkins committed for s^d Offences by John Finleſon Gent to ye Sher[iff] or Goaler of this County be remanded from this Barr to ye County Goal untill he shall enter into Recognizance of [illegible] together with two securitys each in ye fine of £10 Ster[ling] to be of the [illegible] and good behavior for one year & a Day to to all his Majesties Subjects but especially unto ye Roger Tapp.

DERELICTION OF DUTIES ✤ It is difficult to say exactly how many of the 186 men in Orange County (excluding Frederick and Augusta Counties), who were appointed constables between 1735 and 1769, actually performed their constabulary duties. It is curious that the 186 constables appointed to these ten Orange County precincts, who served a total of 238 years between 1735 and 1769, were credited in the annual county levy for viewing tobacco fields only 148 times.[63] Seven constables, who were never credited for viewing tobacco fields did, however, serve attachments or summon juries or report planters who tended tobacco seconds.[64] Did the other constables shirk their constabulary duties? The 1730 Tobacco Inspection Acts imposed a fine of 1,000 pounds of tobacco on a constable who did not inspect the tobacco fields in his precinct. In Spotsylvania County, between November 1732 and November 1733, five constables were charged "for not executing [their] office in searching after Tobacco Suckers between the last of July 1732 and the 10th of Augt. & the 20th of Augt. and the 10th of September in the said year" and "for not doing [their] Duty in viewing tobacco succors as the Law provides." Two of these constables gave the excuse "that [they] never knew or ever was told that [they] had any precincts to view & that [they] never demanded any satisfaction of ye County as ye Law directs for ye same." Of these five constables, one was fined 50 pounds of tobacco, another was fined 130 pounds of tobacco, and the others were excused. Between 1735 and 1769, the Orange County court charged only three constables "for not looking after suckers and causing them to be cut down according to Law." These charges were all made on 25 November 1736, and all three charges were dismissed four months later. In 1742, the court ordered the sheriff to summon Colvert Anderson to appear at the next court "to Shew Cauſe why he being Conſtable will not execute these precepts delivered to him." When Anderson failed to appear at court, he was again summoned, then two months later, the court issued an attachment against him. However, one month later, he was discharged without a fine.[65] And in another case, William McDonough, 1750 constable of Orange III, was ordered to appear in court to answer charges for refusing to take a runaway into his custody, but nothing else appears in the court order books about the prosecution of this charge.

THE LISTS OF TOBACCO PLANTERS

The 1730 Tobacco Inspection Acts directed constables "to discover whether any slips or suckers shall be turned out or tended, from the stalks from which any tobacco-plant hath been before cut or taken, above the height of nine inches from the ground" on all tobacco plantations in his precinct. If any owner or overseer tending seconds on his or her plantation "shall refuse or fail to cut up and destroy such slips and suckers, [the] constable is hereby impowered and required to cut up and destroy, or cause the same to be cut up and destroied."[66] In 1736, the legislature revised this law and ordered the constable to report the planting of slips or seconds to his county court rather than destroy them.

Constables were not required to count the number of tobacco plants on each plantation, since the 1730 Tobacco Inspection Acts did away with "stinting" regulations like those passed in 1728, which limited slave owners to 6,000 plants for each worker in his fields. Accounts of this tobacco counting appear in the St. George's Parish vestry books. In June 1729, St. George's vestry divided the parish into eight precincts and appointed sixteen men "to Count all the Tobacco plants" in their precinct. Benjamin Cave and Richard Cheek were ordered to "Examin and Enquire of the name and number of persons allowed to tend tobacco according to a Late act of the assembly made for the Better and more Effectual Improving the staple of Tobacco and the Crops of the several planters and the number of plants growing on any and Every plantation or plantations with in part of the same precincts."[67]

The Tobacco Inspection Acts said nothing about constables making a list of the tobacco fields they had visited. These lists were a constable's invoice, which he presented to the court in order to be paid his 1 pound of tobacco for each tithable recorded on his list. Sixty-five of the seventy Orange County lists of tobacco planters are from the Orange I, II, III, IV and V precincts (today's Orange and Greene Counties), one is from Culpeper I and four are from Madison I and II. There are one to five lists every year from 1735 to 1769, except 1740–1748 and 1750.

What appeared on these lists varied from constable to constable: most wrote only the name of each planter and the number of his or her tithables, but Anthony Golding, Orange V (1769), submitted a seven-page list, which detailed the number of seconds found and destroyed on six of the ninety-nine fields he visited. Of all the lists, those of John Williams, constable of Orange I from 1755 to 1764, stand out as particularly conscientious work: his tabulations are always correct or near correct, his spelling is better than average, and he went to the trouble of listing the planters in alphabetical groups on four of his eight lists.

All but seven of the seventy lists of tobacco planters were signed by the constable, and a little more than half of them were dated.[68] Constables were to view tobacco fields ever year when suckers appeared on the tobacco stalk and before the tobacco stalks were cut, "between the last day of July, and the tenth day of August, and between the twentieth day of August and the tenth day of September, and at such other times as any constable shall think proper." Unpredictable weather conditions may explain why the legislature allowed constables the leeway to inspect the tobacco fields at "such other times as any constable shall think proper." The date at the top of six tobacco planter lists may have been the date the constable finished viewing the fields in his precinct. Philip Bush, Orange IV, dated his list "Sept 16 1749." Two weeks later, on 28 September, Bush informed the court that John Eubank was tending seconds, something he would have learned only after viewing the tobacco fields. Other lists were dated "Ju 1737," "Jul ye 20^t 1756" and "august 1st 1766."[69]

Almost all constables labeled their list in some way: "Claim for seeing the cutting up Suckers within his precincts," "Looking of Secons," "Sucker hunting," "List of Titheables in my precincts of Soucor fees," "Account for suceers," "afrucker hunting," "Sucker hunting" and an "acco^t due for viewing tob^o fields." More than half of the lists are titled a variation of "A List of the Tithables Within the precints Whereof I am Constable." But this was a misnomer, since constables only recorded the names of the tobacco planters and the number of tithables in their household. The actual "List of Tithables" was the list of names of all tithables in a precinct, which was collected by justices in June (see Appendix).[70] Between 1736 and 1741, the court described this duty in the county levy as viewing or counting tobacco suckers; after 1743, it was simply called viewing tobacco fields.

Not everyone living in the county would have appeared on these tobacco planter lists, since not everyone—like the clergy, innkeepers, craftsmen and lawyers—made their living from tobacco.[71] But, in fact, almost everyone did grow at least some tobacco to pay county and parish levies and for some extra income. The 1730 Tobacco Inspection Acts made no distinction between full- and part-time tobacco-growers when it directed constables to inspect "all the several fields and places whereon tobacco shall be planted or tended." Reverend John Becket, who resided at the St. Mark's Parish glebe near Lignum in today's Culpeper County from 1733 to 1740, and Reverends Mungo Marshall and James Marye, who resided at the St. Thomas' Parish glebe on Glebe Run during their tenures, 1750–1757 and 1760–1768, all appeared on the lists of tobacco planters. Charles Curtis, who built the new courthouse in today's Town of Orange in 1751, appeared on lists in 1749 and 1754. Timothy Crosthwait, whose ordinary near that new courthouse must have been most profitable and time-consuming, appeared on one tobacco planter list. But Zachary Lewis, the first prosecuting attorney of Orange County, does not appear on any of the tobacco planter lists.[72] At least in 1756, almost all tithables living in today's Orange and Greene Counties cultivated tobacco: the five constables of Orange I–V reported a total of 1,514 tithables engaged in tobacco growing, and the 1756 county levy recorded 1,595 tithables living in the county (see Appendix and table 2). Some constables included their own name and number of their tithables on their lists. On twenty-eight lists, the constable included the number of his tithables in his total of tithables, which was probably illegal. John Williams included his one tithable on his list but subtracted it from his total; Thomas Graves included his one tithable on his list but crossed it out; and William Cook included his one tithable in his total, but the court credited him one less than his total.[73]

It is logical to assume that constables listed the names of the tobacco planters in the order in which they visited them.[74] Sometimes there is a clustering of the same names over the years in a precinct; however, since the same names do not appear together often enough, this evidence can only confirm or suggest, it cannot be used independently to identify a planter's neighbors.

Some constables added titles to the names of some planters: Thomas White added a title to almost everyone on his 1755 Orange III list, but no titles appear on Ben Cave's 1757 Orange II list. Three titles of courtesy were used for men: Mr., Gent. and Esq. The most common was Mister, an eighteenth century mark of some status but used haphazardly by most of the constables: Alexander McDaniel called William Talliaferro, "Mr," on his Orange I list in 1753, but not in 1752. Educated men who were wealthy enough to be free from work and any man appointed a justice were called "Gentleman." Curiously, the title Esquire was used only once by William Price, Orange I (1765), to describe Joseph Jones, a comfortably prosperous planter of no more distinction or wealth than other distinguished Orange County planters. The professional titles of Reverend and Doctor also appear, but also randomly: James Marye, reverend of St. Thomas' Parish from 1760 to 1768, was called "Rev" four of the five times he appeared on a tobacco planter list when he was the acting reverend of the parish. The militia ranks of Lieutenant, Captain, Major and Colonel were frequently used. The small number of women who owned tobacco plantations were usually, but not always, called "Miss," "Mrs," "Madam" or "Widow." The four women who were sometimes called "Madam" (Madams Spencer, Winslow, Taylor and Talliaferro) were widows of prominent and wealthy Orange County men. Finally, two planters were called "old," and several constables added "dcd" after a planter's name to note the planter's recent death.[75]

Constables usually noted the quarters—property of an absentee landlord—and the names of the overseer or overseers who managed the quarter. In 1764, Constable Robert Bickers, Orange III, identified thirteen of the fifty tobacco fields he visited as quarters and named all of their overseers. A number of constables appended "Est" to a planter's name. In most cases, the constable was probably identifying the plantation as the estate of a recently deceased planter; for example, Benjamin Cave died in 1762, and that year "Est" was added to his name. Finally, the location of two plantations on "Mine Run" was noted on one tobacco planter list.[76]

THE TABULATIONS ~ The totals of the number of tithables on 64 percent of the tobacco planter lists are incorrect: most by as little as one, some by as much as forty-seven (most errors were an undercount in the county's favor). More often than not, the total on each list was the amount the court entered in the county levy. However, for some unexplained reason, the court credited twelve constables as much as 90 pounds of tobacco less than they had claimed (see table 2). Sometimes a constable inexplicably subtracted a number or series of numbers from his total; for example, John Bryant wrote on his list, "In all 153 32 ded^{d}" (153 minus 32 = 120) and was credited 120 pounds of tobacco. Several constables added fees for other tasks they had performed or for reimbursement of their levy: Manoah Singleton added 11 pounds of tobacco for "1 Levy over pd" and 35 pounds of tobacco for summoning a coroner's jury to his total of 386 (386+11+35=432) and was credited the 432 pounds of tobacco he claimed.[77]

Constables crossed out some names or some tithable numbers or both on a number of tobacco planter lists. Henry Rice, Orange II (1739), crossed out and did not include in his total the tithables of seven planters; four of these planters with the same number of tithables as on Rice's list appear on Elijah Daniel's 1739 Orange III tobacco planter list. The same confusion about which planters belonged in which precinct is seen on Ben Cave's 1763 Orange II-A list: Cave crossed out the number of tithables of seventeen planters; four of these planters—with different numbers of tithables—appear on Thomas Price's 1763 Orange IV list and eleven on Manoah Singleton's 1763 Orange II-B list.[78]

The sixty-five lists compiled by the constables of Orange I, II, III, IV and V reveal, as would be expected, a fairly consistent growth of planters and their tithables from one year to the next. However, sometimes there were extreme increases or decreases in the number of tithables from one year to the next. In some cases, this was because the court enlarged or reduced the precinct; for example, when Orange IV was reduced by the formation of Orange III in 1738 and the formation of Orange V in 1739, the number of tithables went from 233 to 79 to 38. Sometimes the constable misunderstood (intentionally or not) the boundaries of his precinct and included tobacco fields in a neighboring precinct; for example, in 1767, Edmund Burrus, constable of Orange II, included most of the large Orange III planters on his list, which resulted in a count of 743 tithables compared with his total of 457 tithables on his 1768 tobacco planter list. But sometimes the large increase or decrease of totals is a mystery: Thomas White, Orange III constable from 1755 to 1758, listed 58 planters with 432 tithables in 1755, 62 planters with 407 tithables in 1756, but then 36 planters with 253 tithables in 1757, and in 1758, he listed 61 planters with 407 tithables.

WHEN DID CONSTABLES TURN IN THEIR LISTS? ~ A constable probably delivered his list to the courthouse as soon as it was completed so it could be included in the county levy, which, from 1735 to 1769, was laid between 19 October and 29 November. A date appears at the top or at the bottom of more than half of the lists of tobacco planters, but only eleven have the full date with the day, month and year. The date at the top of the list, as noted earlier, was probably the date the constable compiled his list. The date at the bottom of five of the lists may have been the date the constable delivered his list to the court. Some of these dates—"acco Nov. Levy" and "27 October 1737" (the date of the 1737 county levy) and "Papers Relating October Court 1764"—could have been added by either the constable or by a court officer.[79] As described in a 1762 court order, sometime after a constable submitted his list of tobacco planters to the court, the court "Ordered the Sheriff to pay Benj^a Cave Constable 396 l^b Tobacco for his Account for Viewing Tob^o out of the the Deposit in the Sherifs hands." Constable Robert Deering, Orange IV (1751), was not paid for his tobacco-viewing until three years after he submitted his list to the court.

Several constables turned in their tobacco planter lists late. In one case, "Ben. Cave Constable [of Orange II] who was sick & could not come at the laying the County Levy Now Produced his Accot for Viewing Tobo fields . . . [on] 24 March 1763." And Constable John Goodall, Orange V (1756), appended a note to his list asking the court's understanding for delivering his list on the 23rd of November (the levy was laid on the 25th), explaining that he was incapacitated "being Crippled by my Horse & not able to Attend Your Worships." Constable John Griffin, Orange IV (1768, 1769), was appointed constable on 22 September 1768—twelve days after the legislature directed constables to view tobacco fields—and presented his tobacco planter list for 1768 together with his 1769 list. He reported 314 tithables in 1768 and 336 tithables in 1769 with a total of 650, but the court credited him 490. Was he fined 160 pounds of tobacco for turning in his list late? And Constable David Phillips, Madison I (1736, 1737), was not credited by the court in 1736 for the 165 tithables on his list. In 1737, he submitted a list with 172 tithables and the court credited him 237½ pound of tobacco, a number explained by Phillip's tabulation on his 1737 list: 165 + 172 = 337 - 100½ = 237½. The 100½ deduction might be explained by a 25 November 1736 court order stating that a grand jury charged David Phillips "for not looking after suckers . . . this present Year."

CHARGES FOR TENDING TOBACCO SUCCORS OR SECONDS

The first charge for tending tobacco suckers in Spotsylvania County, after passage of the 1730 Tobacco Inspection Acts, was brought by Constable Robert Williams on 5 September 1733 against "John Wests Plantation [where] there were a certain number of Suckers or Slips of tobacco contrary to Law topt and hilled on the eighth day of August last."[80] Between 1737 and 1766, eleven Orange County constables informed the court that twenty-one planters had "turned out and tended Succors" or tended "tobacco Slips Seconds & Succurs." These charges were turned over to the county "Attorney for our Soverign Lord the King [to] prosecute them according to Law." In one case, Constable Alexander McDaniel, Orange I, reported Thomas West (related to John West?) for tending Seconds on 27 September 1750. Over a year later, on 29 September 1751, in the case of Rex. vs Thomas West, the defendant pleaded not guilty, and the trial was referred to the next Court. Finally, on 26 April 1753—in an example of the wheels of justice turning slowly—a jury found West guilty and fined him 1,500 pounds of tobacco plus costs. On the same day the jury found West guilty, McDaniel, "a witness . . . against Thomas West, ordered said West pay him four hundred fifty pounds of tobacco for eighteen days attendance at this Court." Of the twenty-one charges for tending seconds in the Orange County order books, juries found eight planters guilty, three not guilty, and the cases against three were dismissed. Nothing appears in the court records about the resolution of the other seven cases.[81] Anthony Golding, Orange V (1769), turned in one of the last tobacco planter lists and noted six plantations where he found seconds; on one plantation he found "seccond about 50 or 60 & they was Destroyd Before me Anthony Golding." However, nothing appears in the Orange County order books in 1769 or 1770 about the prosecution of these planters for tending seconds.

The 1730 Tobacco Inspection Acts stated that planters found guilty of tending seconds were to be fined "five hundred pounds tobacco, for every person emploied in making tobacco on his or her plantation." Thus, Edward Price with five tithables was fined 2,500 pounds of tobacco. The charges brought by constables for tending seconds usually noted the number of tithables in the household of the accused: "over Seven tithables tended Tobacco Succors" or "William Crawford having two tithables & his Wife in family did tend Tobacco Succors." Charges against four planters noted "persons above seven"—too young to be tithables—who had tended seconds (see p. 2). John Kendall "having three tithables & one above Seven years on the plantation" was found guilty and fined 2,000 pounds of tobacco since, as stated in the Tobacco Acts, he was fined for "every person emploied in making tobacco on his or her plantation."[82]

In 1770, a year after the Virginia legislature repealed that part of the Tobacco Inspection Acts ordering constables to inspect tobacco fields and report planters tending seconds, the Orange County court charged two planters for tending seconds. Thomas Cluten informed on (his neighbor?) Thomas Wilmoth, who appears on the 1768 Orange V tobacco planter list. The informant against John Vivion, who appears on the 1768 Orange II list, is not noted, but it may have been Edmund Burrus, who was credited for viewing the Orange II tobacco fields in the 1769 and 1770 county levies.[83]

TOBACCO VIEWING IN FREDERICK AND AUGUSTA COUNTIES

It is curious that there are no lists of Frederick County or Augusta County tobacco planters and that the Orange County court did not credit any of the constables of these western precincts for viewing tobacco fields. It is hard to imagine that tobacco planters in Frederick and Augusta Counties were exempt from inspections and fines for growing seconds and equally hard to believe that if these constables rode from plantation to plantation to inspect the plantations, they did not claim payment for their work. Did these constables submit their lists to the Orange County justices who lived in Frederick or Augusta Counties, and did these justices have their own funds for paying constables for this duty?[84] Another peculiarity about the Augusta precincts was that the Orange County court often ordered from two to eight Augusta men to be sworn constables in one order, and justices living in Augusta county—rather than the Orange County court—were often ordered to lay off the constable precincts in Augusta County.[85] In addition, as noted previously, no orders for rolling roads or any mention of tobacco warehouses appear in the Frederick County and Augusta County court orders.

Residents of these distant precincts were, however, not exempt from turning in their annual lists of tithables (see Appendix). On 28 September 1738, the Orange County court ordered "that ye Sheriff of Sharrando gives publick Notices to all that have not given in their Lists of tithables at Sherando & the Irish Tract do give 'em in by next Court or deliver 'em to W^m Ru/sell, Gent [a justice living in Augusta] in order for him to deliver them at ye next Court." And on 29 November 1745 (ten days after a court was constituted in Augusta County), the Orange County court "Ordered that Each Tithable Person in Augusta pay to the Same persons appointed and Directed by Law to receive and collect the Tax or Levy . . . and that the Collector pay the same to the Justices of Frederick County according to the Act of A/sembly." In 1738, 1739 and 1740, the "Shurando Sheriff" and the deputy sheriff of Frederick County submitted delinquent lists—people who had not turned in their list of tithables—to the Orange County court.[86]

THE ORANGE COUNTY, VIRGINIA, CONSTABLE PRECINCTS, 1735–1769

Between 1735 and 1769, the Orange County court appointed over 200 constables to some forty precincts in Orange County, which encompassed today's Orange, Culpeper, Rappahannock, Madison and Greene Counties and the original counties of Frederick and Augusta. I have designated these precincts Orange I–V, Culpeper I and II, Rappahannock, Madison I and II, Frederick I–IX and Augusta I–XX. All available information about the constables appointed to these precincts is quoted from the 1735–1770 Orange County Order Books 1 to 8 (OCOB) and Barbara Vines Little's *Orange County, Virginia, Tithables 1734–1782* (Little).[87] Paraphrased orders are italicized, and the names of men who served as constables are underlined.

THE ORANGE PRECINCTS

The area which encompassed today's Orange and Greene Counties was divided into five constable precincts: Orange I in the northeast, Orange II in the southeast, Orange III in the center, Orange IV inside the western border of "Orange" County, and Orange V—today's Greene County—in the west (see Map 2). Sixty-five lists of tobacco planters, compiled by constables between 1735 and 1769, record the names of planters living in these five precincts. In one year, 1756, there are lists from all five of these precincts and, theoretically, record all tobacco planters who resided in "Orange" and "Greene" Counties in that year.

ORANGE I

Constable precinct Orange I was described by the Orange County court in 1735 as "Northside of the Mountain Road from the Wilderness Bridge up to the Chappel." In 1750, the court described Orange I as "extending from the Mouth of the Robinson, down between the road from the said Robinson and the River as low as the old Trap." Although these two descriptions are very different, they both describe the same boundaries; however, the 1750 order clarified the location of the precinct's western boundary. Orange I was bordered on the north by the "[Rapidan] River," on the south by the "[Southwest] Mountain Road" (approximating Route 20), on the east by the "Wilderness Bridge" (the Spotsylvania County line) and on the west by a road from the Rapidan near the mouth of the Robinson River—the northeast corner of James Taylor's property—to below the Southwest Mountain Road at the "[Southwest Mountain] Chappel."[88] The boundary marker, "as low as the old Trap," described the southern border of the precinct; the Old Trap was north of Locust Grove on or near the Southwest Mountain Road.[89]

The names of tobacco planters on the nineteen Orange I lists, which date from 1735 to 1769, show the population changes to be expected from one year to the next in the precinct: some planters leave or die, some arrive, and some—like the Branhams who lived near Raccoon Ford—appear on almost all lists. Over these thirty-five years, the number of planters in Orange I grew from 62 to 139, with as many as 151 planters in 1766. From 1 to 45 tithables lived in the households of these planters, averaging 3 to 4.4 tithables per household. The total number of tithables of tobacco planters in Orange I, recorded in thirty annual county levies, increased from 190 in 1735 to 552 in 1769 (see table 2). In 1756, 27 percent of the tithables of tobacco planters in "Orange" and "Greene" Counties lived in Orange I.

ORANGE I (1735–1769)
This precinct was described as "Northside of the Mountain Road from the Wilderness Bridge up to the Chappel" in 1735 and "extending from the Mouth of the Robinson, down between the road from the said Robinson and the River as low as the old Trap" in 1750.

1735   Ambrose Jones is hereby appointed Constable on the Northside of the Mountain Road from the Wilderneſs Bridge up to the Chappell & it is ordered that the Sheriff Summon the said Jones to the next Court to be held for this County to be Sworn unto the said Office – 18 February 1734/35 (OCOB 1:5; Little, 152)

Ambrose Jones is on his petition discharged from being Constable as soon as Edmund Manion who is hereby appointed Constable in his Stead shall be sworn into the said office, for which purpose it is ordered that the said Ambrose Jones summon the said Edmund Manion before a Justice of this County to be sworn accordingly – 20 May 1735 (OCOB 1:13; Little, 152)

LIST: Y^e Tithables in the perſinks of Edm^d Manion Constable for the year 1735 – 190 (Little, 1–2)

1736   County Levy (1736): To Edmund Manion for viewing tob^o Succors: 190
To Edmund Manion Constable for repaying him his Levy paid Last Year: 15 – 19 October 1736 (OCOB 1:123; Little, 154)

We [the Grand Jury] present Edward Manion Constable for not looking after tobacco Succors and causing them to be cut up according to the Law this present year – 25 November 1736 (OCOB 1:127; Little, 154)

The Grand jury presentment ag^t Edmund Manion Constable for not looking after Tobacco Suckers and causing them to be cut up according to Law this present Year is $dismis^d$ – 25 March 1737 (OCOB 1:152; Little, 154)

1737   Ordered that Samuel Pound be Constable in room of Edmund Manion and its further ordered that the s^d Manion Sumons y^e s^d Pound before a Justice of y^e Peace for this County to be Sworn into y^e s^d Office accordingly – 26 May 1737 (OCOB 1:171; Little, 155)

On the information of Samuel Pound that John Hawkins Overseer of fourteen tithables for Rebecca Conway, John Kendall Overseer of three tithables for John Willis, Edward Price Overseer of five tithables for Joseph Molton & Stephen Wells one tithable & one above seven years old had turned out and tended Succours Its ordered that $Zach^y$ Lewis Gent Attorney for our Sovereign Lord the King prosecute them according to Law – 22 September 1737 (OCOB 1:213; Little, 155)

On the Information of Zachary Lewis Gent Attorney for our Sovereign Lord the King that John Kendall . . . Stephen Wells, Edward Price . . . John Hawkins [and others] had tended Succors Its ordered that the said persons be Summoned by the Sheriff to the next court to answer the s^d Information – 27 October 1737 (OCOB 1:225)

The case against John Hawkins:

In the Suit of Information brought by Zachary Lewis Gent Attorney for our Sovereign Lord the King ag^t John Hawkins for tending tobacco Succors the said Hawkins being called appeared and pleaded not guilty which I∫sue the said Zachary Lewis Gent joyned and the tryal thereof is referred untill the next Court – 25 November 1737 (OCOB 1:254)

In the Suit of Information . . . in behalf of . . . the King ag^t John Hawkins Deft for tending tobacco Succours a Jury . . . after hearing all Evidences . . . find the Deft guilty & that he had two tithables & no more on the plantation . . . and its Considered by the Court that the said John Hawkins be fined One thousand pounds of Tobacco according to Law . . . together with Costs – 24 February 1737/38 (OCOB 1:261)

On the Motion of Samuel Pound who made oath that he had attended two days as an Evidence for . . . the King ag^t John Hawkins for tending tobacco Succors Its ordered that the said John Hawkins [pay Samuel Pound for appearing as a witness] according to Law – 24 March 1738/39 (OCOB 1:453)

The case against John Kendall:

In the Suit of Information brought . . . for the King ag^t John Kendal for tending tobacco Suckers the Deft being called and failing to appear and the Sheriff having [illegible] the Summons & [illegible] the said John Kendal Its Ordered that an Attachment i∫sue ag^t the body of the said John Kendal for his personal appearance at the next Court to answer the said Information – 25 November 1737 (OCOB 1:253)

In the Suit of Information brought . . . in behalf of . . . the King ag^t John Kendall Deft for tending tobacco Suckers A Jury . . . heard all Evidence . . . find the Deft guilty having three tithables & one above Seven years on the plantation . . . wherefore its considered by the Court that the said Deft be fined Two thousand pounds of tobacco according to Law . . . together with Costs – 24 February 1737/38 (OCOB 1:264)

The case against Edward Price:

In the Suit of Information . . . in behalf of . . . the King ag^t Edward Price for tending tobacco Succors the said Price being called appeared & pleaded not Guilty which I∫sue . . . Zachary Lewis Gent joyned and the tryal thereof is referred untill the next Court – 25 November 1737 (OCOB 1:254)

In the Suit of Information . . . in behalf of . . . the King ag^t Edward Price for tending tobacco Succors a Jury . . . having heard all Evidence . . . find the Deft guilty five tithables . . . wherefore its considered by the Court that the said Deft be fined two thousand five hundred pounds of tobacco according to Law . . . together with Costs –

24 February 1737/38 (OCOB 1:265 [and repeated 1:268])

On the Motion of Samuel Pound who made oath that he had attended two days as an Evidence for our Sovereign Lord the King ag^t Edward Price for tending tobacco Succors Its ordered that the said Edward Price [pay Samuel Pound for appearing as a witness] according to Law – 24 March 1738/39 (OCOB 1:453)

The case against Stephen Wells:

In the Suit of Information brought . . . for . . . the King ag^t Stephen Wells for tending tobacco Succors the said Stephen Wells appeared and pleaded not guilty which Ifsue . . . Zachary Lewis Gent joyned & the trial thereof is referred untill next Court – 25 November 1737 (OCOB 1:254)

In the Suit of Information brought . . . in behalf of . . . the King ag^t Stephen Wells Deft for tending tobacco Suckers A Jury . . . having heard all Witnessses find the Deft Guilty . . . whereupon its considered by the Court that the said Deft be fined One thousand pounds of tobacco according to Law . . . together with Costs – 24 February 1737/38 (OCOB 1:262)

On the Motion of Samuel Pound who made oath that he had attended two days as an Evidence for our Sovereign Lord the King ag^t Stephen Wells for tending tobacco Succors Its ordered that the said Stephen Wells [pay Samuel Pound for appearing as a witness] according to Law – 24 May 1739 (OCOB 1:453)

County Levy (1737): To Samuel Pound [Constable for viewing tobacco]: 162 – 27 October 1737 (OCOB 1:233; Little, 155)

LIST: The List of Tithables in the pro*f*inks of Samuel pound Constable – 162 (Little, 7–8)

1738 LIST: Saml pound – 216 (Little, 13)

On the information of Samuel Pound Constable that Eliz^a Ro*f*er has tended Succors on her plantation and had three persons above the age of seven Years living on ye s^d pl^t its ordered that Zachary Lewis Gent Attorney for our Sovereign Lord the King prosecute her according to Law[90] – 28 September 1738 (OCOB 1:378; Little, 157)

County Levy (1738): To Samuel Pound Constable for counting tobacco Succours & for repaying his Levy: 216 – 26 October 1738 (OCOB 1:394; Little, 158)

1739 Samuel Pound took the oaths prescribed by Acts of Parliament & the oaths prescribed by a late act of A*f*sembly Subscribed the Tests & was Sworn Constable accordingly – 24 May 1739 (OCOB 1:479)

LIST: For the year 1739 p me Samuel Pound Constable (Little, 18)

County Levy (1739): To Saml Pound [Constable for Succors]: 192 – 25 October 1739 (OCOB 2:80; Little, 160)

1740 County Levy (1740): To Saml Pound Constable: 175 – 23 October 1740

To Saml Pound for Attending Eleven days on [prisoners] Sweeny & four days on Sanders: 375 – 23 October 1740 (OCOB 2:274, 275; Little, 163)

1741 County Levy (1741): To Samuel Pound for Viewing tobacco Succors: 130½
To Samuel Pound for Summoning a Jury of Inquest on Negro Harry: 50 – 22 October 1741 (OCOB 3:49; Little, 165)

County Levy (1742): To Samuel Pound for Summoning a Jury of Inquest on Wm Mathews: 35 – 25 November 1742 (OCOB 3:294)

1742 James Whiting is hereby appointed Conſtable in ye room of Samuel Pound who being called appeared & having taken the oaths appointed by Law Subscribed ye Test & was Sworn Conſtable accordingly – 25 March 1742 (OCOB 3:113; Little, 165)

Wm Husk is hereby appointed Conſtable in the room of James Whiting & its ordered that he go before a Justice of ye Peace of this County to be ſworn in the said office & appear at next Court to take the oaths appointed by a late Act of Aſsembly – 24 June 1742 (OCOB 3:163; Little, 166)

Thomas Wharton is hereby appointed Conſtable in the room of James Whiting in the Lower part of his precinct & its ordered that he be ſummoned to appear at the next Court to be ſworn in the said Office, Wm Husk being discharged[91] – 22 July 1742 (OCOB 3:167; Little, 166)

County Levy (1742): To Thos Wharton Conſtable: 189 – 25 November 1742 (OCOB 3:294; Little, 167)

1743 Thomas Wharton *executed an attachment against the estate of Samuel Pound* – 25 February 1742/43 (OCOB 3:372)

County Levy (1743): To Thomas Wharton for viewing tob^o fields as Constable: 199 – 24 November 1743 (OCOB 4:27; Little, 169)

James Minor having taken the Oaths Prescribed by Act of Parliament instead of the Oaths of Allegiance and Supremacy and the Abjuration Oath and [illegible] the Oath of a Constable was constituted Constable[92] – 25 November 1743 (OCOB 4:29; Little, 169)

1744 County Levy (1744): To James Minor as Pr Constable for Viewing Tob^o Fields: 295 – 25 October 1744 (OCOB 4:224; Little, 171)

1745 County Levy (1745): To James Minor Constable for Viewing Tobacco Fields which is to be lodged in the Sheriſs Hands: 224 – 29 November 1745 (OCOB 4:448; Little, 174)

1746 James Minor

1747 John Smith Junr having Taken the several Oaths to his Majesties Person & Governm^t & took & Subscribed the Abjuration Oath & the Test & the Oath Appointed by the Tob^o Law & also the Oath Appointed by Act of Aſsembly for the Preservation of the Breed of Deer was sworn Constable of that part of This County called The Neck[?][93] – 28 February 1746/47 (OCOB 4A:119)

John Morton [Little has John Wooton] having made Oath to his Majesty's Person and Government and took the Abjuration Oath and subscribed the Test was sworn Constable in the room of John Smith, Junr. and took the Oath appointed by the Tobacco Law – 27 August 1747 (OCOB 5:39; Little, 176)

Elijah Morton is by the Court appointed Constable in this county in the room of John Booten [Little has "Boston [?Wooten]"] and it is ordered that he be sworn into his said Office at the next Court[94] – 28 November 1747 (OCOB 5:84; Little, 177)

1748　County Levy (1748): To Elijah Morton for [viewing Tobacco Fields]: 258 – 24 November 1748 (OCOB 5:158; Little, 178)

1749　John Harvey is appointed Constable in the room of Elijah Morton, who is discharged from that Office – 23 March 1748/49 (OCOB 5:177; Little, 178)

1750　John Morton is appointed Constable and ordered the Sheriff summon him to appear at next Court to be sworn to his said Office[95] – 28 June 1750 (OCOB 5:260; Little, 179)

Alexander McDaniel as a Constable in this County took the Oaths required &c. and that he have for his Precincts the same that Elijah Morton had Extending from the Mouth of the Robinson, down between the road from the s^d Robinson and the River as low as the old Trap[96] – 26 July 1750 (OCOB 5:272; Little, 179)

Upon the Information of Alexander McDaniel, Constable, it is ordered the Attorney for the King enter a Prosecution against Thomas West for tending Seconds – 27 September 1750 (OCOB 5:282)

Rex ag^t Thomas West Deft On an Information The Deft. saith he is Not Guilty in manner and form as in the Information against him is alledged and of this he puts himself upon the Country and the Attorney for our Lord the King likewise. Therefore the Tryal of the issue is referred till next Court – 29 November 1751 (OCOB 5:337)

Our Sovereign Lord the King ag^t Thomas West, Deft. On an Information for Tending Seconds – The Deft. saith he is Not Guilty . . . a Jury . . . say the Deft is Guilty . . . Therefore it is considered by the Court the Deft . . . pay fifteen hundred pounds of tobacco . . . according to the Act of General Assembly . . . and also pay the costs – 26 April 1753 (OCOB 5:421)

Alexander McDaniel, a witness in behalf of our Sovereign Lord the King against Thomas West . . . ordered said West pay him four hundred fifty pounds of tobacco for eighteen days attendance at this Court according to Law – 26 April 1753 (OCOB 5:422)

County Levy (1750): To Alexander McDaniel Constable for [Viewing Tobacco fields]: 303 – 22 November 1750 (OCOB 5:285; Little, 180)

1751　County Levy (1751): To Alex^r McDaniel Constable by Acco^t: 320 – 29 November 1751 (OCOB 5:388; Little, 181)

1752　LIST: A List of Tythes for the year 1752 – Total 325 (Little, 28)

Alexander McDaniel added to his list two duties he had performed and the fees due him:
For Summoning an Inquest Jury at Arnolds House p^r 50
For Searching Margaret Bruce by an Order 7[97]

County Levy (1752): To <u>Alexander McDaniel</u> Constable for looking over Tobacco fields: 325
To Alexander McDaniel for summoning a Jury of Inquest on Abraham Direetson: 35 – 24 November 1752 (OCOB 5:395; Little 182)

1753 LIST: A List of Tithables for ye year 1753 – <u>Alex^r McDaniel</u> – 347 (Little, 30)
Alexander McDaniel added to his list two duties he had performed and the fees due him:
To summonsing a Jury upon Andrew Mannens P Servt fellow Natt 50 w^t Tobacco
To Summoning a Jury on a Inquest Erofs Nath^t 35

County Levy (1753): To Alex^r McDaniel [Constable] for [Viewing Tob^o fields]: 347 – 23 November 1753 (OCOB 5:512; Little, 184)

County Levy (1754): To Alex^r McDaniel for two County & Public Levys when Constable: 32 – 28 November 1754 (OCOB 6:56; Little, 185)

1754 On the Petition of Alexander McDaniel he is discharged from the Office of Constable and <u>John Morton</u> is appointed in his room and thereupon John Morton took the Oaths appointed by Law to his Majesty's person and government and repeated and subscribed the Test and took the Oaths required to be taken by Constables – 1 March 1754 (OCOB 5:514; Little, 184)

1755 On the Petition of John Morton, who has served as Constable for one year, <u>John Williams</u> is appointed Constable in his room and it is ordered that the Sheriff summon him to appear at next Court to be sworn into the Office – 27 February 1755 (OCOB 6:71; Little, 185)

John Williams took the Oaths to his Majesty's person and government and took and subscribed the Oath of Abjuration and Test and took all the Oaths required to be taken by Constables and is appointed Constable in the room and precinct of John Morton – 27 March 1755 (OCOB 6:78)

LIST: John Williams Constable His List of Tithables within His Per/inks (Little, 36–37)

County Levy (1755): To John Williams Constable for [Viewing tob^o fields]: 415 – 27 November 1755 (OCOB 6:184; Little, 186)

1756 <u>John Williams</u> *executed an attachment against the estate of William Williams* – 23 September 1756 (OCOB 6:266)

LIST: John Williams Consta^l Audit 418 (Little, 42–43)

County Levy (1756): To John Williams Constable for Viewing Tob^o fields: 418 – 25 November 1756 (OCOB 6:300; Little, 187)

1757 LIST: Account for suceers – <u>John Williams</u> C – In all 4-1-7 (Little, 46–47)

County Levy (1757): To John Williams Constable for [viewing Tobacco fields]: 417 – 24 November 1757 (OCOB 6:358; Little, 188)

1758   John Plunket being brought before the court by the Complaint of <u>John Williams</u>, Constable setting forth that John Plunket has resqued goods out of his hands after they had been seized by Execution and Williams and Plunket heard, John Plunket is discharged[98] – 27 April 1758 (OCOB 6:367)

LIST: A List of Tithables in the Precincts of John Williams Constable Orange 1758 – in all 380 (Little, 52–53)

County Levy (1758): To John Williams [Constable] for [Viewing Tob° fields]: 380 – 24 November 1758 (OCOB 6:442; Little, 188)

1759   LIST: A List of Tithes for y^e year 1759 – <u>John Williams</u> Constable $acco^t$ – In all 415 [*at the bottom of this list, the sum of the four columns is "410"*] (Little, 58–59)

County Levy (1759): To John Williams Constable for Viewing Tobacco fields: 410 – 22 November 1759 (OCOB 6:506; Little, 189)

1760   County Levy (1760): To <u>John Williams</u> Constable for viewing Tob° fields: 400 – 23 October 1760 (OCOB 6:547; Little, 190)

1761   <u>John Williams</u> . . . as Constable took the Oaths appointed by Act of Parliament instead of the Oaths of Allegiance and Supremacy and also repeated and subscribed the Test and the said Williams . . . took the several Oaths required by Constables – 25 June 1761 (OCOB 6:580)

LIST: A List of Tithables in the Precincts of John Williams Constable in $Orang^e$ – 1761 – W^ms Accot as Constable 417 (Little, 62–63)

County Levy (1761): To John Williams Constable for Viewing Tobacco fields: 417 – 27 November 1761 (OCOB 6:607; Little, 191)

1762   LIST: <u>John Williams</u> List of Tithables 1762 – John Williams Accot. 423 (Little, 64–65)

County Levy (1762): To John Williams Constable for Viewing Tob° fields: 423 – 28 October 1762 (OCOB 6:685; Little, 192)

1763   County Levy (1763): To <u>John Williams</u> Constable for Viewing Tob° fields: 443 – 22 October 1763 (OCOB 7:61; Little, 193)

1764   LIST: A List of tiths in my porsinct for the year 176[torn] – Papers Relating October Court 1764 – 491 (Little, 74–75)

County Levy (1764): To <u>John Williams</u> as Constable for [viewing Tob° Fields]: 491 – 25 October 1764 (OCOB 7:228; Little, 195)

<u>Arjalon Price Junr</u> as Constable in the Room of Manoah Singleton Took the Oaths to his Majestys Person and Goverment and repeated and subscribed the Test & Took the Several Oaths required to be taken by a constable[99] – 25 October 1764 (OCOB 7:231; Little, 195)

1765   <u>William Price</u> as Constable in the room of Arjalon Price j^r took the oaths to his Majestys person & Repeated and Subscribed the Test & Took the Several Oaths required to be Taken by a Constable – 23 May 1765 (OCOB 7:309; Little, 195)

LIST: A List wherein I have Viewed the Several Fields of Tobacco in the Precincts of which I am Appointed Constable, October 23^d 1765 – 427 (Little, 76–77)

County Levy (1765): To William Price [Constable] p^r acco^t: 427 – 28 November 1765 (OCOB 7:366; Little, 196)

1766   LIST: <u>William Price's</u> *Lift* for 1766 – 501 (Little, 82–83)

County Levy (1766): To [William Price] as Constable for viewing Tobacco fields & c: 501 To William Price for Guarding John Morgan one night: 20 – 27 November 1766 (OCOB 7:403)

1767   LIST: Orange County D^r to <u>Wm Price</u> Constable for Viewing tob^a fields – 568 Tithables (Little, 92–93)

Henry Field produced into Court a Certifiate for Hemp under the hand of Wm Price Constable – 22 October 1767 (OCOB 7:457)

County Levy (1767): To William Price [Constable] for [Viewing Tobacco Fields]: 568 – 27 November 1767 (OCOB 7:462; Little, 197)

1768   James Clark Overseer for Joseph Jones Esq produced into Court [two] Certificate[s] under the hand of <u>William Price</u> Constable . . . [for] hemp – 28 April and 27 October 1768 (OCOB 7:482, 528)

LIST: Wm Price – 524 (Little, 96–97)

County Levy (1768): To William Price [Constable] for [Viewing Tobacco Fields]: 524 – 24 November 1768 (OCOB 7:537; Little, 198)

1769   LIST: <u>William Prics</u> List of Tiths for the y^r 1769 – 552 (Little, 100–101)

County Levy (1769): To William Price [Constable] p^r [Account for Viewing Tob^o fields &c]: 552 – 26 October 1769 (OCOB 8:39; Little, 199)

On 7 November 1769, the Virginia legislature repealed the acts ordering constables to view tobacco fields.

ORANGE II

The constable precinct in southeast "Orange" County—what I call Orange II—was described as "from the Southside of the Mountain Road up to the Chappel" in 1735 and "from the Wilderness Run along the South side of the South West Mountain Road up to the Plantation of James Coleman, Gent, extending to the County Line" in 1749. In 1753, 1760 and 1763, the court divided Orange II into two precincts; then, in 1756, 1761, 1764 and 1768, these subprecincts were reunited. The first division of Orange II, in 1753, was from the "South Side the North Fork of the North anna up to the Mountain Road & to the County line" (Orange II-A). Roger Bell, constable of this precinct, called it the "forck of permunkey" on his 1753 tobacco planter list. The remaining part of Orange II (Orange II-B) was between the North Fork of the Northanna (the Pamunkey River), the Southwest Mountain Road and the Spotsylvania County line. In 1760, the court appointed Samuel Faulconer constable "all between the Mountain Road down by Capt Caves & the Pamunkey Road down by John Pendletons down to the County Line" (Orange II-B). In 1763, Manoah Singleton was appointed constable "all below the Pamunkey road about a mile below the Church down over Terry's Run to the County Line and between the said Line and the Road that passes by Cave's Ordinary" (Orange II-B).

All these orders describe the same boundaries using different landmarks (see Map 2). The northern border, "Southside of the Mountain Road" and "the Mountain Road down by Capt Caves" (Capt. Benjamin Cave lived below the Southwest Mountain Road near Rhoadesville), was the Southwest Mountain Road (approximating Route 20).[100] The eastern border, "Wilderness Run," was the Spotsylvania County line. The "County Line" was understood by the constables in 1749 and 1753 to be the Louisa County line, and in 1760 and 1763 it was understood to be the Spotsylvania County line. The western border of Orange II was described as the "[Southwest Mountain] Chappel" in 1735, "up [west] to the Plantation of James Coleman" in 1749, "up to the Mountain Road" in 1753 and "the Pamunkey Road about a mile below the [Middle] Church" in 1763. The Southwest Mountain Church (renamed the Middle Church in 1744) was built in 1735 a little north of the older Southwest Mountain Chapel in the vicinity of Church Run below the Southwest Mountain Road.[101] The "Mountain Road"—one of several in Orange County—ran east of today's Route 15 along the eastern foot of the Southwest Mountains, from the Albemarle or Louisa County line to the Middle Church to the Southwest Mountain Road. James Coleman's land, on the head of Negro Run, was near this Mountain Road.[102] So the western border of Orange II was along or near the Mountain Road which ran from the head of Negro Run on the county's southern border north to the Southwest Mountain Road above the Southwest Mountain (Middle) Church.

The dividing line between Orange II-A and Orange II-B was "the North Fork of the North anna" (the Pamunkey River) or "the Pamunkey Road," which ran a little north of the river and joined the Southwest Mountain Road above the Middle Church.[103] That the same tobacco planters appear on the Orange II-A and on the Orange II-B lists in 1753, 1760 and 1763, confirms these subprecincts were always divided by the same boundary line.

The names of the tobacco planters on the twenty Orange II lists, dating from 1737 to 1768, show the population changes to be expected from one year to the next: some planters leave or die, some arrive and some—like Roger Bell, Joseph Reynolds, Malachi Chiles, John Stevens—appear on all, or almost all, Orange II lists. Over these 31 years, the number of planters in the precinct grew from 44 to 131. From 1 to 17 tithables lived in the households of these planters, averaging 2.5 to 4.2 tithables per household. The total number of tithables of tobacco planters in Orange II, recorded in twenty-nine annual county levies, increased from 102 in 1737 to 498 in 1770 (see table 2). In 1756, 22 percent of the tithables of tobacco planters in "Orange" and "Greene" Counties lived in Orange II.

ORANGE II (1735–1752)

This precinct was described as "on Pamunkey . . . from the Southside of the Mountain Road up to the Chappell" in 1735 and "from the Wilderness Run along the South side of the South West Mountain Road up to the Plantation of James Coleman, Gent, extending to the County Line" in 1749.

| 1735 | John Henderson on Pamunkey is hereby appointed Constable from the Southside of the Mountain Road up to the Chappell & it is ordered that the Sheriff Summons the said Henderson to the next Court to be held for this County to be Sworn into the said Office – 18 February 1734/35 (OCOB 1:5; Little, 152) |

1736   Ordered that George Smith be Constable in the room of John Henderson and that he Summon the said Smith before a Justice to be sworn accordingly into the said Office – 16 March 1735/36 (OCOB 1:58; Little, 153)

1737   LIST: A Lift of Tithables Within the precints Whereof I am Conftable – Geo Smith – pr 102 – 27 Oct 1737 (Little, 9)

County Levy (1737): To George Smith [Constable for viewing tobacco]: 102 – 27 October 1737 (OCOB 1:233; Little, 155)

1738   George Smith

1739   Henry Rice is hereby appointed Constable in the room of Robert [George] Smith and its ordered that the Sheriff Sumon the s^d Rice to appear at ye next Court to be Sworn into ye s^d Office according to Law[104] – 24 May 1739 (OCOB 1:463; Little, 158)

LIST: A List of the Tithables in my Precinct – p me Henry Rice Constable – 117 (Little, 21)

County Levy (1739): To Henry Rice Constable: 117 – 22 November 1739 (OCOB 2:85; Little, 160)

1740   John Mallory having taken ye oaths appointed by Act of Parliament & Subscribed ye Test took ye oaths appointed by a late Act of Afsembly was Sworn Constable in ye room of Henry Rice – 22 May 1740 (OCOB 2:165; Little, 161)

County Levy (1740): To John Mallory Constable: 125 – 23 October 1740 (OCOB 2:275; Little, 163)

1741   John Mallory

1742   Malachy Chiles is hereby appointed Constable in the room of John Mallory & its ordered that he be fummoned to appear at the next Court to be Sworn into the said Office – 25 February 1741/42 (OCOB 3:99; Little, 165)

Malachi Chiles [and another] having taken the oaths appointed by Acts of Parliament & Subscribed the Test were Sworn Conftables accordingly – 25 March 1742 (OCOB 3:113)

County Levy (1742): To Malachi Chiles Conſtable: 135 – 25 November 1742 (OCOB 3:294; Little, 167)

1743 Robert Bickers is hereby appointed Conſtable in the room of Malachi Chiles and its ordered that the said Chiles ſummon him to appear before a Justice of ye Peace of this County to be ſworn in the s^d Office accordingly[105] – 26 May 1743 (OCOB 3:426; Little, 168)

County Levy (1743): To Robert Bickers for viewing tob^o fields as Constable: 139 – 24 November 1743 (OCOB 4:27; Little, 169)

1744 County Levy (1744): To Robt Bickers as p^r Constable for Viewing Tobacco Fields: 201 – 25 October 1744 (OCOB 4:224; Little, 171)

1745 John Mallory is by the Court appointed Constable in the room of Robert Bickers who is discharged from that office and the said Mallory was sworn into his said office and Took the Oaths appointed by the Tobacco Law – 23 May 1745 (OCOB 4:328; Little, 172)

County Levy (1745): To John Mallory Constable for Viewing Tobacco Fields: 208 – 29 November 1745 (OCOB 4:448; Little, 174)

1746 County Levy (1746): To John Mallery Constable for viewing Tob^o Fields: 99 – 27 November 1746 (OCOB 4A:103; Little, 175)

1747 Thomas Gahagan is by the Court Appointed Constable in This County in the Room of John Mallory Who is Discharged from that Office & it is Ordered that he be sworn into his said Office at the next Court – 28 May 1747 (OCOB 4A:150; Little, 176)

Thomas Gahagan having taken the usual Oaths to his Majesties Person and Government & Took & subscribed the Abjuration Oath & the Test was sworn Constable in this County in the room of John Mallory & took the Oath Appointed by the Tobacco Law – 25 June 1747 (OCOB 4A:173; Little, 176)

County Levy (1747): To Thomas Gahagan for Viewing Tobacco Fields: 133 – 27 November 1747 (OCOB 5:81; Little, 176)

County Levy (1750): To Thomas Gahagon for viewing Tob^o fields in 1748 [*sic*] omitted to be Levied – 100[106] – 22 November 1750 (OCOB 5:285; Little, 180)

1748 John Henderson took the Oaths to his Majesty's Person & Government and took the Oath of Abjuration and subscribed the Test and was sworn a Constable in this County then took the Oath appointed by the Tobacco Law[107] – 26 May 1748 (OCOB 5:117; Little, 177)

John Chapman is by the Court appointed Constable in the room of Thomas Gahagan and thereupon he took the Oaths to his Majesty's Person & Government and the Oath of Abjuration and subscribed the Test and was sworn Constable, and then took the Oath appointed by the Tobacco Law – 23 June 1748 (OCOB 5:135)

County Levy (1748): To John Chapman for [viewing Tobacco Fields]: 241 – 24 November 1748 (OCOB 5:158; Little, 178)

1749	Stephen Smith Noblet is by the Court appointed Constable in the room of John Chapman and it is ordered that he be sworn into the s^d Office at the next Court[108] – 25 February 1748/49 (OCOB 5:175; Little, 178)

James Mitchell [Little has James Mikhell] is by the Court appointed Constable from the Wilderness Run along the South side of the South West Mountain Road up to the Plantation of James Coleman, Gent., extending to the County Line. Whereupon he took the Oaths to his Majesty's Person and Government, the Abjuration Oath and subscribed the Test was sworn Constable and took the Oaths appointed by the Tobacco Laws[109] – 22 June 1749 (OCOB 5:182; Little, 178)

LIST: Acount of thes Tithabell In my presPe – p^r me James Mitchull – 312 (Little, 25)

County Levy (1749): To James Mitchel for [viewing Tobacco Fields]: 312 – 24 November 1749 (OCOB 5:233; Little, 179)

1750	James Cox is appointed Constable in the Precincts and room of James Mitchel [Little has James Mikhel] who has served in that Office above a year, and it is ordered the Sheriff summon said Cox to appear at the next Court to be sworn to his said Office accordingly – 28 June 1750 (OCOB 5:260; Little, 179)

James Cox as a Constable in the County in the room and Precincts of John Mitchel took the Oaths to his Majesties Person and Government and the Oath of Abjuration and subscribed the Test and then took the Oath of a Constable and the Oath appointed by the Tobacco Law – 26 July 1750 (OCOB 5:272; Little, 179)

County Levy (1750): To James Cox Constable for Viewing Tobacco fields: 318 – 22 November 1750 (OCOB 5:285; Little, 180)

1751	County Levy (1751): To James Cox Constable by Acco^t: 232 – 29 November 1751 (OCOB 5:338; Little, 181)

Joseph Chandler is appointed Constable in this County in the Room of James Cox, who is discharged from that Office, and it is ordered said Joseph be summoned to appear at the next Court to be sworn into his Office – 26 September 1751 (OCOB 5:322; Little, 180)

Joseph Chandler as a Constable in this County in the room of James Cox took the Oaths to his Majesty's Person and Government and the Oath of Abjuration and subscribed the Test and then took the Oath of a Constable and also the Oath appointed by the Tobacco Law – 29 November 1751 (OCOB 5:337; Little, 181)

1752	Joseph Chandler

ORANGE II-A AND ORANGE II-B (1753–1755)
In 1753, the court divided Orange II into two precincts: Orange II-A, "on the South side the North Fork of the North anna up to the Mountain Road & to the County line"; and Orange II-B, the remainder of Orange II, between the North Fork of the North Anna (Pamunkey River), Southwest Mountain Road and the Spotsylvania County line.

ORANGE II-A (1753–1755)

1753   Roger Bell is appointed Constable in this County on the South side the North Fork of the North anna up to the Mountain Road & to the County line and ordered the Sheriff summon him to appear at next Court to be sworn into his Office[110] – 22 February 1753 (OCOB 5:411; Little, 182)

Roger Bell . . . as Constables took the Oaths to his Majesty's Person and Government and the Abjuration Oath and repeated and subscribed the Test . . . and . . . the Oaths of a Constable and the Oath appointed by the Tobacco Law and Preservation of the Breed of Deer – 26 April 1753 (OCOB 5:413)

LIST: A list of the tythables in the forck of permunkey 1753 – p^r Roger Bell Constable – In all 197[111] (Little, 31)

County Levy (1753): To Roger Bell Constable for Viewing Tob^o fields: 197 – 23 November 1753 (OCOB 5:512; Little, 184)

1754   Thomas Graves is appointed Constable in the room and Precincts of Roger Bell and it is ordered Thomas Graves be summoned to appear at next Court to be sworn into his Office – 25 April 1754 (OCOB 6:2; Little, 184)

Thomas Graves as Constable took the Oaths to his Majesty's person and government and repeated and subscribed the Test and also took all the Oaths required to be taken by him as Constable and hath for his Precincts the same that Roger Bell was late Constable of – 23 May 1754 (OCOB 6:4; Little, 185)

LIST: A list of tythables in the Sub^{es} perints – Thomas Graves Con^{ble} – In all 221 (Little, 32)

County Levy (1754): To Thomas Graves Constable for Viewing Tob^o fields: 221 – 28 November 1754 (OCOB 6:56; Little, 185)

1755   On the motion of Thomas Graves, who has served as Constable for one year last past, Reubin Daniel is appointed in his room and it is ordered that the Sheriff summon him to appear at next Court to be sworn into his Office – 25 April 1755 (OCOB 6:110; Little, 186)

John Henderson is appointed Constable in the room of Thomas Graves and it is ordered the Sheriff summon him to next Court to be sworn into the Office – 26 June 1755 (OCOB 6:123; Little, 186)

LIST: A Memorandum of The List of Titheables in my precincts of Soucor fees – 236 (Little, 35)

County Levy (1755): To Thomas Graves Constable for Viewing tob^o fields: 236 – 27 November 1755 (OCOB 6:184; Little, 186)

ORANGE II-B (1753–1755)

1753   John Gollorthun is appointed Constable in this County in the room of Joseph Chandler who is discharged from that Office and it is ordered the Sheriff summon said Gollorthun to appear at the next Court to be sworn into his Office – 23 May 1752 (OCOB 5:391; Little, 182)

> John Gollorthun as a Constable in this County in the room and Precinct of Joseph Chandler, late Constable, took the Oaths to his Majesty's Person and Government and the Oath of Abjuration and repeated and subscribed the Test and then took the Oath of a Constable and also the Oath appointed by the Tobacco Law – 22 February 1753 (OCOB 5:411; Little, 182)

1754 Lawrence Harrison is appointed Constable in this County in the room of John Gollorthun who hath removed himself out of this County, and it is ordered that the Sheriff summon Lawrence Harrison to appear at next court to be sworn into his Office – 1 March 1754 (OCOB 5:522; Little, 184)

Charles Harrison as Constable took the Oath to his Majesty's person and government and repeated and subscribed the Test and also took all the Oaths required to be taken as a Constable and hath for his Precinct the same that John Gollorthun lately had[112] – 28 March 1754 (OCOB 5:528; Little, 184)

LIST: February 1754 – 203 (Little, 33)

County Levy (1754): To Charles Harrison [Constable] for [Viewing Tob^o fields]: 203 – 28 November 1754 (OCOB 6:56; Little, 185)

1755 Joseph Reynolds is appointed Constable in the room of Charles Harrison, and it is ordered the Sheriff summon him to next Court to be sworn into the Office – 26 June 1755 (OCOB 6:124; Little, 186)

Ordered that Joseph Rennolds be summoned to appear at next Court to be sworn Constable in the room of Charles Harrison[113] – 25 July 1755 (OCOB 6:148)

ORANGE II (1756–1759)
In 1756, Benjamin Cave replaced Thomas Graves, constable of Orange II-A; however, there is no mention in the court orders about the replacement of either Joseph Reynolds or Charles Harrison, the 1755 Orange II-B constables. Even though there was no court order to reunify Orange II in 1756, the fact that Cave reported almost the same number of tithables in 1756 and in 1757 (332 and 382) as the combined number of tithables reported by the Orange II-A and Orange II-B constables in 1754 (221 + 203) and the fact that almost all the names on the 1754 Orange II-A and Orange II-B tobacco planter lists appear on the 1756, 1757, 1758 and 1759 Orange II lists, prove this to be the case.

1756 Benjamin Cave ju^r is Appointed Constable in the room of Thos Graves – 26 February 1756 (OCOB 6:201; Little, 186)

Benjamin Cave, Junr. as Constable took the Oaths appointed to be taken by Act of Parliament instead of the Oaths of Allegiance and Supremacy and took and subscribed the Oath of Abjuration and subscribed the Test and . . . all the Oaths required to be taken as Constable – 26 February 1756 (OCOB 6:203)

LIST: A List of the tythables in the Sub^{es} percints 1756 – Ben Cave Constab^l acco^t 332 (Little, 40)

County Levy (1756): To Benjamin Cave Constable for [Viewing Tob° fields]: 332 – 25 November 1756 (OCOB 6:300; Little, 187)

1757   LIST: The above is acco^t due for view.g tob° fields – 1757 – Ben Cave – Total 382 (Little, 49–50)

County Levy (1757): To Benjamin Cave Constable for viewing Tobacco fields: 382 – 24 November 1757 (OCOB 6:358; Little, 188)

1758   William Cook as Constable took the Oaths to his Majesty's person and government and repeated and subscribed the Test and . . . the Oaths required as Constable and is in the room and Precinct of Benjamin Cave – 27 April 1758 (OCOB 6:367)

LIST: A List of Tithables in the Subscribers precincts 1758 – William Cooke Con^t – in all 437 (Little, 54–55)

County Levy (1758): To William Cook Constable for Viewing Tob° fields: 436 – 24 November 1758 (OCOB 6:442; Little, 188)

1759   LIST: 1759 – in all 430 – Cr^t Ex^{ed} p^r Wm Cooke (Little, 57–58)

County Levy (1759): To William Cook Constable for Viewing Tobacco fields: 396 – 22 November 1759 (OCOB 6:506; Little, 189)

ORANGE II-A AND ORANGE II-B (1760)

In 1760, the court again divided Orange II when they appointed Samuel Faulconer constable "all between the Mountain Road down by Capt Caves & the Pamunkey Road down by John Pendletons down to the County Line" (Orange II-B). William Cooke, the 1759 constable of Orange II, continued as constable of the remainder of Orange II (Orange II-A). Because the same planters appear on the 1755 and 1760 Orange II-A lists and the 1754 and 1760 Orange II-B lists, the court ordered the same division of Orange II in 1753 and 1760.

ORANGE II-A (1760)

1760   LIST: Will Cook constable accot – 172 (Little, 61)

County Levy (1760): To William Cook [Constable] for [viewing Tob° fields]: 172 – 23 October 1760 (OCOB 6:547; Little, 190)

ORANGE II-B (1760)

1760   Ordered that Samuel Faulkner be summoned to appear at next Court to be sworn a Constable – 25 April 1760 (OCOB 6:531)

Samuel Faulconer as Constable took the Oaths to be taken by Act of Parliament instead of the Oaths of Allegiance and Supremacy and took and subscribed the Oath of Abjuration and repeated and subscribed the Test and . . . took the several Oaths required as Constable – 22 May 1760 (OCOB 6:533)

Ordered that Saml Faulconer Constable have for his precincts all between the Mountain Road down by Capt Caves & the Pamunkey Road down by John Pendletons down to the

County Line – 22 May 1760 (OCOB 6:533; Little, 190)

LIST: 1760 – Sworn to by Sam¹ Faulkner Constable – 150 (Little, 60)

County Levy (1760): To Samuel Faulkner Constable for Viewing Tob° fields: 150 – 28 November 1760 (OCOB 6:549; Little, 190)

ORANGE II (1761–1762)

In 1761, Benjamin Cave was again constable of Orange II. Although the court directed Cave to replace only William Cook and not both Cook and Samuel Faulconer and there was no order to reunite Orange II-A and Orange II-B, the fact that almost the same number of tithables were reported by Cave in 1761 (396) as were reported by Cook and Faulconer in 1760 (Orange II-A: 172 + Orange II-B: 150), shows the precinct was reunited in 1761.

1761   Benjamin Cave as Constable took the Oaths appointed by Act of Parliament instead of the Oaths of Allegiance and Supremacy and also repeated and subscribed the Test and the said . . . Cave took the several Oaths required by Constables and the said Cave is in the Precincts whereof William Cook was late Constable – 25 June 1761 (OCOB 6:580)

Ordered that the Sheriff pay to Benjamin Cave, Constable, three hundred and ninety six pounds of tobacco for his Account for viewing tobacco fields out of the Deposit in the said Sheriffs hands – 25 February 1762 (OCOB 6:614; Little, 191)

1762   Benjamin Cave, Constable, who was sick and could not come at the laying the County Levy now produced his Account for viewing tobacco fields amounting to four hundred and eleven pounds of Tobacco and being sworn to the services, it is ordered that the Sheriff pay that sum of tobacco to him out of the Deposit in his hands – 24 March 1763 (OCOB 6:696; Little, 192)

ORANGE II-A AND ORANGE II-B (1763)

In 1763, the court appointed Manoah Singleton constable "all below the Pamunkey road about a mile below the Church down over Terry's Run to the County Line and between the said Line and the road that passes by Cave's Ordinary" (Orange II-B), and Benjamin Cave continued as constable of the remainder of Orange II (Orange II-A). The names of tobacco planters on the 1763 Orange II-A and Orange II-B tobacco planter lists are the same as the names on the earlier Orange II-A and Orange II-B lists, therefore the boundary between the two precincts was the same.

ORANGE II-A (1763)

1763   LIST: Ben Cave acco – 257 – Nov Levy Levied 1763 (Little, 69)

County Levy (1763): To Benja^n Cave [Constable] for [Viewing Tob° fields]: 257 – 26 November 1763 (OCOB 7:82; Little, 194)

ORANGE II-B (1763)

1763   Manoah Singleton as Constable took the Oaths to be taken by Act of Parliament instead of the Oaths of Allegiance and Supremacy and repeated and subscribed the Test and also took the Oath of Abjuration and the several Oaths required as Constable and has for his Precinct all below the Pamunkey road about a mile below the Church down over Terry's Run to the County Line and between the said Line and the Road that passes by Cave's Ordinary – 28 April 1763 (OCOB 6:716; Little, 192)

John Conner, Junr. as Constable took the Oaths appointed to be taken by Act of Parliament instead of the Oaths of Allegiance and Supremacy and repeated and subscribed the Test and the said Conner took the Oath of Constable and has for his Precinct the bounds of Capt. Daniel's [militia] Company[114] – 25 August 1763 (OCOB 7:33)

LIST: aliſt of tiths for Manoah Singleton in his pirſinks aſrucker hunting in orange county – 141 (Little, 68)

County Levy (1763): To Manoah Singleton Constable for Viewing Tob^o fields: 141 – 26 November 1763 (OCOB 7:82; Little, 194)

ORANGE II (1764–1766)
In 1764, Manoah Singleton replaced Benjamin Cave. Since no one replaced Singleton, and the 432 tithables on Singleton's 1764 tobacco planter list almost equals the total of tithables on the 1763 Orange II-A (257) and Orange II-B (141) lists, and since almost all the names on Singleton's 1764 list appear on the 1763 Orange II-A and Orange II-B lists, it is clear that the court again reunited Orange II.

1764   Ordered that Manoah Singleton Constable have for his precincts the Same that Benjamin Cave late Constable had – 24 November 1763 (OCOB 7:64; Little, 193)

LIST: Manoah Singleton's Liſt tithes – 432 (Little, 72–73)
Manoah Singleton added to his list a duty he had performed and the fee due him:
Sum[mon] of jury on inquest 35

County Levy (1764): To Manoah Singleton as Constable for [viewing Tob^o Fields]: 432 – 25 October 1764 (OCOB 7:228; Little, 195)

Arjalon Price Junr as Constable in the Room of Manoah Singleton Took the Oaths to his Majestys Person and Goverment and repeated and subscribed the Test & Took the Several Oaths required to be taken by a constable[115] – 25 October 1764 (OCOB 7:231; Little, 195)

1765   John Oaks as Constable in the Room of Arjalon Price Junr Took the oaths to his Majestys Person and Government and repeated and subscribed the Test and Took the Several Oaths required to be Taken by a Constable – 28 March 1765 (OCOB 7:271; Little, 195)

LIST: 1765 John Oakes Constable – A List of Tithes in my Percintes – in all 371 [361 is written as the total of his four columns] (Little, 79–80)

County Levy (1765): To John Oaks Constable p^r Accot.: 361 – 28 November 1765 (OCOB 7:366; Little, 196)

1766   LIST: John Oakes List of Tiths in my percincts 1766 – 402 (Little, 86–87)

County Levy (1766): To John Oakes for [viewing Tobacco fields & c]: 402 – 27 November 1766 (OCOB 7:403; Little, 196)

ORANGE II AND ORANGE III (1767)

In 1767, Edmund Burrus, who replaced John Oakes, compiled a list of tobacco planters with almost twice as many tithables as were reported for Orange II in 1766. The names on Burrus' list are the same as those on John Oakes' 1766 Orange II list plus about twenty names of planters—large landowners like the Taylors, James Madison, John Baylor, Richard Beale—who lived west and northwest of Orange II and who had previously been counted on the Orange III tobacco planter lists. There is nothing in the court orders about Burrus expanding his precinct to include these Orange III landowners. (In 1767, the court did not credit the Orange III constable, William Leak, for viewing the tobacco fields in his precinct.)

1767 Edmund Burrus as Constable in the Room of John Oaks Took the Oaths to his Majestys person and Government and repeated and Subscribed the Test and took the Several Oaths required to be taken by a Constable – 26 February 1767 (OCOB 7:410; Little, 197)

LIST: Edmon Burrus Et 1767 – 743 (Little, 88–89)

County Levy (1767): To Edmund Burrus Constable for Viewing Tobacco Fields: 743 – 27 November 1767 (OCOB 7:462; Little, 197)

ORANGE II (1768–1770)

In 1768, only tobacco planters living in the Orange II precinct appear on Edmund Burrus' list: the same names appear on Burrus' 1768 and John Oakes' 1766 tobacco planter lists.

1768 LIST: 1768 – p^r Edward Burrus 453 – Edm^d Burrus 453 (Little, 94–95)

County Levy (1768): To Edmund Burrus [Constable] for [Viewing Tobacco Fields]: 453 – 24 November 1768 (OCOB 7:537; Little, 198)

1769 County Levy (1769): To Edmund Burris Constable for Viewing Tobacco Fields 476 ^{pd} Tobo to be paid out of the Deposit that is in the Sheriffs hands – 23 November 1769 (OCOB 8:46; Little, 199)

Although the Virginia legislature repealed the acts ordering constables to view tobacco fields on 7 November 1769, Edmund Burrus (and the constables of Orange III and Orange IV) was credited for performing this duty in 1770.

1770 County Levy (for 1770): To Edmund Burrus [as Constable] by Account: 498 – 28 March 1771 (OCOB 8:105; Little, 200)

ORANGE III

The Orange III constable precinct, in the center of what is now Orange and Greene Counties, was formed in 1738 when the court ordered William Bell "to look after Succors from James Taylors Quarter to ye County Line." The names on the 1738 and 1739 Orange III tobacco planter lists show that this precinct was formed from Orange IV and a small part of Orange I and included the huge land patents of Henry Willis, William Todd, Thomas Chew, James Madison, John Baylor and James Taylor, some of whom did not appear on any of the earlier lists of tobacco planters. The only other description of this precinct was in 1761 when Joseph Rogers was appointed constable "all above John Williams up to Blue Run between the Precincts of Benjamin Cave and the River." So the boundaries of Orange III were from the Rapidan River in the north ("from James Taylors Quarter") to the "[Hanover] County line" in the south and from the Blue Run east to the borders of Orange I ("all above [west of] John Williams," the 1761 constable of Orange I) and Orange II ("the Precincts of Benjamin Cave," the 1761 constable of Orange II). The eastern border ran from the Rapidan at the mouth of the Robinson River, down an unidentified road east of James Taylor's property to the Southwest Mountain Road above the Middle Church, then continued along the eastern foot of the Southwest Mountains to the Hanover County line near the head of Negro Run.[116] The oldest and largest Orange County land patents, which were granted the prosperous families of John Baylor, David Bray, Thomas Chew, James Madison, James Taylor, William Todd and Henry Willis, were in this precinct. "These patents, the last of which came six years before Orange County was formed, locked up almost all of the best soil in the area."[117]

In 1763, the boundaries of Orange III changed when the court ordered the boundaries of neighboring Orange IV be "from the great Run the boundary Between Capt Bells & Capt Scotts Company down to the Blue Run & thence along the road by Mr Madisons to his Mill & thence up the road by Mr Colemans & all on the West side the s^d Road." This transferred the southern half of Orange III—below a line running east-west from Madison's Mill on Madison Run through James Madison's property to the Blue Run then to the Rapidan in the vicinity of Liberty Mills—to Orange IV (see Map 2).

But the names on many of the Orange III tobacco planter lists show that there was often confusion about the borders of this precinct. The large properties above the Southwest Mountain Road—Baylor, Taylor and Taliaferro—appear on all Orange III tobacco planter lists. However, many of the planters who lived below this road appear, disappear and reappear one year to the next on the Orange III lists. For example, James Madison, Capt. John or Johnny Scott, and the Beale family, who lived south of the Southwest Mountain Road in the center of Orange III, appear on seventeen tobacco planter lists between 1738 and 1769: half of the time they appear on Orange III lists and the other half they appear on Orange II or Orange IV lists. In 1739, James Coleman and three other planters, who lived on the western border of Orange II, appear on both the Orange II and the Orange III tobacco planter lists, but their tithable numbers are crossed out on the Orange II list. James Madison appears on two tobacco planter lists in 1753: on the Orange III list with twenty tithables and on the Orange II-A list with seven tithables; he appears on two lists in 1764: Orange III with four tithables and Orange IV with twenty-five tithables; and he appears on two lists in 1768: Orange II with six tithables and Orange IV with nine tithables. (On the 1766 and the 1769 Orange III tobacco planter lists, James Madison has, respectively, forty-two and thirty-three tithables.) And, in 1767, more than half of the Orange III tobacco planters—all the large landowners—appear on the

Orange II tobacco planter list, but there was no court order for the Orange II constable to so expand his tobacco viewing territory.

Even though the boundaries of Orange III changed over the years, and the constables were often confused about which tobacco fields were in their precinct, the twelve Orange III tobacco planter lists show that over a period of thirty-one years, the number of planters in this precinct ranged from 27 to 66. From 1 to 56 tithables lived in the households of these planters, averaging 5 to 9 tithables per household. The total number of tithables of tobacco planters in Orange III, recorded in eighteen annual county levies, ranged from 170 to 588 (see table 2). This precinct had the smallest number of tobacco planters—many of whom were very prosperous—with the largest average number of tithables in their households. In 1756, 26 percent of the tithables of tobacco planters in "Orange" and "Greene" Counties lived in Orange III.

ORANGE III (1738–1762)
This precinct was described as "from James Taylors Quarter to ye County Line" in 1738 and "all above John Williams up to Blue Run between the Precincts of Benjamin Cave and the River" in 1761.

1738 Wm Bell is hereby appointed Constable and its ordered that he look after Succors from James Taylors Quarter to ye County Line And its further ordered that he go before a Justice of ye Peace for this County to be Sworn into ye said Office accordingly – 27 April 1738 (OCOB 1:300; Little, 156)

LIST: A list of tithables in my precint – p^r Me W Bells, Conſtable 170 (Little, 14)

County Levy (1738): To William Bell Constable for counting tobacco Succours: 170 – 26 October 1738 (OCOB 1:393; Little, 157)

1739   Elijah Daniel is hereby appointed Constable in the room of Wm Bell who is hereby ordered to Sumon ye s^d Elijah before some Justice of ye Peace for this County to be Sworn into ye s^d Office accordingly – 22 March 1738/39 (OCOB 1:437; Little, 158)

Elijah Daniel having taken the oaths & Subscribed the Test was Sworn Constable then took the oaths prescribed by a Late Act of Aſsembly – 24 May 1739 (OCOB 1:479)

LIST: The Liſt of tithes wherin I am Conſtable for the year 1739 – In all the Liſt of tithes coms to 250 by me Elijah Daniel conſtable (Little, 19)

County Levy (1739): To Elijah Daniel [Constable for Succors]: 196 – 25 October 1739 (OCOB 2:80; Little, 160)

1740 Wm Bell is hereby appointed Constable in ye room of Elijah Daniel & its ordered that he be Sumoned by the Sheriff to ye next Court to be Sworn in ye s^d Office accordingly – 27 March 1740 (OCOB 2:133; Little, 160)

Robert Bickers having taken ye oaths appointed by Act of Parliament & Subscribed ye Test took ye oaths appointed by a late Act of Aſsembly & was Sworn Conſtable in ye room of Elijah Daniel & Wm Bell who last Court was appointed is discharged having lately been Constable[118] – 22 May 1740 (OCOB 2:165; Little, 161)

County Levy (1740): To Rob{{t}} Bickers Constable: 193

To Rob{{t}} Bickers for guarding Sweeny & Johnſton three days: 75 – 23 October 1740 (OCOB 2:275; Little, 163)

1741 <u>Robert Bickers</u>?

1742 <u>Solomon Ryon</u> is hereby appointed Conſtable in the upper part of James Whitings precinct & its ordered that he be ſummoned to appear at next Court to be ſworn in the said office accordingly[119] – 22 July 1742 (OCOB 3:167; Little, 166)

Solomon Ryon Conſtable came into Court & took the oaths appointed by a late Act of Aſsembly – 26 August 1742 (OCOB 3:201)

County Levy (1742): To Solomon Ryon Conſtable: 217 – 25 November 1742 (OCOB 3:294; Little, 166)

Solomon Ryon *executed an attachment against the estate of Benjamin Horn* – 27 November 1742 (OCOB 3:304)

1743 County Levy (1743): To <u>Solomon Ryon</u> for viewing tob^o fields as Constable: 237 – 24 November 1743 (OCOB 4:27; Little, 169)

1744–45 <u>Solomon Ryon</u>

1746 <u>Peter Rucker</u> is by the Court appointed Constable in this County in the Room of Solomon Ryon who is Discharged from that Office and it is Ordered that he be sworn into his said office at the Next court – 26 February 1745/46 (OCOB 4:457; Little, 174)

Peter Rucker [and another] took the Usual Oaths to his Majesty's Person & Government and took & Subscribed the Abjuration and Test and took the Oaths appointed by the Tobacco Law and Swore into the Office of Constable – 26 June 1746 (OCOB 4:489; Little, 175)

County Levy (1746): To Peter Rucker [Constable for viewing Tobacco Fields]: 416 – 27 November 1746 (OCOB 4A:103; Little, 175)

1747 William M{{c}}Donaugh is by the Court Appointed Constable in this County in the room of <u>Peter Rucker</u> who is Discharged from that office and it is ordered that he be sworn into his said Office at the next Court – 28 May 1747 (OCOB 4A:150; Little, 176)

1748 <u>Zachary Gibbs</u> is by the Court appointed Constable in the room of Peter Rucker who is discharged from that Office, and it is ordered that he be sworn into his said Office before a Justice of this County and be summoned to take the other Oaths at next Court – 23 June 1748 (OCOB 5:140)

1749 <u>John Moran</u> as a Constable in this County in the room of Zachary Gibs took the Oaths to his Majesty's Person and Government and the Oath of Abjuration and subscribed the Test and took the Oath of a Constable and the Oath appointed by the Tobacco Laws – 26 January 1748/49 (OCOB 5:159; Little, 178)

Dunkin Bohannan is by the Court appointed Constable in the room of John Morin who is discharged from that Office and it is ordered that Dunkin be sworn into his Office at the next Court – 22 June 1749 (OCOB 5:182; Little, 178)

1750   William McDonough is appointed Constable – 28 June 1750 (Little, 179)

William McDonough as a Constable in the Precincts whereof Peter Rucker was Constable, took the Oaths to his Majesties Person and Government and the Oath of Abjuration and subscribed the Test and then took the Oath of a Constable and the Oath appointed by the Tobacco Law[120] – 26 July 1750 (OCOB 5:272; Little, 179)

County Levy (1750): To William McDonough Constable for [Viewing Tobacco fields]: 253 – 22 November 1750 (OCOB 5:285; Little, 180)

1751   John Grigsby came into Court and informed the Court that pursuant to Certificate from a Justice he carried a runaway to William McDonough, Constable, who refused to take the runaway into his custody. Its therefore ordered the Sheriff summon said McDonough to appear at next Court to answer the Complaint[121] – 24 January 1750/51 (OCOB 5:287)

The Pet[ition] of William Donaught Humbly Begs that your Worships will allow me my Tobacco for Sucker Hunting Last year according to the list I sent your worships[122] – undated (Orange County Judgments)

Ordered William McDonaugh be allowed two hundred thirty nine pounds of tobacco for viewing Tobacco Fields as Constable in the year 1751 to be paid out of the Deposit now in the Sheriff's hands – 27 April 1753 (OCOB 5:423)

1752   William McDonough

1753   John Bohannon is appointed Constable in this County in the room of William McDonaugh and ordered the Sheriff summon him to appear at the next Court to be sworn into his Office – 22 February 1753 (OCOB 5:411; Little, 182)

John Bohannon as Constable took the Oaths to his Majesty's Person and Government and the Abjuration Oath and repeated and subscribed the Test and then . . . took the Oaths of a Constable and the Oath appointed by the Tobacco Law and Preservation of the Breed of Deer – 26 April 1753 (OCOB 5:413)

LIST: Orange County D^r 1753 ?____? – Errors Excepted ^{pr} John Bohannon – 245[123] (Little, 31)

County Levy (1753): To John Bohanon [Constable] for [Viewing Tob^o fields]: 245 – 23 November 1753 (OCOB 5:512; Little, 184)

1754   Thomas White is appointed Constable in the room and Precincts of John Bohanon and it is ordered that the Sheriff summon him to appear at the next Court to be sworn into his Office – 25 April 1754 (OCOB 6:2; Little, 184)

Thomas White as Constable took the Oaths to his Majesty's person and government and repeated and subscribed the Test and took all the other Oaths required to be taken by Constables and hath for his Precincts the same as that John Bohannon was late Constable of – 27 June 1754 (OCOB 6:33; Little, 185)

1755   LIST: A List of What Tithes in in Thos Whits constable pursinks – 441[124] (Little, 38)

County Levy (1755): To Thomas White Constable for [Viewing tob^o fields]: 441 – 27 November 1755 (OCOB 6:184; Little, 186)

1756   LIST: A List of The Tithes that is in Thos Whits purcinks – Thos White Consta^{ble} – 397 (Little, 39)

County Levy (1756): To Thomas White Constable for Viewing Tob^o fields: 397 – 25 November 1756 (OCOB 6:300; Little, 187)

William Finnel is appointed Constable in the room of Thomas White and it is ordered the Sheriff summon him to appear at the next Court to be sworn into his Office[125] – 25 November 1756 (OCOB 6:300; Little, 187)

1757   LIST: Thos White acco^t – 1757 – 233 (Little, 51)

County Levy (1757): To Thomas White Constable for [viewing Tobacco fields]: 233 – 24 November 1757 (OCOB 6:358; Little, 188)

1758   LIST: The List of the Tithes Belonging To the Pursinks That I the Subscribor is Cunstabill of – 405 (Little, 56)

County Levy (1758): To Thomas White [Constable] for [Viewing Tob^o fields]: 405 – 24 November 1758 (OCOB 6:442; Little, 188)

1759   Thomas White

1760   Timothy Burgess is appointed Constable in the room of Thomas White and it is ordered he be summoned to appear at next Court to be sworn into his said Office[126] – 28 August 1760 (OCOB 6:538; Little, 190)

Timothy Burgess as Constable took the Oaths to his Majesty's person and government and repeated and subscribed the Test and also took the several Oaths required as Constable and is in the Precincts where Thomas White was lately Constable – 25 September 1760 (OCOB 6:542; Little, 190)

1761   John Terrell is appointed Constable in the room of Timothy Burgess . . . and it is ordered that the Sheriff summon [him] to appear at next Court to be sworn into the said Office – 25 June 1761 (OCOB 6:579; Little, 191)

Joseph Rogers as Constable having taken the Oaths appointed to be taken by Act of Parliament instead of the Oaths of Allegiance and Supremacy and taken and subscribed the Oath of Abjuration and also subscribed the Test took the several Oaths required to be taken by Law as Constable and hath for his Precinct all above John Williams up to Blue Run between the Precincts of Benjamin Cave and the River being the same Precinct that Timothy Burgess was late Constable in[127] – 27 November 1761 (OCOB 6:606)

1762   Elijah Fennell is appointed Constable in this County in the room of Joseph Rogers who is discharged from that Office and it is ordered that he be summoned to the next Court to be sworn into his said Office – 24 June 1762 (OCOB 6:645)

Elijah Fennel as a Constable took the Oaths appointed to be taken by Act of Parliament instead of the Oaths of Allegiance and Supremacy and repeated and subscribed the Test and the said Fennel took the several Oaths required as Constable and is in the Precincts whereof Joseph Rogers was late Constable – 26 August 1762 (OCOB 6:669; Little, 192)

LIST: An Acco^t of the Tith^s at at the Several plantations in my Precincts – Elijah Finnell – The Whole 207 (Little, 66)

County Levy (1762): To Elijah Finnel Constable for [viewing Tobacco fields]: 207 – 25 November 1762 (OCOB 6:687; Little, 192)

ORANGE III (1763–1770)
In 1763, Orange III was reduced by the enlargement of Orange IV.

1763   County Levy (1763): To Elijah Finnel [for Guarding the Prison] 8 Nights on [White & Glasgow]: 120 – 22 October 1763 (OCOB 7:61)

1764   Robert Bickers as Constable in the Room of Elijah Finnel Took the oaths to his Majestys Person & Government & Repeated & Subscribed the Test and Took the Several Oaths required to be Taken by a Constable – 26 April 1764 (OCOB 7:111; Little, 194)

LIST: 1764 – A List of the Quantity of Tithes in my presinks – p^r mr robert Bickers Constable – In all 379 (Little, 70)

County Levy (1764): To Robert Bickers as Constable for viewing Tob^o Fields: 342 – 25 October 1764 (OCOB 7:228; Little, 195)

1765   William Leek as Constable in the room of Robert Bickers Took the Oaths to her Majestys Person & Government and Repeated and Subscribed the Test and Took the Several Oaths required to be Taken by a Constable – 23 May 1765 (OCOB 7:309; Little, 195)

LIST: William Leek – 471 (Little, 78)

County Levy (1765): To William Leek [Constable] p^r acco^t: 471 – 28 November 1765 (OCOB 7:366; Little, 196)

1766   LIST: A memorandom of Tithes in Subscribers Precinct – Wm Leak Constable – 1760 – 588[128] (Little, 81)
William Leek added to his list three additional duties he had performed and the fees due him:
To Summoning a Coroner's Jury on Bettey Sellers Child N 35
To 5 days & 4 nights attendance on John Morgan 90
To 4 Days & 3 nights [attendance] of Wm Mallory 70

Ordered that John Grigsby be Summoned to the next Court to Answer an Information made by Wm Leek Constable against him for Tending Tob^o Seconds – 25 September 1766 (OCOB 7:390)

William Leek Plt. against John Grigsby Dft. } On Information } Is dismissed – 28

November 1766 (OCOB 7:407)

County Levy (1766): To William Leek Constable for Viewing Tobacco Fields & c: 588 – 27 November 1766 (OCOB 7:402; Little, 196)

1767 William Leek

In 1767, Edmund Burrus, constable of Orange II, produced a list of 162 tobacco planters with 743 tithables, which included the large landowners of Orange III (see p. 41).

William Finnell appointed Constable in the Room of Wm Leak and that he be Sworn before Some Majestrate of this County – 28 November 1767 (OCOB 7:466; Little, 197)

1768 William Finnell

1769 LIST: Orange County D^r to William ~~Finn~~ Finnell 263 ^lb Tob° for Lineing the ~~Sev~~ Several Feilds of Tob^a (Little, 106)

County Levy (1769): To William Finnell [Constable] p^r [Account for Viewing Tob° fields &c]: 263 – 26 October 1769 (OCOB 8:39; Little, 199)

Although the Virginia legislature repealed the acts ordering constables to view tobacco fields on 7 November 1769, William Finnell (and constables of Orange II and Orange IV) was credited for performing this duty in 1770.

1770 County Levy (for 1770): To Wm Finnell as Constable by Account: 285 – 28 March 1771 (OCOB 8:105; Little, 200)

ORANGE IV

In 1735, the Orange County court appointed Henry Downs constable "from the Chappel upwards." This precinct, which I have designated Orange IV, encompassed the area from the "[Southwest Mountain] Chapel" west to the Blue Ridge Mountains and from the Rapidan River south to the Hanover County line (see Map 2). As noted in the previous section, for some reason, the large plantations between the Blue Run and the Southwest Mountain Chapel did not appear on the first 1736 Orange IV tobacco planter list.

In 1738, Orange III was formed from Orange IV when the court appointed William Bell constable "from James Taylors Quarter to the County line." This moved the eastern border of Orange IV from the Southwest Mountain Church (which replaced the Southwest Mountain Chapel) east to the Blue Run. This new eastern border was described in 1753, when the court appointed John Eubank constable of Orange IV "above [west of] Blue Run."

In 1739, another new precinct, Orange V, was formed from Orange IV when the court appointed Thomas Callaway constable of the "Upper Precinct of James River Mountains"; in other words, the western precinct up to the Blue Ridge Mountains.[129] The names of the tobacco planters on the 1739 Orange V list show that the eastern border of Orange V was in the vicinity of the Great (also Big or White) Run in east "Greene" County. So, in 1739, Orange IV's western border moved from the Blue Ridge Mountains east to the Great Run.

In 1763, the court again changed the borders of Orange IV when it appointed Thomas Price constable of Orange IV "from the great Run the boundary Between Capt Bells & Capt Scotts Company down to the Blue Run & thence along the road by Mr Madisons to his Mill & thence up the road by Mr Colemans & all on the West side the s^d Road." This nearly doubled the size of Orange IV. "[T]o the Blue Run & thence along the road by Mr Madisons to his Mill" describes the southern half of Orange III below a line running east-west from Madison's Mill on Madison Run (probably near the Mountain Road approximating today's Route 15) to the vicinity of Liberty Mills. "[U]p the road by Mr Colemans" describes the western border of Orange II (in 1749, Orange II was described "up to the Plantation of James Coleman"). Initially, there was some confusion about Orange IV's new eastern border: in 1763 and 1764, the Orange IV constables inspected the fields of James Coleman and several other planters who lived east of this border and who normally appeared on the Orange II lists.

Although most of the tobacco planters on the eight Orange IV tobacco planter lists, dating from 1736 to 1769, are the same one year to the next, confusion about the eastern and western borders of this precinct resulted in some tobacco planters appearing one year in Orange IV and the next in Orange III or Orange V. For instance, more than half of the planters on the 1756 Orange IV tobacco planter list appeared on earlier Orange IV lists, four appeared previously on Orange V lists, two appear on both the 1756 Orange IV and Orange V lists, one appears on both the 1756 Orange IV and Orange III lists, and ten tobacco planters—who appear on Orange IV lists before and after 1756—appear this year on the Orange III list. Over the thirty years covered by the eight Orange IV lists of tobacco planters, the number of planters in this precinct ranged from 47 to 96. From 1 to 25 tithables lived in the households of these planters, averaging 3.2 to 4.3 tithables per household. The total number of tithables of tobacco planters, recorded in fifteen annual county levies, grew from 147 in 1735 to 339 in 1770 (see table 2). In 1756, 10 percent of the tithables of tobacco planters in "Orange" and "Greene" Counties lived in this precinct.

ORANGE IV (1735–1737)

This precinct was described as "from the Chappel upward" in 1735.

1735   Henry Downs is hereby appointed Constable from the Chappel upward and it is ordered that the Sheriff Summon the said Downs to the next Court to be held for this County to be Sworn into the said Office – 18 February 1734/35 (OCOB 1:5; Little, 152)

County Levy (1735): To Henry Downs Constable for viewing Tobacco Suckers: 147 – 18 November 1735 (OCOB 1:41; Little, 152)

1736   LIST: Henry Downs Constable his Claim for seeing the cutting up Suckers within his precincts – 233 – Errors Excepted p me Henry Downs – October court papers Au^{ts} C^{cr} (Little, 4)

County Levy (1736): To Henry Downs Constable for repaying him his Levy paid Last Year: 15 To Henry Downs for Viewing Succors: 233 – 19 October 1736 (OCOB 1:122, 123; Little, 153, 154)

Abraham Bletsoe jun^r is hereby appointed Constable in the Room of Henry Downs who for that purpose is ordered to Summon the s^d Bledsoe before a Justice of the Peace for this County to be Sworn into the said Office accordingly – 19 October 1736 (OCOB 1:118; Little, 153)

1737   Abraham Bledsoe, Jr.

Ordered that John Cleaveland be hereby appointed Constable in the room of Abraham Bletsoe Junr and it is further ordered that the said Bledsoe Sumon ye s^d John Cleaveland before a Justice of the Peace for this County to be Sworn into the said office accordingly – 27 October 1737 (OCOB 1:227; Little, 155)

ORANGE IV (1738)

In 1738, Orange IV was reduced by the formation of Orange III to the east.

1738   County Levy (1738): To John Cleaveland Constable for counting tobacco Succours: 79 – 26 October 1738 (OCOB 1:393; Little, 157)

ORANGE IV (1739–1762)

In 1739, Orange IV was again reduced by the formation of Orange V to the west. In 1753, it was described as "above Blue Run."

1739   County Levy (1740): To [John Cleveland Constable] for ye year 1739: 38 – 23 October 1740 (OCOB 2:275; Little, 163)

1740   County Levy (1740): To John Cleveland Constable: 41 – 23 October 1740 (OCOB 2:275; Little, 163)

1741   John Cleaveland

1742   John Cleaveland *executed attachments against the estates of Richard Brown and Thomas Williams* – 23 July 1742 (OCOB 3:191)

County Levy (1742): To John Cleaveland Conſtable: 84 – 25 November 1742 (OCOB 3:294; Little, 167)

1743 John Cleaveland

1744–46 County Levy (1747): To John Cleavland for Levies for the years 1744, 1745 & 1746 he being Consble during that time: 46 – 27 November 1747 (OCOB 5:81; Little, 176)

1747 John Cleaveland

1748 John Askew . . . appointed Constable . . . in the room of John Cleveland . . . and it is ordered that [he] be sworn into [his] said Office at the next Court – 26 May 1748 (OCOB 5:115; Little, 177)

Philip Bush is appointed Constable in the room of John Asher [Little has Aſkew] and it is ordered that he be sworn into his said Office at the next Court – 22 September 1748 (OCOB 5:153; Little, 177)

1749 Philip Bush as Constable in this County took the Oaths to his Majesty's Person and Government and also the Abjuration Oath and then . . . the Oath of a Constable and the Oath appointed by the Tobacco Law – 24 November 1748 (OCOB 5:157)

Upon the information of Philip Bush late Constable It is Ordered that the Attorney for the King enter a Prosecution against John Eubank for tending Seconds – 28 September 1749 (Little, 179)

> On the Information of Philip Bush against John Eubank for tending seconds, it's ordered that said Eubank be summoned to appear at next Court[130] – 23 March 1749/50 (OCOB 5:238)

LIST: Sep^ت 16th 1749 A List of the Tithables that Phillip Bush Constable have View'd in his Presinks – Total 187[131] (Little, 26)

County Levy (1749): To Philip Bush Constable for viewing Tobacco Fields: 187 – 24 November 1749 (OCOB 5:233; Little, 179)

Robert Deering is by the Court appointed Constable in the room of Philip Bush who is discharged from that Office and thereupon Robert took the Oaths to his Majesty's Person and Government and the Abjuration Oath and subscribed the Test and was sworn into his Office and took the Oath appointed by the Tobacco Law – 28 September 1749 (OCOB 5:220; Little, 179)

1750 County Levy (1750): To Robert Dearing Constable for [Viewing Tobacco fields]: 201 – 22 November 1750 (OCOB 5:285; Little, 180)

1751 LIST: 1754 – To the worshipfull corts of Orange your humb^l petitioner did serve two full years in the Constables office and has had my Tobb^o for Sucker hunting Levid but one year there is 244 pounds for ye year 1750 that has not been Lev^d Which I hope your worships wont be againsts granting to me now and your petitioner in Duty bound shall Ever pray – Robert Deering[132] (Little, 34)

County Levy (1754): To Robert Dearing for Viewing Tob° fields as Constable in 1751: 244 – 28 November 1754 (OCOB 6:56; Little, 185)

Bently Franklyn is appointed Constable in this County in the room of Robert Dearing who is discharged from that Office and it is ordered the Sheriff summon said Franklyn to appear at the next Court to be sworn into his said Office – 26 September 1751 (OCOB 5:323; Little, 181)

Bradly Kimbrow is appointed Constable in this County in the room and precincts of Robert Dearing, who is discharged from that Office, and it is ordered said Kimbrow be summoned to the next Court to be sworn into the said Office – 29 November 1751 (OCOB 5:337; Little, 181)

1752 John Eubank is appointed Constable in this County in the room of Bradley Kimbrow who was not qualified for that Office and it is ordered said Eubank be summoned to appear at next Court to be sworn into his Office[133] – 28 May 1752 (OCOB 5:369; Little, 181)

1753 John Eubanck [Little has John Eubank] is appointed Constable in this County above Blue Run and ordered he be summoned to next Court to be sworn into his Office – 28 April 1753 (OCOB 5:438; Little, 183)

John Eubank as Constable took the Oaths to his Majesty's Person and Government, subscribed the Abjuration Oath and repeated and subscribed the Test and then took the Oath of a Constable and the Oath appointed by the Tobacco Law and the Law for the preservation of the breed of Deer – 24 May 1753 (OCOB 5:442; Little, 183)

1754 William Lucas Junr is appointed Constable in the room and Precincts of John Eubank and that he be summoned to appear at the next Court to be sworn into his Office – 23 May 1754 (OCOB 6:4; Little, 185)

William Lucas, Junr. as Constable took the Oaths to his Majesty's person and government and repeated and subscribed the Test and also took all the Oaths required to be taken by him as Constable and hath for his Precincts the same that John Eubank was late Constable of – 27 June 1754 (OCOB 6:20; Little, 185)

On the information of William Lucas Constable it is Ordered that the King's Attorney prosecute Darby Haney for tending of Tob° Seconds – 27 September 1754 (OCOB 6:48; Little, 185)

Ordered that the Sheriff summon Darby Haney to appear at the next Court to answer the Information against him for tending seconds[134] – 22 May 1755 (OCOB 6:106)

1755 William Cleveland as Constable took the Oaths to his Majesty's person and government and subscribed the Abjuration Oath and Test and also took all the Oaths required as Constable is in the Precincts of William Lucas – 26 June 1755 (OCOB 6:123; Little, 186)

1756 Josias Bush is appointed Constable in this County in the room and Precincts of William Cleaveland and it is ordered the Sheriff summon him to appear at next Court to be sworn into his Office – 26 February 1756 (OCOB 6:200; Little, 186)

John Bryant is appointed Constable in the room of William Cleveland and it is ordered that the Sheriff summon him to appear at the next Court to be sworn into his Office – 25 March 1756 (OCOB 6:207; Little, 187)

John Bryant took the Oaths appointed to be taken by Act of Parliament instead of the Oaths of Allegiance and Supremacy and took and subscribed the Oath of Abjuration and subscribed the Test and then took all the Oaths required to be taken as a Constable and has for his Precincts that William Cleveland had – 22 April 1756 (OCOB 6:234; Little, 187)

LIST: July ye 20^{ft} 1756 – In all 153 (152-32 ded^t) – John Bryant Consta^b Acco^t 120 (Little, 45)

County Levy (1756): To John Bryant Constable for [Viewing Tob^o fields]: 120 – 25 November 1756 (OCOB 6:300; Little, 187)

1757 Thomas German is appointed Constable in the County in the room of John Bryant and it is ordered that Thomas German be summoned to the next Court to be sworn into his Office – 26 May 1757 (OCOB 6:338; Little, 188)

1758 Joshua Furguson as Constable in the room of John Bryant took the Oaths to his Majesty's person and government and repeated and subscribed the Test and took the several Oaths required to be taken by Constables – 23 February 1758 (OCOB 6:364; Little, 188)

1759 William Ham is appointed Constable in the room of Joshua Farguson and it is ordered the Sheriff summon him to appear at next Court to be sworn into the Office – 24 May 1759 (OCOB 6:459; Little, 189)

William Ham took the Oaths to his Majesty's person and government and the Oath of Abjuration and repeated and subscribed the Test and then took the several Oaths required as Constable and is to act in the room and Precinct whereof Joshua Farguson was late Constable – 26 July 1759 (OCOB 6:486)

1760 Anthony Foster is appointed Constable in the room of William Ham and it is ordered that he be summoned to appear at next Court to be sworn into his said Office – 28 August 1760 (OCOB 6:538; Little, 190)

William Coursey is appointed Constable in the room of William Ham and it is ordered that he be summoned to appear at the next Court to be sworn to the said Office – 25 September 1760 (OCOB 6:542; Little, 190)

1761 Joseph Smith [is appointed Constable] in the room of William Coursey and it is ordered that the Sheriff summon [him] to appear at next Court to be sworn into the said Office – 25 June 1761 (OCOB 6:579; Little, 191)

Ordered that the Sheriff summon . . . Thomas Shackleford . . . appointed Constable to appear at next Court to be sworn into [his] Office – 27 November 1761 (OCOB 6:607; Little, 191)

1762 William Grant Constable took the Oaths appointed to be taken by Act of Parliament instead of the Oaths of Allegiance and Supremacy and repeated and subscribed the Test and the said ... Grant took the several oaths required as Constables and that the said ... Grant's [Precinct be in the bounds of] Capt. Scott's Company[135] – 25 March 1762 (OCOB 6:618)

County Levy (1762): To Wm Grant Constable for viewing Tobacco fields: 344 – 25 November 1762 (OCOB 6:687; Little, 192)

ORANGE IV (1763–1770)

In 1763, Orange IV was enlarged when it gained the southern half of Orange III; it was described as "from the great Run the boundary Between Capt Bells & Capt Scotts Company down to the Blue Run & thence along the road by Mr Madisons to his Mill & thence up the road by Mr Colemans & all on the West side the s^d Road."

1763   Joseph Phillips, Junr. is appointed Constable in the room of William Grant and it is ordered that the Sheriff summon him to appear at next Court to be sworn into his Office – 24 February 1763 (OCOB 6:691; Little, 192)

John [Thomas] Price [and another] as Constables took the Oaths appointed to be taken by Act of Parliament instead of the Oaths of Allegiance and Supremacy, repeated and subscribed the Test and ... Price [took] the several Oaths as Constables and ... has for his Precinct the same that William Grant was late Constable of – May 1763 (OCOB 7:5)

Ordered that John [Thomas] Price Constable have for his precincts from the great Run the boundary Between Capt Bells & Capt Scotts Company down to the Blue Run & thence along the road by Mr Madisons to his Mill & thence up the road by Mr Colemans & all on the West side the s^d Road – 22 June 1763 (OCOB 7:14; Little, 193)

LIST: 1763 – Tyths in all 3.6.0[136] (Little, 67)

County Levy (1763): To Thomas Price [Constable] for [Viewing Tob^o fields]: 358 – 26 November 1763 (OCOB 7:82; Little, 194)

1764   John Tilly as Constable in the Room of Thomas Price Took the oaths to his Majestys Person & Government & Repeated & Subscribed the Test & Took the Several Oaths Required to be Taken by a Constable – 26 April 1764 (OCOB 7:119; Little, 194)

LIST: John Tilly Cunstable list for my presints of tiths 1764 – Total 414 (Little, 71)

County Levy (1764): To John Tilly as Constable for [viewing Tob^o Fields]: 414 – 25 October 1764 (OCOB 7:228; Little, 195)

1765   Thomas Price?

1766   Mereman Marshall as Constable in the Room of Thomas Price took the Oaths to his Majestys Person & Government & repeated & Subscribed the Test and Took the Several Oaths required to be Taken by a Constable[137] – 27 March 1766 (OCOB 7:371; Little, 196)

County Levy (1767): To Mereman Marshall for Summoning a Jury on Inquest: 35 – 27 November 1767 (OCOB 7:462)

1767   Joseph Martin is appointed a Constable in the Room of Mereman Marshall and it is Ordered that the Sheriff Summon him to appear at next Court to be Sworn into the Said Office – 27 August 1767 (OCOB 7:448; Little, 197)

1768 John Griffen appointed Constable in the Room of Joseph Martin & that he be Sworn before Some Justice of this County – 22 September 1768 (OCOB 7:526; Little, 198)

LIST: A List of The Tithables in The precincts wherein I John Griffin am Constable for the Year 1768 Being in the Whole 314 Tithes[138] (Little, 107, 108)

1769 LIST: A List of the Tithables in The precincts Wherein I John Griffen am Constable for the Year 1769 Being in the Whole 336 Tithes (Little, 108)

County Levy (1769): To John Griffen Constable by Account for Viewing Tob° fields &c: 490 – 26 October 1769 (OCOB 8:39; Little, 199)

Although the Virginia legislature repealed the acts ordering constables to view tobacco fields on 7 November 1769, John Griffen (and constables of Orange II and Orange III) was credited for performing this duty in 1770.

1770 County Levy (for 1770): To John Griffin [as Constable] by Account: 339 – 28 March 1771 (OCOB 8:105; Little, 200)

ORANGE V

Orange V, which encompassed almost all of today's Greene County, was formed from Orange IV in 1739 when the court appointed Thomas Callaway constable of the "Upper Precinct of James River [Blue Ridge] Mountains."[139] In 1762, the court ordered Orange V to "be in the bounds of Capt Bell's [Militia] Company," and in 1763, the boundary between Orange V and Orange IV was described as the "great Run the boundary Between Capt Bells & Capt Scotts [Militia] Company." Capt. William Bell lived in Orange V, and Capt. John or Johnny Scott lived in Orange IV.[140] The eastern border of Orange V was probably always the Great Run (also called the Big Run or White Run), which flows from Ruckersville north into the Rapidan River (see Map 2). A few landowners, who lived on or near the boundary separating Orange IV and Orange V, appear some years on the Orange IV tobacco planter lists and some years on the Orange V lists.

There are six Orange V tobacco planter lists, dating from 1739 to 1769. Over these thirty-one years, the number of planters grew from 33 to 99, with as many as 118 in 1767. From 1 to 15 tithables lived in the households of these planters, averaging 2 to 3 tithables per household. The total number of tithables of tobacco planters in Orange V, recorded in ten annual county levies, grew from 46 in 1739 to 346 in 1768 (see table 2). In 1756, 14 percent of the tithables of tobacco planters in "Orange" and "Greene" Counties lived in this precinct.

ORANGE V (1739–1769)

This precinct was described as the "Upper Precinct of James River Mountains" in 1739 and "in the bounds of Capt. Bell's Company" in 1762.

1739   Thomas Callaway is hereby appointed Constable in the Upper precinct of James River Mountains & its ordered that he be Sworn into ye s^d Office accordingly – 22 March 1738/39 (OCOB 1:442; Little, 158)

Thomas Callaway came into Court and took the oath of a Constable as also the oaths enjoyned by ye Last Acts of A∫sembly – 22 March 1738/39 (OCOB 1:442)

LIST: A List of Tithables in the precincts of Thos Callaway Constables 1739 – per me Thos: Callaway Constabel in all 66[141] (Little, 15)

County Levy (1739): To Thos Callaway Constable for Succors: 46 – 25 October 1739 (OCOB 2:80; Little, 160)

1740   By information of Thomas Callaway we pre∫ent George Douglas and John Fogins[?] for not giving notice to the Church wardens of St Marks Parish according to Law of a bastard Child born in his house[142] – 27 November 1740 (OCOB 2:279)

County Levy (1740): To Thos Calloway Constable: 64 – 27 November 1740 (OCOB 2:281; Little, 163)

1741   Honourias Powell having taken the oaths pre∫cribed by Act of Parliament & Subscribed the Test took the oaths appointed by a late act of Genl A∫sembly was Sworn Con∫table accordingly[143] – 28 August 1741 (OCOB 2:478; Little, 164)

On the Complaint of Honorias Powell Constable that David Williams an Overseer for Mrs Elizabeth Stannard over Seven tithables tended Tobacco Succors Its ordered that ye Kings Attorney prosecute him for ye same according to Law – 25 September 1741 (OCOB 3:13; Little, 165)

The case against David Williams:

Zachary Lewis Gent Attorney for our Sovereign Lord the King having presented into Court an Information ag^t Thomas Wood & David Williams for tending tobacco Succors Its ordered that they be Summoned to answer the said information – 26 March 1742 (OCOB 3:122)

In the suit by Information brought . . . for . . . the King ag^t David Williams for tending succors the Deft failing to appear and the Sheriff having returned on the summons executed at ye Motion of . . . Zach^y Lewis Attorney as afs^d its ordered that an Attachment issue ag^t the Defts body returnable to ye next Court – 27 August 1742 (OCOB 3:212)

In the Suit by Information brought . . . in behalf of . . . the King ag^t David Williams Deft ye Deft appeared and pleaded not guilty & Zachary Lewis Gent Attorney . . . joyning in the issue the tryal thereof is referred untill ye next Court – 29 January 1742/43 (OCOB 3:339)

In the suit by Information made . . . in behalf of . . . the King ag^t David Williams Def^t for tending tobacco Slips Seconds & Succurs a Jury . . . heard all Evidences and Arguments . . . brought in their Verdict . . . ye jury find the Deft not guilty . . . and the s^d suit is dismissed – 27 May 1743 (OCOB 3:437; Little, 168)

On the Compl^t of Honorias Powell Constable that Thomas Wood being a Master of a family tended tobacco succors Its ordered that the Kings Attorney prosecute him for ye Same according to Law – 25 September 1741 (OCOB 3:13)

The case against Thomas Wood:

Zachary Lewis Gent Attorney for our Sovereign Lord the King having presented into Court an Information ag^t Thomas Wood & David Williams for tending tobacco Succors Its ordered that they be Summoned to answer the said information – 26 March 1742 (OCOB 3:122)

In the suit by Information brought . . . for . . . the King ag^t Thomas Wood for tending of Succors the Deft appeared & prayed a Special imparlance [illegible] was granted him untill the next Court – 27 August 1742 (OCOB 3:212)

In the suit of Information brought . . . for . . . the King ag^t Thomas Wood Deft for tending tobacco succors, Judg^t is awarded our . . . King ag^t the said Thomas Wood by [illegible] for what of y^e [illegible] for in ye Declaration Shall appear Justly due unless the s^d Deft appear at ye next Court to answer the said Information – 25 September 1742 (OCOB 3:276)

In the ∫uit of Information brought . . . in behalf of . . . the King ag^t Thomas Wood Deft the Deft appeared and pleaded not Guilty & . . . the Attorney . . . joyning in the i∫sue the tryal thereof is referred untill the next Court – 29 January 1742/43 (OCOB 3:339)

In the ∫uit of Information brought . . . for . . . the King ag^t Thomas Wood Deft for tending tobacco seconds slips & ∫uccors a Jury . . . having heard all Evidences and arguments . . . find the Deft guilty . . . and its Considered by the Court that the s^d Deft be fined one thousand pounds of tobacco for ye s^d Offence to his Majesty and its ordered that the Sheriff of this County on refusal of payment Levy the s^d fine . . . and . . . all the Co∫ts of this Information & pro∫ecution – 27 May 1743 (OCOB 3:436)

Honorias Powell having made oath that he had attended five days as an Evidence for our . . . King ag^t Thos Wood its on his Motion ordered that the said Thos Wood pay him for y^e ∫ame one hundred & twenty five pounds of tobacco according to Law – 27 May 1743 (OCOB 3:436)

County Levy (1741): To Honourias Powell as Constable: 58 – 26 November 1741 (OCOB 3:56; Little, 165)

1742   Honorias Powell

1743   County Levy (1743): To Honorias Powell for viewing tobacco ground as Constable: 65 – 25 November 1743 (OCOB 4:29; Little, 169)

1744   County Levy (1744): To Honorias Powell for Viewing Tobacco fields: 103 – 22 November 1744 (OCOB 4:227; Little, 171)

1745   Honorias Powell

Barnard [Barnett] Crawford is hereby appointed Constable in this County in the Room of Honorias Powel who is Discharged from that office and it is ordered that the said Barnard Crawford be Sworn into his Said office at the next Court – 26 July 1745 (OCOB 4:397)

1746-47   Honorias Powell

1748   David Zachary is appointed Constable in the room of Honourias Powell who is discharged from that Office, and thereupon he took the Oaths to his Majesty's Person & Government, subscribed the Abjuration Oath and Test and was sworn Constable, and then took the Oath appointed by the Tobacco Law – 28 July 1748 (OCOB 5:149; Little, 177)

1749   David Zachary

1750   John Goodall is appointed a Constable in this County in the Room of David Zachary and that he be summoned to appear at the next Court to be sworn into his Office – 22 March 1749/50 (OCOB 5:236; Little, 179)

John Goodall as Constable in the room and Precincts of David Zachary took the Oaths to his Majesties Person and Government and the Oath of Abjuration and subscribed the Test, and then took of a Constable and the Oath appointed to be taken by the Tobacco Law – 26 July 1750 (OCOB 5:274; Little, 179)

1751–52　John Goodall

1753　Upon the Attachment obtained by Francis Williams against the Estate of William Watkins for one pound, twelve shillings directed to any Sheriff or Constable in Virginia and John Goodall, the Constable having made return he had executed the same on one Cow Calf, iron pott, old side saddle, old bedstead and cowhide, and Deft. tho' solemnly called failed to appear to replevy the same . . . Constable Goodall deliver the attached effects to the Sheriff of this County and said Sheriff to make sale of them according to Law and pay the money arising therefrom to said Williams towards satisfying this Judgment [except five shillings to be first paid to said Goodall for wintering and taking care of the yearling] and that he make return of his proceedings thereon – 28 June 1753 (OCOB 5:457)

1754–55　John Goodall

1756　LIST: To the Worshipful Court of Orange County the petition of the Subscribe Humbly Sheweth that whereas he being Constable have Viewed the Several Tob⁰ fields in my precincts & being Crippled by my Horse & not able to Attend Your Worships; prays to be Allowed for the same as followeth (Viz – John Goodal Constable Novem^r the 23rd 1756 – In all 214 Tythables[144] (Little, 44)

County Levy (1756): To John Goodall Constable for [Viewing Tob⁰ fields]: 214 – 25 November 1756 (OCOB 6:300; Little, 187)

1757–60　John Goodall?

1761　Ordered that the Sheriff Sumon James Coursey [and another] who are appointed Constables to appear at next Court to be sworn into their Office – 27 November 1761 (OCOB 6:607; Little, 191)

1762　James Coursey [and another] Constables took the Oaths appointed to be taken by Act of Parliament instead of the Oaths of Allegiance and Supremacy and repeated and subscribed the Test and the Said Coursey [and another] took the several oaths required as Constables and that the said Coursey's Precinct be in the bounds of Capt. Bell's Company[145] – 25 March 1762 (OCOB 6:618)

1763　Robert Cave [and another] as Constables took the Oaths appointed to be taken by Act of Parliament instead of the Oaths of Allegiance and Supremacy, repeated and subscribed the Test . . . and the said Cave [and another] the several Oaths as Constables . . . and the said Cave [has for his Precinct] in that of James Coursey – May 1763 (OCOB 7:5)

1764　Robert Cave

1765　Richard Bruce as Constable in the Room of Robert Cave took the Oaths to his Majestys Person and Government and repeated and Subscribed the Test and took the Several Oaths required to be taken by a Constable – 26 September 1765 (OCOB 7:345; Little, 196)

1766　LIST: A List of the Number of Tithes In my Percincts august 1st 1766 – Richd Bruce – 286 (Little, 84–85)

	County Levy (1766): To Richard Bruce for [Viewing Tobacco Fields & c]: 286 – 27 November 1766 (OCOB 7:402; Little, 196)
1767	Jere Bryant as Constable took the Oaths to his Majestys Person & Government and repeated and Subscribed the Test . . . and took the Several Oaths of a Constable[146] – 28 July 1767 (OCOB 7:446; Little, 197)
	LIST: A List in my Bounds & Number of Tiths p^r me Jerem^h Bryan – 312 (Little, 90–91)
	County Levy (1767): To Jeremiah Bryant [Constable] for [Viewing Tobacco Fields]: 312 – 27 November 1767 (OCOB 7:462; Little, 197)
1768	LIST: 1768 Jeremiah Bryan his List of Sucker hunting tiths – Jer Bryant – in all 346 (Little, 98–99)
	County Levy (1768): To Jeremiah Bryan Constable for Viewing Tobacco Fields: 346 – 24 November 1768 (OCOB 7:537; Little, 198)
1769	Anthony Golding appointed Constable in the Room of Jeremiah Bryan and that he be Sworn into Office by Some Justice of this County – 23 March 1769 (OCOB 7:546; Little, 198)
	LIST: A List of Tiths Anthony G. – 295 (Little, 102–105)
	County Levy (1769): To Anthony Golding [Constable] p^r [Account for Viewing Tob^o fields &c]: 293 – 26 October 1769 (OCOB 8:39; Little, 199)

On 7 November 1769, the Virginia legislature repealed the acts ordering constables to view tobacco fields.

The Culpeper, Rappahannock and Madison Precincts

In 1735 and 1736, the Orange County court divided the area of today's Culpeper, Rappahannock and Madison Counties into five constable precincts. Two precincts were in "Culpeper" County, one in "Rappahannock" County and two in "Madison" County. Constables assigned to these five precincts between 1735 and 1749, the year Culpeper County was formed from Orange County, were credited for viewing tobacco fields thirty-eight times, but only five lists of tobacco planters survive. During the same period, constables in "Orange" and "Greene" Counties were also credited for viewing tobacco fields thirty-eight times, but ten of their lists survive.

Culpeper I

In 1735, the Orange County court appointed Peter Russell constable "from the point of the fork on the South side of the Mountain Run unto crooked Run." This precinct, which I call Culpeper I, was bordered on the east by the Rappahannock River and on the south by the Rapidan River, which flows into the Rappahannock at the "point of the fork"; it was bordered on the north by Mountain Run and on the west by Crooked Run, which forms the border between "Culpeper" and "Madison" Counties. One of the Orange County justices appointed to take the list of tithables in "Culpeper" County in 1737 and 1738 was assigned a precinct with almost the same borders: "from the point of ye fork up ye southside of ye mountain run to ye Great Mountains" (see Map 3 and Appendix, pp. 115, 116).

In 1740, Culpeper I was divided into two subprecincts when the court appointed Simon Miller constable "between the Mountain run bridge & the South River"; William Kelley, who replaced the previous Culpeper I constable, would have been responsible, presumably, for the remaining part of Culpeper I. Today, the only South River in this region is in Greene County, but in the early eighteenth century, the Hazel River and the Rapidan River were also called South River.[147] The southern border of this precinct, "South River," was the Rapidan River. It is curious that only two months later, on 22 May 1740, the court appointed a justice to take the lists of tithables in the same area and described his precinct as "between ye Mountain run & ye rapidan," not South River (see Appendix, p. 117). In 1744, the court redefined the borders of Culpeper I-B: "from the Mouth of Brookes's Run up the same acro∫s to the Mountain, thence to Normans ford & so down to the Point of the Fork." The "Mountain" must be Mountain Run since there is no mountain between the head of Brookes's Run and Norman's Ford. So Culpeper I-B was the southeast finger of "Culpeper" County: from Brookes's Run, northeast to Norman's Ford, then down the Rappahannock to the Point of the Fork, then west along the Rapidan back to Brookes's Run. Culpeper I-A would have been the area from Brookes's Run west to Crooked Run and from Mountain Run south to the Rapidan. The residences of the constables assigned to these two subprecincts confirm that from 1740 to 1745 Culpeper I-A was in the southwest of today's Culpeper County, and Culpeper I-B was in the southeast.[148]

In 1746, James Abbet replaced Roger Topp, constable of Culpeper I-A, and William Nash, the 1745 Culpeper I-B constable, was discharged and not replaced. Abbott was credited with 276 tithable in 1746—far more than the total number credited the Culpeper I-A and Culpeper I-B constables in 1741 and 1742; so it appears that Culpeper I was reunited in 1746.

On 28 November 1747, the court appointed Daniel Carter constable "from Muddy Run to the upper end of Mountponey & from thence to the Courthouse & all the lower end of St Marks Parish." Descriptions of contemporary tithable precincts help to understand the boundaries of this constable precinct. In 1746 and 1747, the court appointed three justices to take the lists of tithables in "Culpeper" County: one justice was assigned the "North Little Fork," another justice was assigned "the upper Part of St Marks Parish" and the third justice was responsible for "the lower Part of St Marks Parish from the mouth of Muddy Run to the upper End of Mountpony and from thence to the Courthouse"—the same description as the 1748 Culpeper I constable precinct (see Appendix, p. 119). The tithable precinct in the "North Little Fork" (the fork formed by the Hazel and Hedgeman's Rivers) was north of the Hazel River and its tributary, Muddy Run. The other two precincts were south of the Hazel River in the "lower" and the "upper" parts of St. Mark's Parish. St. Mark's Parish, reduced by the formation of St. Thomas' Parish in 1740, served the parishioners in the area of today's Culpeper, Rappahannock and most of Madison Counties. The tithable and constable precincts in "the lower Part of St Marks Parish" were in the eastern part of the parish (in the eighteenth century, "lower" meant south or east and "upper" meant north or west).[149] So this 1748 Culpeper I constable precinct, "from Muddy Run to the upper end of Mountponey & from thence to the Courthouse & all the lower end of St Marks Parish," was bordered by the Rapidan and Rappahannock Rivers and a line running southwest from the mouth of Muddy Run to Raccoon Ford on the Rapidan.[150] These new boundaries of Culpeper I encroached on the boundaries of the precinct to the north, Culpeper II. These two precincts were formerly divided by the Mountain Run, but now Culpeper I included a section of Culpeper II from the mouth of Muddy Run to the Mountain Run above Mount Poney.

One list of tobacco planters, dating 1737, survives for Culpeper I. More than half of the men who served as constables of Culpeper I, I-A and I-B appear on this list. Sixty-six tobacco planters with 1 to 11 (an average of 3) tithables in their households lived in this precinct in 1737. The total number of tithables of tobacco planters in Culpeper I, recorded in three annual county levies, grew from 119 in 1735 to 276 in 1746 (see table 2).

CULPEPER I (1735–1739)
This precinct was described as "from the point of the fork on the South side of the Mountain Run unto crooked Run" in 1735.

1735 Peter Russell is hereby appointed Constable from the point of the fork on the South side of the Mountain Run unto crooked Run & it is ordered that the Sheriff Summon the s^d Peter Russell to the next Court to be held for this County to be Sworn into the said Office – 21 January 1734/35 (OCOB 1:4; Little, 152)

County Levy (1735): To Peter Ruſsell Constable for viewing tobacco Suckers: 119 – 18 November 1735 (OCOB 1:41; Little, 152)

County Levy (1736): To Peter Ruſsell Constable for repaying him his Levy paid Last Year: 15 – 19 October 1736 (OCOB 1:122; Little, 153)

1736 James Kirk is hereby appointed Constable in the room of Peter Russell who is hereby ordered to Summon the said Kirk before a Justice of this County to be sworn into the said Office – 17 February 1735/36 (OCOB 1:54; Little, 153)

We [the Grand Jury] present James Kirk Constable for not looking after Succers of tobacco and causing them to be Cut down according to Law this present Year – 25 November 1736 (OCOB 1:127; Little, 154)

> The Grand jury presentment ag^t James Kirk, Constable, for not looking after tobacco Suckers and causing them to be cut down according to Law this present Year, is dismisd – 25 March 1737 (OCOB 1:152; Little, 154)

1737 Ordered that William Taylor be made Constable in the room of James Kirk decd and that he go to a Justice of the Peace for this County to be sworn into this Office accordingly – 24 February 1736/37 (OCOB 1:141; Little, 154)

Isaac Haddock is hereby made Constable in the room of Wm Taylor deced and it is further ordered that he go to a Justice of the Peace for this County to be Sworn into the s^d Office accordingly – 26 May 1737 (OCOB 1:170; Little, 154)

LIST: The Number of Tithables in My persinct Isaac Hadok – 143 (Little, 6)

County Levy (1737): To Isaac Haddock [Constable for viewing tobacco]: 143 – 27 October 1737 (OCOB 1:233; Little, 156)

1738 Isaac Haddock

1739 Wm Rumsey is hereby appointed Constable in the room of Isaac Haddocks who is hereby ordered to Summon ye s^d Rumsey before Some Justice of the Peace of this County to be Sworn into ye s^d Office accordingly – 22 February 1738/39 (OCOB 1:421; Little, 158)

Robert Rumsey Constable came into Court and took the oath enjoyned by the Last Acts of Afsembly – 22 March 1738/39 (OCOB 1:438; Little, 158)

CULPEPER I-A AND CULPEPER I-B (1740–1745)

In 1740, Culpeper I was divided when Simon Miller was appointed constable "between the Mountain run bridge & the South River" (Culpeper I-B), and James Conner, who replaced the 1739 Culpeper I constable, was responsible for the western end of Culpeper I (Culpeper I-A). In 1744, Culpeper I-B was described as "from the Mouth of Brookes's Run up the same acrofs to the Mountain, thence to Normans ford & so Down to the Point of the Fork."

CULPEPER I-A (1740–1745)

1740 Wm Kelly is hereby appointed Constable in the room of Wm Rumfey & its ordered that the said Kelly appear at ye next Court to be Sworn into the said Office accordingly – 28 February 1739/40 (OCOB 2:106; Little, 160)

James Conner is hereby appointed Constable in ye room of Wm Rumsey Wm Kelly having refused to Swear in ye s^d Office & its ordered that ye s^d Conner be Sumoned by ye Sheriff to appear at ye next court to be Sworn into the said Office accordingly – 27 March 1740 (OCOB 2:134; Little, 161)

James Conner having taken the oaths appointed by Act of Parliament & Subscribed the Test took ye oaths appointed by a late Act of Afsembly & was Sworn Constable in ye room of Wm Rumfey – 22 May 1740 (OCOB 2:165; Little, 161)

James Conner *executed an attachment against the estate of John Davis* – 27 March 1741 (OCOB 2:353)

1741　Wm Nash is hereby appointed Constable in the room of James Conner & its ordered that the Sheriff Summon him to appear at the next Court to be Sworn into the said Office accordingly – 27 March 1741 (OCOB 2:332; Little, 163)

William Nash [and two others] having Severally taken the oaths prefcribed by Law & Subscribed the Test Severally took the oath of a Constable were Sworn in the s^d Office accordingly – 28 May 1741 (OCOB 2:363)

County Levy (1741): To Wm Nash [for Viewing tobacco Succors]: 100 – 22 October 1741 (OCOB 3:49; Little, 165)

1742　George Underwood is hereby appointed Constable in the room of Wm Nash & its ordered that he be fummoned by the Sheriff to appear at the next court to be fworn into the said Office – 28 January 1741/42 [Little has 27 November 1741] (OCOB 3:96; Little, 165)

1743　John Coleman is hereby appointed Conftable in the room of George Underwood & its ordered that ye s^d Underwood fummon him before a Justice of ye peace for this County to be fworn in ye s^d Office accordingly – 27 January 1742/43 (OCOB 3:348; Little, 167)

Ordered that James Stewart be Sworn before a Justice of this County into the Office of Constable in the Room of John Coleman late constable for this present year – probably 25 August 1743 (OCOB 4:1; Little, 168)

Roger Topp is hereby appointed Constable in ye Room of John Coleman & being Called took the Oaths appointed by Law to be taken & Subscribed the Test was Sworn into the s^d Office accordingly – 23 September 1743 (OCOB 4:10; Little, 169)

1744　Roger Topp Constable having informed the Court that James Hopkins is a Person of Lewd Life and Converfation & a Common Disturber of his Majesties Peace & that s^d Hopkins did afsault & abuse him when in y^e [illegible] of his Office & from the [illegible] threats of the s^d Hopkins & other Enormities declared he is afraid to execute the Precepts committed to him, It is therefor Ordered by the Court that the s^d Hopkins committed for s^d Offences by John Finlefon Gent to ye Sher[iff] or Goaler of this County be remanded from this Barr to ye County Goal untill he shall enter into Recognizance of [illegible] together with two securitys each in ye fine of £10 Ster[ling] to be of the [illegible] and good behavior for one year & a Day to to all his Majesties Subjects but especially unto ye Roger Tapp – 26 January 1743/44 (OCOB 4:44)

Roger Topp *executed an attachment against the estate of "the Deft"* – 25 August 1744 (OCOB 4:216)

1745　Roger Topp

CULPEPER I-B (1740–1745)

1740   Simon Miller is hereby appointed Constable between the Mountain run bridge & the South River & its ordered that he be Sumoned by ye Sheriff to appear at ye next Court to be Sworn into ye s^d Office accordingly – 27 March 1740 (OCOB 2:135; Little, 161)

Simon Miller having taken the oaths appointed by Act of Parliament & Subscribed the Test took ye oaths appointed by a late Act of A∫sembly & was Sworn Constable accordingly – 26 June 1740 (OCOB 2:187; Little, 161)

1741   Thomas Sparks [Parks] [illegible] is hereby appointed Constable in the room of of Simon Miller & its ordered that he be Summoned to the next Court to be Sworn into the said office accordingly – 28 May 1741 (OCOB 2:357; Little, 164)

Thomas Parks having taken the oaths appointed by Act of Parliament and Subscribed the Test took the oaths appointed by a Late Act of General A∫sembly and was Sworn Constable accordingly[151] – 25 June 1741 (OCOB 2:402; Little, 164)

1742   Gerhard Banks is hereby appointed Con∫table in the room of Thomas Parks & its ordered that the Sheriff Summon him to appear at next Court to be Sworn into the said Office – 27 May 1742 (OCOB 3:151; Little, 166)

County Levy (1742): To Gerhard Banks Con∫table: 39 – 25 November 1742 (OCOB 3:294; Little, 167)

1743   Joseph Kirk is hereby appointed Con∫table in the room of Gerhard Banks and its ordered that ye s^d Banks ∫ummon ye s^d Kirk to appear before a Justice of ye Peace for this County to be ∫worn into ye s^d Office accordingly – 26 May 1743 (OCOB 3:429; Little, 168)

1744   On the Petition of Joseph Kirk to be Discharged from the Office of Constable Its ordered that Peter Ru∫sele be ∫ummoned to appear at next Court to be Sworn into Office – 24 May 1744 (OCOB 4:106; Little, 170)

Ordered that Wm Nash ∫erve as Constable in the Room of Peter Ru∫sell lately appointed & not sworn & that the said Nash be ∫ummoned to appear next court to take the Oath of a Constable according to Law & that he Officiate in the Precincts from the Mouth of Brookes's Run up the same acro∫s to the Mountain, thence to Normans ford & so Down to the Point of the Fork – 29 June 1744 (OCOB 4:153; Little, 170)

Ordered that William William Nash appear at Next Court to Swear as Constable and Its Continued until then – 23 August 1744 (OCOB 4:199; Little, 171)

1745   Ordered that William Nash Constable in this County be Discharged from his said Office – 28 November 1745 (OCOB 4:443; Little, 174)

CULPEPER I (1746)

In 1746, Culpeper I was reunited.

1746   James Abbet having taken the Oaths to his Majesty's Person & Government & took & subscribed the Abjuration Oath and the Test took the Oath appointed by the Tobacco Law and was sworn a Constable of this County in the Room of Roger Topp – 24 July 1746 (OCOB 4A:1; Little, 175)

County Levy (1746): To James Abbitt [Constable for viewing Tobacco Fields]: 276 – 27 November 1746 (OCOB 4A:103; Little, 175)

CULPEPER I (1747–1749)

In 1747, Culpeper I was described as "from Muddy Run to the upper end of Mount Poney and from thence to the Courthouse and all the lower end of Saint Mark Parish."

1747 Daniel Carter is hereby appointed Constable in this County in the room of James Abbit, who is discharged from that Office, and it is ordered that he be sworn into his said Office at the next Court – 23 July 1747 (OCOB 5:1; Little, 176)

Daniel Carter is by the Court appointed Constable in this County from Muddy Run to the upper end of Mount Poney and from thence to the Courthouse and all the lower end of Saint Mark Parish and he having taken the Oaths to his Majesties Person and Government and took and subscribed the Abjuration Oath and the Test is sworn in to his said Office and then took the Oath appointed by the Tobacco Law – 28 November 1747 (OCOB 5:85; Little, 177)

1748 John Asher having obtained an Attachment against the Estate of Joseph Phillips who hath privately removed himself out of this County or absconds that Process cannot be served on him for eight hundred pounds of tobacco and cask and twenty five shillings and nine pence, Daniel Carter, a Constable in this County, making return that he hath attached four head of cattle and a young Calf, some Corn, a small parcel of household stuff, one Hog . . . therefore it is ordered that the Sherif take the effects and make sale of them according to law and of so many of the cattle as with the amount of the other things will be of value sufficient to satisfy the Plt the eight hundred pounds of tobacco and costs and make return thereof to the next Court – 26 March 1748 (OCOB 5:111)

1749 George Roberts is appointed Constable in the room of Daniel Carter and it is ordered that he be sworn into his said Office at the next Court – 26 January 1748/49 (OCOB 5:159; Little, 178)

Culpeper County was formed from Orange County and held its first court session on 18 May 1749.

CULPEPER II

In 1735, John Roberts was appointed constable "on the Northside of the Mountain Run from the Mouth of the said Run up the River & Run to the Gourdvine fork from and cro*f*s to the Mountain Run including the little fork." This large precinct extended from the the Rappahannock River west to the Gourdvine Fork and from the Mountain Run north to and including the Little Fork (see Map 3). In 1736, this precinct was described as "in the Great ffork," a vague but technically correct description since the Great Fork is the land between the Rappahannock, Rapidan and Hazel Rivers; however, Culpeper I was also in the Great Fork.

In 1741, Culpeper II was divided into two subprecincts when John Chissum was appointed constable "above Devis's Rowling path and Muddy run" (Culpeper II-B), and Joseph Norman, former constable of Culpeper II, was "continued Constable in the Lower precinct" (Culpeper II-A). In 1742 and 1743, Culpeper II-A constables reported twice as many tithables as the Culpeper II-B constables, so either Culpeper II-A was geographically larger or was more densely populated than Culpeper II-B. Three years later, in 1744, the court ordered the dividing line between these upper and lower precincts of Culpeper II to be "from the head of Muddy run aCro*f*s to Mountain run." The head of Muddy Run, a tributary of the Hazel River, is northwest of the town of Culpeper. Constables assigned to the lower precinct (Culpeper II-A) lived between Mountain Run and Muddy Run.[152] Constables assigned to the upper precinct (Culpeper II-B) lived above Muddy Run in the Little Fork.[153] So "lower" and "upper" meant south and north of Muddy Run.[154] The numbers of tithables of tobacco planters reported by the Culpeper II-A and Culpeper II-B constables in 1745, 1746 and 1747 are strange. In 1745, 202 tithables were reported for Culpeper II-A and 180 for Culpeper II-B; but in 1746 and 1747, the numbers of tithables in Culpeper II-B greatly increased, while those in Culpeper II-A remained almost the same (1746: 197 in Culpeper II-A and 260 in Culpeper II-B; 1747: 200 in Culpeper II-A and 281 in Culpeper II-B).

In 1748, the court appointed James Graves the new constable of Culpeper II-A "from Norman's Ford along Col Carter's Waggon Road to Mountain Run from thence up the said Run to Mr Clayton's Road thence along the Road to Yancy's Mill & from thence to Scott's Road from thence to Indian Run & so to Negro Run & down Negro Run to the North River." This is the most detailed description of a constable precinct written by the Orange County court. The boundaries of this precinct ran along the Rappahannock River from Norman's Ford south to Col. Charles Carter's Wagon Road, then west toward the Mountain Run and continued along the Mountain Run to Mr. Clayton's Road.[155] Philip Clayton's estate was at Catalpa; in 1743, he petitioned for a road from the courthouse near Raccoon Ford to Mount Poney to Mountain Run. This road, which may have been "Mr Clayton's Road," probably crossed Mountain Run above Mount Poney and continued north to the vicinity of Catalpa.[156] From Clayton's Road, the boundary continued to Yancey's Mill. This mill is mentioned only this one time in the Orange County court orders. In 1731, Philemon Cavanaugh deeded his daughter and son-in-law, Winifred and Lewis Davis Yancey, 800 acres in the Great Fork of the Rappahannock; several later deeds describe Yancey's land being on Muddy Run. In 1743, Philemon Cavanaugh gave land "upon the branches of Muddy Run above Yancey's Mill" to one of his children. Yancey family sites and two Works Progress Administration (WPA) reports trace two properties back to Lewis Davis Yancey: Maple Wood and Arlington, which are northeast of Catalpa on Route 625 (also called Yancey Road). So Yancey's Mill was probably on branches of Muddy Run north of Philip Clayton's residence.[157] (James Graves, the constable appointed to this new precinct, also lived on branches of Muddy Run.)[158] From Yancey's Mill the boundary ran northeast to (or along) Scott's Road and on to Indian Run.[159] From Indian Run the boundary continued to Negro Run, then down to the mouth of Negro Run at the North (Hedgeman, Rappahannock) River, then south along the river back to Norman's Ford. The area of this new Culpeper II-A precinct was much larger than the previous Culpeper II-A precincts. (In 1748, 302 tithables were reported in Culpeper II-A compared with 200 in 1747.) Did the court change the boundaries of Culpeper II-A to agree with the new boundaries assigned the Culpeper I constable six months earlier?

On 25 February 1749, three months before the first meeting of the newly formed Culpeper County court, the Orange County court appointed, in two successive orders, John Field and Rowland Cornelius constables "between Mountain Run & the North River in the lower Precincts." Barbara Vines Little suggested that the court clerk made a mistake, and Cornelius' order should have read "upper Precincts" not "lower Precincts."[160] In the early eighteenth century, the Rappahannock, Hedgeman's, Thornton's and Hughes Rivers were sometimes called the North River.[161] This 1749 court order could have referred to any one of these North Rivers in north "Culpeper" and "Rappahannock" Counties. Between 1737 and 1740, the two tithable precincts in "Culpeper" County were "between the Mountain Run & North river"—the same boundaries as the 1749 Culpeper II constable precinct—and "between the Rappadan & Mountain run"; that is, north and south of Mountain Run, which was the original boundary dividing constable precincts Culpeper II and Culpeper I (see Appendix, pp. 115–117). Whether or not the Orange County court was simply going through the motions of appointing constables to an area they knew would shortly be the responsibility of the new Culpeper County court, they appointed two constables to the east ("lower") and west ("upper") parts of the original 1735 borders of Culpeper II.

No lists of tobacco planters survive for Culpeper II. The total number of tithables of tobacco planters in Culpeper II, recorded in nine annual county levies, grew from 110 in 1735 to 453 in 1748 (see table 2).

CULPEPER II (1735–1740)
This precinct was described as "on the Northside of the Mountain Run from the mouth of the said Run up the River & Run to the Gourdvine fork from and cross to the Mountain Run including the little fork" in 1735 and "in the Great ffork" in 1736.

1735   John Roberts is hereby appointed Constable on the Northside of the Mountain Run from the mouth of the said Run up the River & Run to the Gourdvine fork from and cross to the Mountain Run including the little fork, and it is ordered that the Sheriff Summon the said John Roberts to the next Court to be held for this County to be sworn into the said Office – 18 February 1734/35 (OCOB 1:5; Little, 152)

County Levy (1735): To John Roberts Constable for viewing Tobacco Suckers: 110 – 18 November 1735 (OCOB 1:41; Little, 152)

County Levy (1736): To Benj[a] Cave for Jno Roberts a Constable Last Years Levy: 15 – 19 October 1736 (OCOB 1:123; Little, 154)

1736   On the motion of John Roberts he is discharged from being Constable as Soon as William

Wilson Homes who hereby is appointed Constable in his Stead Shall be Sworn into the said Office for which purpose it is ordered that the said John Roberts Summon the said Wm Wilson Homes before a Justice of this County to be Sworn accordingly – 17 February 1735/36 (OCOB 1:54; Little, 153)

Ordered that Nathanael Hillon be appointed Constable in the Great ffork in the room of William Wilson Holmes and that he be Sworn before a Justice of the Peace into the said office accordingly – 21 September 1736 (OCOB 1:108; Little, 153)

1737 On the Information of Nathaniel Hillen that Andrew Glaspee tended Tobacco Suckers and also that Col° Charles Carters Quarter called Barrows Lowgrounds between three or four hundered Seconds were turned out It is ordered that Zachary Lewis Attorney for our Soverign Lord the King prosecute them according to Law[162] – 25 August 1737 (OCOB 1:204; Little, 155)

The case against Andrew Glaspee:

On the Information of Zachary Lewis Gent Attorney for our Sovereign Lord the King that . . . Andrew Glaspee . . . [and others] had tended Succors Its ordered that the said persons be Summoned by the Sheriff to the next court to answer the s^d Information – 27 October 1737 (OCOB 1:225)

In the Suit by Information brought . . . for . . . the King ag^t Andrew Glaspee for tending tobacco Succours the Sheriff having returned that he had Summoned the said Glaspee and he being called and failing to appear Its Ordered that an Attachment i∫sue ag^t the body of the said Andrew Glaspee for his personal appearance at the next Court to answer the said Information – 25 November 1737 (OCOB 1:253)

In the Suit by Information brought . . . in behalf of . . . the King ag^t Andrew Glaspee Deft who who being called appeared & pleaded not guilty & . . . a Jury . . . having heard all Evidences brought in their Verdict . . . find the Deft Guilty in one tithable person & one person above the age of Seven Years . . . Whereupon its Considered by the Court that the said Deft be fined One thousand pounds of tobacco according to Law and . . . with Costs – 24 February 1737/38 (OCOB 1:265)

County Levy (1737): To Nathanial Hillion [Constable for viewing tobacco]: 152 – 27 October 1737 (OCOB 1:233; Little, 155)

1738 County Levy (1738): To Nathanael Hillen Constable for counting tobo Succours: 181 – 26 October 1738 (OCOB 1:393; Little, 157)

County Levy (1739): To Nathanael Hillen for Overpaying a tithable being Con∫table: 11½ – 25 October 1739 (OCOB 2:79; Little, 160)

1739 Thomas Dillard is hereby appointed Constable in the room of Nathaniel Hillen who is hereby orderd to Summon ye s^d Dillard before Some Justice of the Peace of this County to be sworn into ye s^d Office accordingly – 22 February 1738/39 (OCOB 1:421; Little, 158)

1740 Joseph Norman is hereby appointed Constable in the room of Edward [Thomas] Dillard & its ordered that he be Sumoned by ye Sheriff to appear at ye next Court to be Sworn in ye s^d

Office[163] – 23 May 1740 (OCOB 2:185; Little, 161)

County Levy (1740): To Thos Dillard Constable: 213½ – 23 October 1740 (OCOB 2:275; Little, 163)

CULPEPER II-A AND CULPEPER II-B (1741–1747)

In 1741, Culpeper II was divided into two precincts when John Chissum was appointed constable "above Devis's Rowling path and Muddy run" (Culpeper II-B), and Joseph Norman, former constable of Culpeper II, was "continued Constable in the Lower precinct" (Culpeper II-A). In 1744, the court described this division as the "Lower Part" (Culpeper II-A) and "upper part" (Culpeper II-B) "from the head of Muddy run aCro∫s to Mountain run."

CULPEPER II-A (1741–1747)

1741   John Chi∫sum is hereby appointed Constable above Devis's Rowling path and Muddy run who having taken the oaths appointed by Act of Parliament & Subscribed the Test took the oaths of a Constable & was Sworn in the s^d Office accordingly and it is ordered that Joseph Norman be continued Constable in the Lower precinct – 28 May 1741 (OCOB 2:363; Little, 164)

1742   Saml Parks is hereby appointed Con∫table in the Room of Jo∫eph Norman & its ordered that he be ∫ummoned to appear at next Court to be Sworn in ye s^d Office – 28 January 1741/42 [Little dated this November 1741] (OCOB 3:97; Little, 165)

Samuel Parks [and another] having taken the oaths appointed by Acts of Parliament & Subscribed the Test were Sworn Con∫tables accordingly – 25 March 1742 (OCOB 3:113)

On the Information of Samuel Parks Con∫table that David Williams who lived at George Roberts's tended tobacco ∫uccors & its ordered that the Kings Attorney i∫sue proce∫s ag^t him for the Same according to Law[164] – 26 August 1742 (OCOB 3:201; Little, 166)

County Levy (1742): To Samuel Parks Con∫table: 196 – 25 November 1742 (OCOB 3:294; Little, 167)

1743   Alex^r McQueen is hereby appointed Con∫table in the room of Saml Parks and its ordered that ye s^d Parks ∫ummon him before a Justice of ye Peace to be Sworn into ye s^d Office accordingly – 22 March 1742/43 (OCOB 3:395)

County Levy (1743): To Alexander McQueen for viewing tob^o fields as Constable: 191 – 24 November 1743 (OCOB 4:27; Little, 169)

1744   On ye Pet^n of Alex^r McQueen to be Dischg^d from the Office of Constable Its Ordered that Isaac Norman be ∫ummoned to appear next Court to be ∫worn into y^e ∫^{d} Office in the Room of McQueen – 22 March 1743/44 (OCOB 4:59; Little, 170)

John Renolds is hereby appointed Constable in the room of Alex^r McQueen & its ordered that he be Summoned by the Sheriff to appear at ye next Court to be Sworn into the said office – 24 May 1744 (OCOB 4:108; Little, 170)

Ordered that ye precinct where of Alex^r McQueen was Con∫table be divided from the head of

Muddy run aCrofs to Mountain run and that Isaac Norman be appointed Conftable in ye Lower Part and William White in the upper part and that they be fummoned to appear at next Court to be Sworn into ye s^d Office – 26 May 1744 (OCOB 4:138; Little, 170)

The Order for Isaac Norman and Wm White to be summoned to be sworn Constable Cont^d to be ret^d – 26 July 1744 (OCOB 4:190; Little, 171)

1745   Isaac Norman was Sworn Constable in this County and took the Oath appointed by the Tobacco Law – 23 May 1745 (OCOB 4:329; Little, 172)

County Levy (1745): To Isaac Norman [Constable] for [Viewing Tobacco Fields]: 202 – 29 November 1745 (OCOB 4:448; Little, 174)

1746   John Favours is by the Court appointed Constable in this County in the Room of Isaac Norman who is Discharged from that office and It is Ordered that he be sworn into his said Office at the Next Court – 22 May 1746 (OCOB 4:472; Little, 175)

John Favors [and another] took the Usual Oaths to his Majesty's Person & Government and took & Subscribed the abjuration and Test and took the Oaths appointed by the Tobacco Law and Swore into the Office of Constable – 26 June 1746 (OCOB 4:489; Little, 175)

County Levy (1746): To John Favour Constable for viewing Tobacco Fields: 197 – 27 November 1746 (OCOB 4A:103; Little, 175)

1747   John Reynolds is by the Court Appointed a Constable in this County in the room of John Favour who is Discharged from that Office & it is ordered that he be Sworn into his Said Office at the next Court – 28 May 1747 (OCOB 4A:152; Little, 176)

County Levy (1747): To John Reynolds Constable for viewing Tobacco Fields: 200 – 27 November 1747 (OCOB 5:81; Little, 176)

CULPEPER II-B (1741–1747)

1741   John Chifsum is hereby appointed constable above Devis's Rowling path and Muddy run who having taken the oaths appointed by Act of Parliament & Subscribed the Test took the oaths of a Constable & was Sworn in this s^d Office accordingly and it is ordered that Joseph Norman be continued Constable in the Lower precinct – 28 May 1741 (OCOB 2:363; Little, 164)

County Levy (1741): To Jno Chifsum Constable for viewing Tob° Succors: 93½ – 22 October 1741 (OCOB 3:49; Little, 165)

1742   County Levy (1742): To John Chifsum Constable: 85 – 25 November 1742 (OCOB 3:294; Little, 167)

1743   Wm White is hereby appointed Conftable in the room of John Chifsum deced and its ordered that he go before a Justice of the Peace of this County to be fworn in the said Office accordingly – 25 June 1743 (OCOB 3:479)

County Levy (1743): To Wm White for viewing Tob° fields as Constable: 112 – 24 November 1743 (OCOB 4:27; Little, 169)

1744 Ordered that ye precinct where of Alex^r McQueen was Conſtable be divided from the head of Muddy run aCroſs to Mountain run and that Isaac Norman be appointed Conſtable in ye Lower Part and <u>William White</u> in the upper part and that they be ſummoned to appear at next Court to be Sworn into ye s^d Office – 26 May 1744 (OCOB 4:138; Little, 170)

The Order for Isaac Norman and Wm White to be summoned to be sworn Constable Cont^d to be ret^d – 26 July 1744 (OCOB 4:190; Little, 171)

County Levy (1744): To William White for Viewing of Tobacco fields: 185 – 22 November 1744 (OCOB 4:227; Little, 171)

1745 <u>Samuel Scott</u> is appointed Constable in the Room of William White who is discharged from that office & having taken the usual Oaths to his Majesties Person and Government Taken and Subscribed the Abjuration oath and the Test was Sworn into his said office and then took the Oath appointed by the Tobacco Law[165] – 22 August 1745 (OCOB 4:411; Little, 173)

Samuel Scott Constable in this County Pursuant to Law made a return that he found Slips or Seconds growing and tended upon the Plantations of Joseph Caves and John Wilson each of them having one Tithable whereupon it is Ordered that the Attorney for our Sovereign Lord the King Do enter Prosecution against them for the same[166] – 27 September 1745 (OCOB 4:426; Little, 173)

County Levy (1745): To Samuel Scott Constable for Viewing Tobacco Fields: 180 – 29 November 1745 (OCOB 4:448; Little, 174)

1746 County Levy (1746): To <u>Samuel Scott</u> Constable for viewing tobacco fields: 260 – 23 October 1746 (OCOB 4A:100)

1747 <u>William White</u> in the room of Samuel Scott took the Oaths to his Majesty's Person and Government and took and subscribed the Oath of Abjuration and the Test were Constables and took the Oath appointed by the Tobacco Law – 23 July 1747 (OCOB 5:2; Little, 176)

County Levy (1747): To William White Constable for Viewing Tobacco Fields: 281 – 27 November 1747 (OCOB 5:81; Little, 176)

CULPEPER II-A AND CULPEPER II-B (1748)
In 1748, the court changed the boundaries of Culpeper II-A and Culpeper II-B when they appointed James Graves constable "from Norman's Ford along Colo. Carter's Waggon Road to Mountain Run, from thence up the Run to Mr. Clayton's Road, thence along the Road to Yancey's Mill, thence to Scott's Road, from thence to Indian Run and so to Negro Run and down Negro Run to the North River" (Culpeper II-A). William White continued as constable of Culpeper II-B.

CULPEPER II-A (1748)

1748 Charles Kavanaugh [and another] are appointed Constables . . . the said Charles in the room of John Rennolds and it is ordered that they be sworn into their said Offices at the next Court – 26 May 1748 (OCOB 5:115; Little, 177)

James Graves is by the Court appointed Constable from Norman's Ford along Colo. Carter's Waggon Road to Mountain Run, from thence up the Run to Mr. Clayton's Road, thence along the Road to Yancey's Mill, thence to Scott's Road, from thence to Indian Run and so to Negro Run and down Negro Run to the North River, and he having taken the Oaths to his Majesty's Person & Government and the Abjuration Oath and subscribed the Test, was sworn Constable, and then took the Oath appointed by the Tobacco Law – 23 June 1748 (OCOB 5:139; Little, 177)

County Levy (1748): To James Graves for [viewing Tobacco Fields]: 302 – 24 November 1748 (OCOB 5:158; Little, 178)

CULPEPER II-B (1748)

1748   County Levy (1748): To William White Constable for viewing Tobacco Fields: 151 – 24 November 1748 (OCOB 5:158; Little, 178)

CULPEPER II-A AND CULPEPER II-B (1749)
In 1749, the court again changed the boundaries of Culpeper II-A and Culpeper II-B, when they assigned two constables "between the Mountain Run & the North River in the lower [and upper] Precincts."

CULPEPER II-A (1749)

1749   John Field is by the Court appointed Constable between Mountain Run & the North River in the lower Precincts[167] – 25 February 1748/49 (OCOB 5:175; Little, 178)

CULPEPER II-B (1749)

1749   Rowland Cornelius is by the Court appointed Constable between the Mountain Run & the North River in the lower [*sic* upper] Precincts – 25 February 1748/49 (OCOB 5:175; Little, 178)

James Graves is by the Court appointed Constable in the room of Rowland Cornelius who is discharged from that Office – 23 March 1748/49 (OCOB 5:177; Little, 178)

Culpeper County was formed from Orange County and held its first court session on 18 May 1749.

RAPPAHANNOCK

In 1735, Francis Brown was appointed constable "from the point of the Gourdvine fork up to the great Mountains." This was in today's Rappahannock County, which was formed from Culpeper County in 1833 (see Map 3). Only three constables—all of whom lived in the Gourdvine Fork—were appointed to this precinct.[168] This area might have become the responsibility of Culpeper II-B or Madison II after 1739.[169]

No lists of tobacco planters survive for this precinct, and the court did not credit any constable of this precinct for viewing tobacco fields.

RAPPAHANNOCK (1735–1739)

1735   Francis Brown is hereby appointed Constable from the point of the Gourdvine fork up to the great Mountains, and it is ordered that the Sheriff Summon the said Francis Brown to the next Court to he held for this County to be sworn into the said Office – 18 February 1734/35 (OCOB 1:5; Little, 152)

1736–37 Francis Brown

1738   Thos Kennerley is hereby made Constable in the room of ffrancis Brown and its ordered that the said ffrancis Brown Sumon the said Kennerly before a Justice of ye Peace for this County to be Sworn in the said Office accordingly – 25 May 1738 (OCOB 1:327; Little, 157)

1739   Daniel Brown Junr is hereby appointed Constable in the Room of Thomas Kennerley and its ordered that the Sheriff Sumon the said Brown to appear at the next Court to be sworn into the said Office according to Law – 24 May 1739 (OCOB 1:460; Little, 158)

MADISON I

In 18 1735, David Phillips was appointed constable "in the Fork of the Robinson." This precinct, which I call Madison I, covered the land between the Robinson and Rapidan Rivers west to the Blue Ridge Mountains. In 1747, Madison I was divided into two subprecincts when William Henderson was ordered to be "Continued in the office of Constable in that part of the Little Fork lying in Parish of Saint Thomas and William Rice is appointed Constable of the other part of the said Fork." Madison I-A, "in Parish of Saint Thomas," probably extended from the vicinity of today's town of Shelby south to the Rapidan River. (When St. Thomas' Parish was formed in 1740, it encompassed the counties of today's Orange, Greene and this strip of southern Madison.) Madison I-B, covered the remaining area of Madison I to the north (see Map 3).[170]

Three lists of tobacco planters, dating 1736, 1737 and 1739, survive for Madison I. Over these three years, the number of tobacco planters in the precinct grew from 67 to 127. From 1 to 7 tithables lived in the households of these planters, averaging 2.2 to 2.5 tithables per household. The total number of tithables of tobacco planters in Madison I, recorded in eight annual county levies, grew from 99 in 1735 to 366 in 1747 (see table 2).

MADISON I (1735–1747)

This precinct was described as "in the Fork of the Robinson" in 1735.

1735   <u>David Phillips</u> is hereby appointed Constable in the Fork of the Robinson and it is ordered that the Sheriff Summon the said Phillips to the next Court to be held for this County to be Sworn into the said Office – 18 February 1734/35 (OCOB 1:5; Little, 152)

County Levy (1735): To David Phillips Constable for Viewing Tobacco Suckers: 99 – 18 November 1735 (OCOB 1:41; Little, 152)

1736   LIST: In orange County all ye 1736 Tithables in my pircints" – 237½ – <u>David Phillips</u> Constable[171] (Little, 3)

We [the Grand Jury] present David Phillips Constable for not looking after suckers and causing them to be cut down according to Law this present Year – 25 November 1736 (OCOB 1:127; Little, 154)

> The Grand jury presentment ag^t David Phillips Constable for not looking after tobacco Suckers and causing them to be cut down according to law this present Year, is dismis^d – 25 March 1737 (OCOB 1:152; Little, 154)

1737   LIST: 1737 Orange County all ye Tithables In my pircincts – <u>David Phillips</u> Constable – 172 (Little, 5)

County Levy (1737): To David Phillips [Constable for viewing tobacco]: 237½ – 27 October 1737 (OCOB 1:233; Little, 156)

On the information of David Phillips that William Crawford having two tithables & his Wife in family did tend Tobacco Succors & Its ordered that Zachary Lewis Attorney for our Lord the King prosecute him for the Same according to Law – 27 October 1737

(OCOB 1:234; Little, 156)

The case against William Crawford:

On the Information of Zachary Lewis Gent Attorney for our Soverign Lord the King that Nathanael Hedgeman & Wm Crawford had tended Succors its ordered that the said persons be summoned to the next Court to answer the said Information[172] – 24 February 1737/38 (OCOB 1:273; Little, 156)

In the Suit by Information brought . . . in behalf . . . ye King ag^t Wm Crawford for tending tobacco Succors the Deft pleaded not guilty and the Plt joyning in the iſsue the tryal [illegible] referred untill next Court – 24 March 1737/38 (OCOB 1:287)

In the Suit by Information brought . . . in behalf of . . . the King ag^t William Crawford Deft for tending tobacco Succors a Jury . . . having heard all Evidences and arguments of both Parties . . . find the Deft not guilty . . . & its considered by the Court that ye Suit be dismissed – 27 April 1738 (OCOB 1:298–299)

Ordered on the motion of David Phillips that Wm Crawford be hereby appointed Constable in his room & it is further ordered that the said Phillips Sumons the said Wm Crawford before a Justice of the Peace for this County to be Sworn into the said Office accordingly – 27 October 1737 (OCOB 1:234; Little, 156)

1738   County Levy (1738): To Wm Crawford Constable for counting tobacco Succours: 153 – 26 October 1738 (OCOB 1:393; Little, 157)

James Picket is hereby appointed Constable in the room of Wm Crawford [illegible] hereby ordered to Summon the said Picket before a Justice of the Peace of this County to be sworn into the said Office accordingly – 23 November 1738 (OCOB 1:407; Little, 158)

1739   LIST: A List of Tithables in the precincts of James Pickett Constable 1739 [year added] – in all 294[173] (Little, 16–17)

County Levy (1739): To James Picket [Constable for Succors]: 204 – 25 October 1739 (OCOB 2:80; Little, 160)

1740   Wm Jackſon having taken the oaths appointed by Act of Parliament & by a late Act of Aſsembly & Subscribed the test is hereby appointed Constable in the room of James Picket – 28 August 1740 (OCOB 2:237; Little, 162)

1741   Thomas Rucker is hereby appointed Constable in the room of Wm Jackson & he having taken the oaths appointed by Law & Subscribed the Test was Sworn into this s^d office accordingly – 28 May 1741 (OCOB 2:357; Little, 164)

Thomas Rucker *executed attachments against the estates of Thomas Downer and James Stephens* – 22, 23 July 1742 (OCOB 3:172, 179, 191)

Thomas Rucker *executed an attachment against the estate of Thomas Callaway* – 29 January 1742/43 (OCOB 3:338)

1742	John Howard is hereby appointed Conſtable in ye room of Thomas Rucker who being called appeared & was Sworn into ye s^d Office according to Law – 25 March 1742 (OCOB 3:112; Little, 165)
	John Howard *executed attachments against the estates of John Garth and Jacob Stober* – 28 August 1742 (OCOB 3:217–218)
	John Howard *executed an attachment on the corn and tobacco of James Dyer's plantation at Neals Mountain* – 27 November 1742 (OCOB 3:304)
	"Jas. [John] Howard, Constable" *executed an attachment against the estate of James Dyer* – 25 February 1742/43 (OCOB 3:373)
1743	James Picket is hereby appointed Conſtable in the room of John Howard & he having taken the oaths appointed by Act of Parliament to be taken in Stead of ye oath of Allegiance & the Supremacy & the Abjuration oath Subscribed ye test & then took ye oath of a Conſtable & was Sworn in ye s^d Office accordingly – 28 January 1742/43 (OCOB 3:314; Little, 167)
	James Pickett *executed an attachment against the estate of John Howard* – 27 May 1743 (OCOB 3:444)
	County Levy (1743): To James Picket for viewing tob^o Fields as Constable aſsigned to Henry Downs Gent: 119 – 25 November 1743 (OCOB 4:29; Little, 169)
1744	Tully Choice is hereby appointed Constable in the room of James Pickett and his having taken ye oaths preſcribed by Act of Parliament to be taken inſtead of ye oaths of Allegiance & Supremacy & the Abjuration oaths & Subscribed ye Test took ye oaths of a Constable and was Sworn accordingly – 26 May 1744 (OCOB 4:138; Little, 170)
	William Herondon [Henderson] is hereby appointed Constable in the room of James Pickett and it's Ordered that the said Herondon be Summoned to appear at the next Court to Swear into the said Office[174] – 25 August 1744 (OCOB 4:216; Little, 171)
	William Henderson having Taken the Oaths prescribed by Act of Parliament instead of the Oaths of Allegiance and Supremacy & the Abjuration Oath and have Subscribed the Test was Sworn into the Office of a Constable – 27 September 1744 (OCOB 4:219; Little, 171)
1745	County Levy (1745): To William Henderson Constable for viewing Tobacco Fields: 351 – 29 November 1745 (OCOB 4:448; Little, 174)
1746	County Levy (1746): To William Henderson [Constable] for viewing Tobacco Fields: 193 – 27 November 1746 (OCOB 4A:103; Little, 175)
1747	County Levy (1747): To William Henderson for Viewing Tobacco Fields: 366 – 27 November 1747 (OCOB 5:81; Little, 176)

MADISON I-A AND MADISON I-B (1748–1749)
This precinct was divided into "that part of the Little Fork lying in Parish of Saint Thomas" and "the other part of the said Fork" in 1747.

1748–49 William Henderson is by the Court continued in the Office of Constable in that part of the Little Fork lying in Parish of Saint Thomas and William Rice is appointed Constable of the other part of the said Fork and it is ordered that he be sworn into the said Office at the next Court – 27 November 1747 (OCOB 5:82; Little, 177)

Culpeper County, which included today's Madison County, was formed from Orange County and held its first court session on 18 May 1749.

MADISON II

In 1736, the Orange County court ordered John Micall to replace William Rush as constable "at the great [Blue Ridge] Mountains in the fork of Rappahannock." This precinct, Madison II, covered the north of today's Madison County and probably extended into western "Culpeper" County (see Map 3). In 1740, Madison II was divided into two subprecincts when the court appointed Timothy Terril "Constable from the double topp down to white oak run & from the North side down to deep run" (Madison II-B), and Thomas Garrel replaced John Michael, who was constable of Madison II in 1739 (Madison II-A). Doubletop Mountain is in northwest "Madison" County, and White Oak Run and Deep Run flow through the Hebron Valley into the Robinson River. The Hebron Valley stretches along the Robinson River and takes its name from the German Lutherans who were granted some of the oldest land patents in "Madison" County. Richard Burdyne and Zacharias Blankenbaker, two Madison II-B constables, lived in the Hebron Valley.[175] Madison II-A can be identified as the most northern area of "Madison" County by the residences of some of the constables assigned to this precinct.[176]

One list of tobacco planters, dating 1739, survives for Madison II. Fifty-three tobacco planters with 1 to 10 tithables in their households (averaging 1.7 tithables per household) lived in this precinct in 1739. The total number of tithables of tobacco planters in Madison II, recorded in two annual county levies grew from 57 in 1737 to 70 in 1739 (see table 2).

MADISON II (1735–1739)

This precinct was described as "at the great Mountains in the fork of Rappahannock" in 1736.

1735   William Rush[177]

1736   Ordered that John Micall be appointed Constable at the great Mountains in the fork of Rappahannock in the room of William Rush deced and that he be Sworn in the said office before a Justice of the Peace of this County – 21 September 1736 (OCOB 1:108; Little, 153)

1737   On the information of John Michael that John Layton having two tithables Thomas Walker having two tithables and Henry Kendall having three tithables all had turned out and tended Succors Its ordered that Zach^y Lewis Gent Attorney for our Sovereign Lord the King prosecute them according to Law[178] – 22 September 1737 (OCOB 1:214; Little, 155)

On the Information of Zachary Lewis Gent Attorney for our Sovereign Lord the King that . . . John Layton . . . Thomas Walker, Henry Kendall [and others] had tended Succors Its ordered that the said persons be Summoned by the Sheriff to the next court to answer the s^d Information – 27 October 1737 (OCOB 1:225)

The case against John Layton:

In the Suit by Information brought . . . for . . . the King ag^t John Layton for tending tobacco Succors the Deft appeared and pleaded not guilty which I∫sue . . . Zachary Lewis [Attorney] joyned and the tryal thereof is referred untill next Court – 25 November 1737 (OCOB 1:253)

In the Suit by Information brought . . . in behalf of . . . the King ag^t John Layton Deft for tending tobacco Succors A Jury . . . having heard all Evidences . . . find the Deft had two tithables & one person above seven years old & is guilty . . . whereupon its considered by the Court that the said Deft be fined fifteen hundred pounds of tobacco according to Law and . . . Costs – 24 February1737/38 (OCOB 1:261–262)

The case against Thomas Walker:

In the Suit by Information brought . . . for . . . the King ag^t Thomas Walker for tending tobacco Succors who being called appeared & pleaded not guilty which I/sue . . . Zachary Lewis [Attorney] joyned & the trial thereof is referred untill next Court – 25 November 1737 (OCOB 1:254)

In the Suit by Information brought . . . in behalf of . . . the King ag^t Thomas Walker Deft for tending tobacco Succors a Jury . . . having heard all Evidences . . . find for the Deft . . . & the Suit is dismissed – 24 February 1737/38 (OCOB 1:269)

The case against Henry Kendall:

In the Suit by Information brought . . . for . . . the King ag^t Henry Kendal for tending tobacco Succors the said Kendal being called appeared and pleaded not guilty which I/sue . . . Zachary Lewis [Attorney] joyned and the tryal thereof is referred untill the next Court – 25 November 1737 (OCOB 1:254)

In the Suit by Information brought . . . in behalf of . . . the King ag^t Henry Kendall Deft for tending tobacco Succors a Jury . . . having heard all Evidences . . . find for the Deft . . . & the Suit is dismissed – 24 February 1737/38 (OCOB 1:269)

County Levy (1737): To John Michael Constable [for viewing tobacco]: 51½ – 27 October 1737 (OCOB 1:233; Little, 155)

1738   John Michael

1739   John Michaels Constable came into Court and took the oath enjoynd by the Last Acts of A/sembly – 22 March 1738/39 (OCOB 1:438; Little, 158)

LIST: John Mickell His List of Tithables in his Precints – 100 (Little, 20)

County Levy (1739): To John Michael [Constable for Succors]: 70 – 25 October 1739 (OCOB 2:80; Little, 160)

MADISON II-A AND MADISON II-B (1740–1749)
In 1740, Madison II was divided into two precincts when Thomas Garrel replaced John Michael (Madison II-A), and Timothy Terrill was appointed constable "from the double topp down to white oak run & from the North side down to deep run" (Madison II-B).

MADISON II-A (1740–1749)

1740   Thomas Garrel is hereby appointed Constable in the Room of John Michaell and its ordered that the Sheriff Sumon the said Garrel to appear at the next Court to be sworn into the said office according to Law – 24 May 1739 (OCOB 1:460; Little, 158)

1741   Mathew Stanton is hereby made Constable in the room of Thos Garrott who having taken the oaths appointed by Law and Subscribed the Test was Sworn in the s^d Office accordingly – 28 May 1741 (OCOB 2:358; Little, 164)

County Levy (1741): To Mathew Stanton Conſtable for viewing tob^o fuckors: 22½ – 22 October 1741 (OCOB 3:49; Little, 165)

1742   Richard Yarbrough is hereby appointed Constable in the room of Mathew Stanton who being called appeared & having taken the oaths appointed by Law Subscribed the Test & Was Sworn in the s^d Office accordingly – 25 March 1742 (OCOB 3:113; Little, 165)

County Levy (1742): To Richard Yarbrough Conſtable: 89 – 25 November 1742 (OCOB 3:294; Little, 167)

1743   Richard Yarborough *executed attachments on the estates of David Phillips and John Spiller* – 29 January and 26 February 1742/43 (OCOB 3:343, 377)

County Levy (1743): To Richd Yarbough's Levy aſsigned to [Henry Downs Gent]: 17 – 25 November 1743 (OCOB 4:29; Little, 169)

1744–46 Richard Yarborough

1747   Daniel Brown is hereby Appointed Constable in this County in the room of Richd Yarbrough & it is ordered that he be sworn into his said office at the next Court[179] – 28 March 1747 (OCOB 4A:142; Little, 175)

1748   Russell Hill took the Oaths to his Majesty's Person and Government and took and subscribed the Abjuration oath and the Test was sworn Constable in this County in the room of Daniel Brown and then took the Oath appointed by the Tobacco Law – 25 March 1748 (OCOB 5:104)

1749   Beaumont Sutton is appointed Constable in the room of Russell Hill who is discharged from that Office and it is ordered that said Sutton be sworn into his Office at the next Court – 23 March 1748/49 (OCOB 5:177; Little, 178)

Culpeper County, which included today's Madison County, was formed from Orange County and held its first court session on 18 May 1749.

MADISON II-B (1740–1749)

1740   Timothy Terril is hereby appointed Constable from the double topp down to white oak run & from the North Side down to deep run and its ordered that he appear at ye next Court to be sworn into the said Office accordingly – 28 February 1739/40 (OCOB 2:107; Little, 160)

Timothy Terrill having taken the oaths appointed by Act of Parliament & by a late act of Aſsembly & Subscribed the Test was Sworn Constable accordingly – 27 March 1740 (OCOB 2:134)

Ordered that the Kings Attorney prosecute Leonard Ziegler for refusing to obey and aſsist

Timothy Terrill a Constable in conveying a prisoner that had broken out of Goal & was retaken by the said Constable[180] – 27 February 1740/41 (OCOB 2:312)

1741 Richard Burdine is hereby appointed Constable in the room of Timothy Terrill and its ordered that he be Sumoned by the Sheriff of this County to appear at the next Court to be Sworn into the said Office accordingly – 28 May 1741 (OCOB 2:357; Little, 164)

Richard Burdine being last Court appointed Constable this day being called appeared and having taken the oaths appointed by Act of Parliament & Subscribed the Test Took the oaths appointed by a late Act of Afsembly & was Sworn Constable accordingly – 25 June 1741 (OCOB 2:398; Little, 164)

1742 County Levy (1742): To Richard Burdine for Summoning a Jury on Waggoner: 35 – 25 November 1742 (OCOB 3:294)

1743–45 Richard Burdyne

1746 Ordered that Zachary Blakenpecker do serve as Constable in this County in the Room of Richard Burdyne who is Discharged from that office – 28 August 1746 (OCOB 4A:25; Little, 175)

1747 Zachary Blankenbeckler [Little has Zacharyas Blakenbukler] as a Constable in this County in the room of Richard Burdyne [and another] took the Oaths to his Majesty's Person and Government and took and subscribed the Oath of Abjuration and the Test were Constables and took the Oath appointed by the Tobacco Law – 23 July 1747 (OCOB 5:2; Little, 176)

County Levy (1747): To Zachariah Blankenbeker for viewing Tobacco Fields: 99 – 27 November 1747 (OCOB 5:81; Little, 176)

1748 Robert Hutcheson is by the Court appointed Constable in the Room of Zacharias Blakenbecker and it is ordered that he be sworn into his said Office at the next Court – 25 August 1748 (OCOB 5:152; Little, 177)

County Levy (1748): To Zachary Blakenbecker [for viewing Tobacco Fields]: 102 – 24 November 1748 (OCOB 5:158; Little, 178)

1749 Robert Hutcheson?

Culpeper County, which included today's Madison County, was formed from Orange County and held its first court session on 18 May 1749.

THE FREDERICK PRECINCTS

Frederick County was formed from Orange County in 1738, but was governed by Orange County until a court was constituted in the new county and held its first session on 11 November 1743. When formed, Frederick County stretched from the Potomac River south to the northern border of today's Rockingham County and from the Blue Ridge Mountains west to "the utmost limits of Virginia."[181] Between 1754 and 1866, twelve counties were formed from Frederick County; seven of these counties became part of West Virginia when it attained statehood in 1863 (see Maps 1 and 4).

Between 1735—three years before the formation of Frederick County—and 1743, the Orange County court appointed over fifty constables to precincts in Frederick County. These men can be identified as constables of Frederick County by the description of their precinct or—absent that—by road orders, land grants and deeds which place them in the county at the time of their appointment. In 1735, the Orange County court divided Frederick County into four precincts; in 1740, it was divided into six precincts; and by 1743, Frederick County was divided into eleven precincts. These eleven precincts covered the county from the Potomac River in the north to Funk's Mill in the south and from the Shenandoah River in the east to the Cacapon River in the west. (These precincts were located in today's counties of Frederick, Shenandoah, Warren and Clarke in Virginia; and Jefferson, Berkeley, Morgan and Hampshire in West Virginia.) At the first meetings of the newly formed Frederick County court in late 1743 and early 1744, twelve men were appointed constables; unfortunately, the court did not describe the boundaries of their precincts.[182]

Constable precincts in Frederick County were described as being on waterways: the Shenandoah River, the Potomac River, "Cape Cappurie," Opequon Creek, Tuscarora Creek, Bullskin Run, "Stapy" Creek and the "fourth branch of Potomack"; and near man-made sites: Chester's (Ferry), Scott's Mill, "Yunks [Funk's] Mill," and the residences of Morgan Morgan and Jost Hite. Two precincts were described as "at Gerundo" and "at Sherundo."

The Shenandoah River is formed at the confluence of the North and South Forks of the Shenandoah above Fort Royal and flows into the Potomac near Harper's Ferry.[183] "Cape Cappurn" was one of many variant spellings of the Cacapon River, a tributary of the Potomac River in the west of Frederick County.[184] Opequon Creek is a tributary of the Potomac River,[185] Tuscarora Creek is a tributary of Opequon Creek,[186] and Bullskin Run is a tributary of the Shenandoah River.[187]

The precinct "from Stapy Creek to ye fourth branch of Potomack" is not easy to identify. A clue might be found in a deed and a road order which place Patrick Dougharty, the constable appointed to this precinct, living east of the Cacapon River near Sleepy Creek and Warm Branch, tributaries of the Potomac River.[188] It is possible that "Stapy Creek" was the court clerk's miswriting of Sleepy Creek. Which of the many tributaries of the Potomac River was understood in the eighteenth century to be the "fourth branch" needs research.[189]

"Chesters" was Thomas Chester's ferry, which the Orange County court granted him permission to operate "from the mouth of Happy Creek to the fork of Sherundo a Cross the Main River" on 19 October 1736. This ferry was located where the North and the South Forks of the Shenandoah enter the Shenandoah River.[190] Scott's Mill may have been on Long Marsh Run, which flows into the Shenandoah River north of Berryville in today's Jefferson County. Between 1744 and 1746, the Frederick County court issued six orders for a road from "Scots [or Johnston's] mill on Sharando to the Courthouse [at Winchester]." By 1745, Scott's Mill had been renamed: "Road from [George]

Johnstons Mill /: formerly Scots :/ to the Courthouse." George Johnston's plantation was described in the road orders as being on "Long Marsh [Run]." The proximity of Scott's Mill to Winchester plus the precincts "Scott's Mill to Chesters" and "from Bullskin to Scott's Mill" support Scott's Mill having been between Chester's Ferry and Bullskin Run on or near Long Marsh Run.[191] "Yunks Mill," a misspelling of Funk's Mill, was owned by John Funk and was located on Funk's Mill Run, which flows into the west side of the North Fork of the Shenandoah River near Strasburg in today's Shenandoah County.[192]

Morgan Morgan was granted 1,000 acres between Tuscarora Creek and Mill Creek, tributaries of Opequon Creek, in 1735. Morgan's residence was west of Bunker Hill on Torytown Run, a branch of Mill Creek, in today's Berkeley County. Roads to Morgan's Chapel in Bunker Hill were ordered laid and maintained by the Orange County and the Frederick County courts from as early as 1742.[193] Jost Hite lived in today's Frederick County on Opequon Creek near Bartonville, south of Winchester. Several roads from (John) Funk's Mill to (Jost) Hite's Mill are mentioned in the Orange County and Frederick County court orders.[194]

Two precincts in eastern Frederick County were described as "at Gerundo" and "at Sherundo" (two precincts in the Beverley Manor in Augusta County were also described as "in Sherandoe"). These variant spellings of Shenandoah referred to the general area of the Shenandoah Valley, which spreads from today's Jefferson County, West Virginia, in the former Frederick County, south to Rockbridge County, Virginia, in the former Augusta County.[195] Similarly, the deputy sheriff of Frederick County was called the deputy sheriff of "that part of the County called Sherundo," and the Augusta County sheriff was called "the Sheriff of Sharrando."[196]

No lists of tobacco planters survive for Frederick County, and the Orange County court did not credit any of the Frederick County constables for viewing tobacco fields (see p. 22).

FREDERICK I (1735–1743)

This precinct was described as "at Opeckon" in 1736 and "from Morgan Morgans to Just Hites" in 1742.

1735   Abraham Wiseman [and three others] are appointed Constables & ordered to repair to Some Justice to be Sworn accordingly – 17 June 1735 (OCOB 1:19; Little, 152)

1736   Peter Stephens is hereby appointed Constable in the room of Abraham Wiseman who is hereby ordered to Summon the s^d Stephens before a Justice of the Peace for this County to be Sworn into the said Office – 18 May 1736 (OCOB 1:74; Little, 153)

Lewis Stephen is hereby made a Constable at Opecken in the room of Peter Stephen therefore it is ordered that the said Peter Stephen Sumon the said Lewis before a Justice of this County to be Sworn into the said Office accordingly – 20 July 1736 (OCOB 1:93; Little, 153)

[A jury found] that Samuel Hews on the 30th of October 1736 imported into the Government of Virginia 79 gallons of rum and entered the Same with Capt Morgan Morgan and failing to pay the duty as the Law directs twenty gallons of the said rum was Seized on the tenth day of November by the order of the Deft Collector and the broad arrow put on by Lewis Stephens Constable and *if* the Law before the Plt we find for him Eight pound Curr^t Money damage otherwise we find for the Deft . . . and the Suit is continued till the next Court for the matters of Law arising upon the s^d Verdict to be argued[197] – 28 July 1737 (OCOB 1:198)

1737   Ordered that <u>George Boman</u> be made a Constable in the room of Lewis Stevens and it is further ordered that the said Stevens Sumons ye s^d Boman before a Justice of the Peace for this County to be Sworn into the Said office accordingly – 28 July 1737 (OCOB 1:198; Little, 155)

1738   <u>Robert Worfe</u> is hereby appointed Constable in the room of Lewis Stephens who is hereby ordered to Sumon the said Worfe before a Justice of the Peace to be Sworn into ye s^d Office accordingly and its further ordered that ye s^d Stephens do not leave the s^d office till ye s^d Worf be Sworn into it – 28 September 1738 (OCOB 1:378; Little, 157)

A List of Delinquents Over Sharandore for ye year 1738 . . . Constables Refuſeth to pay . . . Robert Warth (Little, 12)

1739   <u>Robert Warf</u>

1740   <u>John McQuin</u> is hereby appointed Constable in the room of Robert Warf & its ordered that ye s^d McQuin appear at ye next Court to be Sworn into the said Office accordingly – 28 February 1739/40 (OCOB 2:111; Little, 160)

John Quin having taken the oaths appointed by Act of Parliament and by a late act of Aſsembly & Subscribed the Test was Sworn Constable accordingly – 27 March 1740 (OCOB 2:134)

Whereas the Constable that was appointed in the room of Robert Warf being aloofe man is absconded & the precinct is left without a Constable Its ordered that Jacob Niswanger be appointed in his room & that he be Sworn before a Magistrate in the office of Constable and be Summoned to appear at ye next Court to be Sworn according to the Late Act of Aſsembly[198] – 28 August 1740 (OCOB 2:238; Little, 162)

1741   <u>John McDowell</u> is hereby appointed Conſtable in the room of John Quin and its ordered that the Sheriff Summon him to appear at the next Court to be ſworn into the said Office – 23 July 1741 (OCOB 2:427; Little, 164)

1742   <u>Joseph Vaunce</u> is hereby appointed Conſtable from Morgan Morgans to Just Hites & its ordered that the Sheriff Summon him to appear at next Court to be Sworn in the said Office[199] – 27 May 1742 (OCOB 3:152; Little, 166)

The Frederick County court was constituted on 11 November 1743.

FREDERICK II (1735–1743)

This precinct was described as "at Opeakon" in 1738 and "the northern part of Bulskin precinct" in 1743.

1735   <u>John Petite</u> [and three others] are appointed Constables & ordered to repair to Some Justice to be Sworn accordingly[200] – 17 June 1735 (OCOB 1:19; Little, 152)

Its ordered that the Sheriff of this County take Providence Williams into his Custody for his

Contempt or abuse of John Petite Constable in executing his Office and him Safely keep untill he enter into bond in twenty pounds Current Money for his appearance at the next Court to answer the said Complaint[201] – 15 July 1735 (OCOB 1:28)

1736   John Petite

1737   On the petition of John Petite to be discharged from being Constable it is ordered that Thos Low be made Constable in his room and it is further ordered that the said Petite Summon the said Low before a Justice of the Peace for this County to be Sworn into the said Office accordingly – 25 March 1737 (OCOB 1:156; Little, 154)

1738   Andrew Hampton is hereby made Constable at Opeckon in the Room of Thomas Low who is orderd to Sumon the said Hampton before a Justice of ye Peace for this County to be Sworn into the said Office accordingly & its further ordered that the said Low be not discharged from being Constable till ye s^d Hampton be Sworn into ye s^d Office – 23 March 1737/38 (OCOB 1:275; Little, 156)

Ordered that the Sheriff Sumon Abraham Wiseman to appear at the next Court to answer the Complaint of George Thurston Constable for refusing to aſsist him with two runaway Negroes[202] – 22 June 1738 (OCOB 1:329)

George Thurston is hereby appointed Constable in the room of Andrew Hampton who is hereby ordered to Sumon the said George Thurston to appear before a Justice of the Peace for this County to be sworn in the said Office accordingly – 27 July 1738 (OCOB 1:346; Little, 157)

Abraham Wiseman being brought before the Court by Virtue of an Order of last June Court, to answer ye Compl^t of George Thurston Constable for refusing to aſsist him to carry two Runaway Negroes to their Master, said he had been a long while Sick & that he was not able to aſsist him its ordered that he be dismissed paying fees – 27 July 1738 (OCOB 1:350)

1739   George Thurston

1740   Colvert Anderſon is hereby appointed Constable in the room of George Thurston and its ordered that ye s^d Anderſon appear at ye next Court to be Sworn into the said Office accordingly – 28 February 1739/40 (OCOB 2:111; Little, 160)

Colvert Anderſon having taken the oaths appointed by Act of Parliament & Subscribed the Test took ye oaths appointed by a late Act of Aſsembly & was Sworn Constable Accordingly – 27 March 1740 (OCOB 2:134)

1741   Jacob Bruks is hereby appointed Constable in the room of Colvert Anderſon and its ordered that the Sheriff Summon the said Bruks to appear at the next court to be Sworn into the said Office accordingly – 26 March 1741 (OCOB 2:325; Little, 163)

1742   Ordered that the Sheriff of this County Summon Colvert Anderſon to appear at next Court to Shew cauſe why he [illegible] being Constable will not execute precepts delivered to him – 27 May 1742 (OCOB 3:150)

Ordered that Colvert Anderſon be again Summoned to appear at next Court to Shew Cauſe why he being Conſtable will not execute these precepts delivered to him – 24 June 1742 (OCOB 3:164)

John Hampton is hereby appointed Conſtable in the room of Colvert Anderſon and its ordered that he be ſummoned to appear at next Court to be ſworn into the said Office – 23 July 1742 (OCOB 3:178; Little, 166)

The order for Sumoning Culvert Anderſon being returned by the Sheriff Executed & the s^d Anderſon being called and failing to appear to Shew cauſe why he had refused to execute precepts delivered to him being conſtable Its ordered that an Attachment iſsue ag^t him returnable to the next Court[203] – 28 August 1742 (OCOB 3:223)

Ordered that Culvert Anderſon the Late Conſtable Summon John Hampton who is hereby appointed Conſtable in his room to appear before a Justice of ye Peace to be sworn in the said Office accordingly – 24 September 1742 (OCOB 3:240; Little, 167)

1743   George Thurston is hereby appointed Conſtable & he having taken the oaths prescribed by Law & Subscribed the Test was Sworn Conſtable for ye northern part of Bulskin precinct accordingly – 22 March 1742/43 (OCOB 3:395)

The Frederick County court was constituted on 11 November 1743.

FREDERICK III (1735–1743)

This precinct was described as "at Gerundo" in 1736 and "Sharandore" in 1738 and "from Scott's Mill to Chesters" in 1742.

1735   John Wood [and three others] are appointed Constables & ordered to repair to Some Justice to be Sworn accordingly – 17 June 1735 (OCOB 1:19; Little, 152)

1736   Thomas Postgate is hereby appointed Constable in the Stead of John Wood who is hereby ordered to Summon the s^d Postgate before a Justice of the Peace for this County to be Sworn into the said Office[204] – 18 May 1736 (OCOB 1:74; Little, 153)

Ordered that William Routfrors be appointed Constable in the Room of John Wood at Gerundo and that he be Sworn into the s^d office accordingly – 21 September 1736 (OCOB 1:108; Little, 153)

1737   Ordered that Peter Woolf be Constable in the Room of William Rentfrow and that the s^d Rentfrow Summon the s^d Woolf before a Justice of the Peace for this County to be sworn into the s^d Office accordingly – 26 May 1737 (OCOB 1:170; Little, 154)

1738   Hugh Gilder is hereby appointed Constable in the room of Peter Wolf and its ordered that ye s^d Peter Wolf Summon ye s^d Hugh Gilder before a Justice of ye Peace for this county to be Sworn in ye s^d office accordingly[205] – 25 May 1738 (OCOB 1:327; Little, 157)

A List of Delinquents Over Sharandore for ye year 1738 . . . Constables Refuſeth to pay . . . Hutzin Gilder (Little, 12)

1739	James McKee is hereby appointed Constable in the room of Hugh Guilder and its further ordered that the Sheriff Summon the said James McKee to appear at the next Court to be Sworn in to the said Office according to Law – 28 June 1739 (OCOB 2:2; Little, 159)
	James McKay having taken the oaths appointed by Law & Subscribed the Test then took the oath of a Constable was Sworn in the s^d Office accordingly – 23 August 1739 (OCOB 2:63; Little, 160)
	"Constable McKay" *executed an attachment against the estate of Richard Wood* – 23 November 1739 (OCOB 2:102–103)
1740	Leonard Helms is hereby appointed Constable in ye room of James McKee & its ordered that he be Sumoned by the Sheriff to appear at ye next Court to be Sworn in ye s^d Office accordingly – 27 March 1740 (OCOB 2:133; Little, 161)
	Leonard Helms having taken the oaths appointed by Acts of Parliament & Subscribed the Test took ye oaths appointed by a late Act of Aſsembly & was Sworn Constable accordingly – 26 June 1740 (OCOB 2:187; Little, 161)
1741	John Alford is hereby appointed Constable in the room of Leonard Helms & its ordered that the Sheriff Summon the s^d Alford to appear at the next court to be Sworn into the s^d Office accordingly – 26 March 1741 (OCOB 2:325; Little, 163)
	John Alford [and two others] having Severally taken the oaths preſcribed by Law & Subscribed the Test Severally took the oath of a Constable were Sworn in the s^d Office accordingly – 28 May 1741 (OCOB 2:363)
	John Nation is hereby appointed constable in John Alford's precinct and its ordered that he be Summoned to appear at the next Court to be sworn in the said Office and its further ordered that the s^d John Alford be also continued in this s^d office in the said precinct – 25 September 1741 (OCOB 3:7; Little, 165)
1742	The order for Summoning John Nation to be ſworn conſtable is continued untill the next Court to be executed – 26 February 1741/42 (OCOB 3:106; Little, 165)
	John Nation is hereby appointed Conſtable from Scotts Mill to Chesters who being called appeared and having taken the Oaths prescribed by Law & Subscribed the Test – 27 May 1742 (OCOB 3:152; Little, 166)
1743	Ralph Craft is hereby appointed Conſtable in the room of John Nation and its ordered that the said Nation ſummon him to appear before a Justice of the Peace for this County to be Sworn into the said Office accordingly – 24 June 1743 (OCOB 3:474)

The Frederick County court was constituted on 11 November 1743.

FREDERICK IV (1735–1743)
This precinct was between the Potomac River and Bullskin Run. It was described as "on Potomack" in 1737, "at Sherundo" in 1738, "from Opecken to Bullskin" in 1742 and "Southern part of Bullskin Precinct" in 1743.

1735	Samuel Murris [and three others] are appointed Constables & ordered to repair to Some Justice to be Sworn accordingly – 17 June 1735 (OCOB 1:19; Little, 152)
1736	On the petition of Samuel Morris Isaac Pennington is appointed Constable in his room and it is ordered that the said Samuel Summon the said Isaac Pennington before a Justice of this County to be Sworn into the said Office – 18 May 1736 (OCOB 1:74; Little, 153)
1737	Ordered that John Pitts be Constable in room of Isaac Pennington and it is further ordered that the s^d Pennington Summon the s^d Pitts before one of his Majestys Justice of the Peace for this County to be Sworn into the s^d Office accordingly[206] – 26 May 1737 (OCOB 1:169; Little, 154)
	Ordered that Thomas Sheppard be constable on Potomack and it is further ordered that he go to a Justice of the Peace for this County to be Sworn into the s^d Office accordingly[207] – 26 May 1737 (OCOB 1:169; Little, 154)
1738	Thos Sheppard is on his petition discharged from being Constable at Sherundo as soon as Richard Morgan who is hereby appointed Constable in his Stead Shall be sworn into the said Office for which purpose it is ordered that the said Thomas Sheppard Summon the said Richard Morgan before a Justice of this County to be Sworn accordingly – 26 February 1737/38 (OCOB 1:257; Little, 156)
	A List of Delinquents Over Sharandore for ye year 1738 . . . Constables Refuſeth to pay . . . Richard Morgan (Little, 12)
1739	Wm Myers is hereby appointed Constable in the room of Richard Morgan and its further ordered that the Sheriff Summon the said Wm Myers to appear at the next Court to be Sworn into the said Office according to Law – 28 June 1739 (OCOB 2:2; Little, 159)
	Ordered that Wm Myers who last Court was appointed Constable be summoned to appear at ye next Court to be Sworn in the s^d Office according to Law and that he be fined if he fails to appear – 26 July 1739 (OCOB 2:29; Little, 159)
	Wm Myers having taken ye oaths appointed by Acts of Parliament and Subscribed the Test took the oath of a Constable & was Sworn in the s^d Office accordingly – 23 August 1739 (OCOB 2:49; Little, 160)
1740	John Tradan is hereby appointed Constable in the room of Wm Myer & its ordered that he be Sumoned by the Sheriff to appear at ye next Court to be Sworn in ye s^d Office accordingly – 27 March 1740 (OCOB 2:133; Little, 161)
	John Tradan being last Court appointed Conſtable in ye room of Wm Moyers & being Summoned appeared and refused to Swear alledging that he was Roman Catholick, wherefore William Johnston is hereby appointed Constable in the room of John Tradan & its ordered that ye Sheriff Summon ye s^d Johnston to appear at ye next Court to be Sworn into ye s^d Office accordingly – 26 June 1740 (OCOB 2:189; Little, 161)
1741	Peter Hilton is hereby appointed Constable in the room of Wm Johnſon and its ordered that the Sheriff Summon the s^d Hilton to appear at the next Court to be Sworn into the said Office

accordingly – 26 March 1741 (OCOB 2:325; Little, 163)

Peter Hilton [and two others] having Severally taken the oaths preſcribed by Law & Subscribed the Test Severally took the oath of a Constable were Sworn in the s^d Office accordingly – 28 May 1741 (OCOB 2:363)

Peter Hilton *executed an attachment against the estate of Thomas Rennicks* – 23 July 1742 (OCOB 3:190)

1742 Thomas Hart is hereby appointed Conſtable in the room of Peter Hilton & its ordered that he be ſummoned to the next Court to be ſworn into the said Office accordingly – 25 March 1742 (OCOB 3:113; Little, 165)

Thos Heart is hereby appointed Conſtable from Opccken to Bullskin who being called appeared and having taken the oaths prescribed by Law & Subscribed the Test was Sworn in ye s^d Office accordingly – 27 May 1742 (OCOB 3:152; Little, 166)

1743 Robert Worthington is hereby appointed Conſtable of ye Southern part of Bullskin Precinct who having taken ye oath prescribed by Law & Subscribed the Test was Sworn in ye s^d office accordingly[208] – 22 March 1742/43 (OCOB 3:395; Little, 168)

The Frederick County court was constituted on 11 November 1743.

FREDERICK V (1740–1743)

This precinct was described as "in Bulskin precinct" in 1740 and "from Bullskin to Scotts Mill" in 1742.

1740 Henry Robinſon is hereby appointed Constable in Bulskin precinct & its ordered that he be Sumoned by the Sheriff to appear at ye next Court to be Sworn into ye s^d Office accordingly – 27 March 1740 (OCOB 2:134; Little, 161)

Henry Robinſon having taken the oaths appointed by Act of Parliament & Subscribed the Test took ye oaths appointed by a late Act of Aſsembly & was Sworn Constable of Bulskin precinct – 22 May 1740 (OCOB 2:166; Little, 161)

1741 Abraham Yeates is hereby appointed Constable in the room of Henry Robinson & its ordered that the Sheriff Sumon him to appear at the next Court to be sworn into the s^d Office accordingly – 27 March 1741 (OCOB 2:332; Little, 163)

Abraham Yates failing to appear at Court to be Sworn in the office of Constable [illegible] its ordered that he be again Sumoned to appear at the next Court to be sworn into the s^d Office – 28 May 1741 (OCOB 2:357; Little, 164)

William Davis is hereby appointed Constable in the room of Henry Robinſon & its ordered that the Sheriff Sumon him to appear to the next Court to be ſworn in the s^d Office & that if he fail to appear he be fined – 26 June 1741 (OCOB 2:408; Little, 164)

Gilbert Gilder is hereby appointed Conſtable in the room of Henry Robinſon & it is ordered that the Sheriff Summon him to appear at the next Court to be Sworn in the s^d Office accordingly – 23 July 1741 (OCOB 2:427; Little, 164)

Gilbert Gilder having taken the oaths appointed by Act of Parliament & Subscribed the Test & taken the oaths appointed by a late act of Genl Aſsembly was Sworn Conſtable – 27 August 1741 (OCOB 2:461)

1742 John Osborn is hereby appointed Conſtable in ye room of Huckill Guilder & its ordered that he be ſummoned to appear at next Court to be ſworn in the said Office[209] – 25 March 1742 (OCOB 3:113; Little, 165)

John Osborn is hereby appointed Conſtable from Bullskin to Scotts Mill who being called appeared and having taken the oaths preſcribed by Law & Subscribed the Test was Sworn in the said Office accordingly – 27 May 1742 (OCOB 3:152; Little, 166)

1743 Daniel McDaniel is hereby appointed Conſtable in the room of John Osborn who is hereby ordered to ſummon him to appear before a Justice of ye Peace for this County to be ſworn in ye s^d Office accordingly – 24 June 1743 (OCOB 3:475; Little, 168)

The Frederick County court was constituted on 11 November 1743.

FREDERICK VI (1740)
This precinct at "Cape Cappurn," in west Frederick County, was in the area of the Cacapon River.

1740 John Welton Junr is hereby appointed Constable at Cape Cappurn [Little has Cappurie] & its ordered that he be Sumoned by the Sheriff to appear at ye next Court to be Sworn into ye s^d Office accordingly[210] – 27 March 1740 (OCOB 2:134; Little, 161)

FREDERICK VII (1742)
This precinct was described as "from Potomack to Tuscarora" in 1742.

1742 Job Curtis is hereby appointed Conſtable from Potomack to Tuscarora & its ordered that the Sheriff Summon him to appear at the next Court to be Sworn in ye s^d Office – 27 May 1742 (OCOB 3:152; Little, 166)

The order to ſummon Job Curtis to be sworn in the office of Constable continued untill ye next Court to be returned – 28 August 1742 (OCOB 3:223; Little, 166)

The order that ſummon Job Curtis to be ſworn Conſtable is dismised – 25 September 1742 (OCOB 3:272; Little, 167)

FREDERICK VII-A AND FREDERICK VII-B (1743)
In 1743, this precinct was divided when the court appointed two constables to replace Job Curtis: one "at Tuscorara" and the other "from Stapy Creek to ye fourth branch of Potomack."

FREDERICK VII-A (1743)

1743 Cornelius Newkirk is hereby appointed Conſtable at Tuscorora in the room of Job Curtis and its ordered that he ſummon him before a Justice of ye Peace of this County to be Sworn in ye s^d Office accordingly – 26 May 1743 (OCOB 3:426; Little, 168)

The Frederick County Court was constituted on 11 November 1743.

FREDERICK VII-B (1743)

1743   Patrick Dougharty is hereby appointed Conſtable from Stapy Creek to yᵉ fourth branch of Potomack & its ordered that Job Curtis ſummon him to appear before a Justice of yᵉ Peace of this County to be Sworn in yᵉ Office accordingly – 26 May 1743 (OCOB 3:426; Little, 168)

The Frederick County court was constituted on 11 November 1743.

FREDERICK VIII (1742)

This precinct was described as "Tuscarora to Morgan Morgans" in 1742. It may have been a subdivision of Frederick II.

1742   Ralph Low is hereby appointed Conſtable from Tuscarora to Morgan Morgans & it is ordered that the Sheriff Summon him to appear at next Court to be Sworn in yᵉ sᵈ Office – 27 May 1742 (OCOB 3:152; Little, 166)

The Frederick County court was constituted on 11 November 1743.

FREDERICK IX (1742)

This precinct was described as "from Just Hites to Yunks [Funks] Mill" in 1742.

1742   John Denton is hereby appointed Conſtable from Just Hites to Yunks Mill & its ordered that the Sheriff Summon him to appear at next Court to be Sworn in the said Office – 27 May 1742 (OCOB 3:152; Little, 166)

The order to ſummon John Denton to be ſworn in the office of Constable is continued untill the next Court to be returned – 28 August 1742 (OCOB 3:223; Little, 166)

Ordered that the Sheriff Summon [John] Denton to appear before a Justice of yᵉ Peace to be Sworn in yᵉ office of Conſtable – 25 September 1742 (OCOB 3:272; Little, 167)

The Frederick County court was constituted on 11 November 1743.

FREDERICK UNIDENTIFIED PRECINCT (1742–1743)

1742   The Order for Summoning John [Joseph] Edwards to be ſworn Conſtable is continued untill the next Court to be executed[211] – 26 February 1741/42 (OCOB 3:106)

The order to ſummon John Edwards to be Sworn Conſtable is continued to be returned – 23 July 1742 (OCOB 3:180; Little, 166)

Ordered that Joseph Edwards be ſummoned by the Sheriff before a Justice of yᵉ Peace to be Sworn Constable – 24 September 1742 (OCOB 3:249)

1743   On the Information of Morgan Morgan Gent one of his [Majesty's] Justices of the Peace for this County that Joſeph Edwards Constable hath ſeized nine Deer Skins which were in yᵉ hands & poſseſion of John Pearcy who was found travelling with the ſame in order to carry them out of the Colony without paying any duty for yᵉ same according to yᵉ Act of Aſsembly . . . . And that the said Skins had remained in the hands of the said Morgan Morgan above the Space of two Months and that the Owner of ye s^d Skins hath never made proof being made before this Court at any time that the said Duty hath been paid Therefore its conſidered by the Court that the said Skins are forfeited and its ordered that the Sheriff Sell the said Skins according to the Act of Aſsembly & make return of his proceedings to y^e next Court – 24 February 1742/43 (OCOB 3:354)

The Frederick County court was constituted on 11 November 1743.

FREDERICK UNIDENTIFIED PRECINCT (1743)

1743   Mathias Seltzer [Little has Mathias T_l_y] is hereby appointed Constable & its ordered that he be ſummoned to appear before [?] James Patton to be ſworn into the s^d Office accordingly[212] – 23 June 1743 (OCOB 3:464; Little, 168)

The Frederick County court was constituted on 11 November 1743.

The Augusta Precincts

Augusta County was formed from Orange County in 1738 but was governed by Orange County until a court was constituted in the new county and held its first session on 9 December 1745. Augusta County covered a vast area—larger than the rest of the Virginia colony—from the Blue Ridge Mountains to the Mississippi River and from the Great Lakes to Tennessee (see Maps 1 and 5). Twenty-six Virginia counties and the states of Michigan, Illinois, Indiana, Ohio, West Virginia and Kentucky were formed from Augusta County.[213]

From 1736—two years before the Virginia Assembly created Augusta County—to 1745, the Orange County court appointed over one hundred men to constable precincts in Augusta County. I identified twenty precincts (Augusta I–XX) where about eighty men were appointed constables; another seventeen men were appointed to unidentified precincts. These men can be identified as constables of Augusta County by the description of their precinct or—absent that—road orders, land grants and deeds that place them in the county at the time of their appointment. In 1736, the Orange County court appointed one constable to serve in Augusta County; in 1743, seventeen constables were appointed; and by 1745, on the eve of Augusta County assuming responsibility for constable appointments, the Orange County court appointed thirty-two constables to this enormous area. (In 1745 thirteen constables served in the Orange, Culpeper and Madison precincts in 1745.) During the year following the first meeting of the Augusta County court, on 9 December 1745, the Augusta justices appointed twenty-nine constables; ten of these twenty-nine appointees replaced constables appointed by the Orange County court.[214]

The Orange County court described very few of the precincts in Augusta County, and—unique to Augusta County—in 1743, 1744 and 1745, the court ordered justices living in Augusta County to lay out the precincts of thirty constables appointed to the area.[215] The court used waterways to describe all but two—Borden's Tract and Beverley Manor—precincts: the "north River of Gerundo," the "South River of Sharrando River," the "Second ffork of Sherundo," the James River, the "Cow Pasture," the "Calf Pasture," "Linwell's Creek" and "Christee's Creek." Some constables were appointed to simply "Augusta" or "that part of Orange County called Augusta" or "at Sherundo County" or "in Sherandoe."[216]

The "north River of Gerundo" was the North Fork of the Shenandoah River, an area on the northern border of Augusta County in today's Rockingham County.[217] I identified six precincts in this area, which I designated Augusta I–VI; Augusta I was the oldest precinct in the county. The "South River of Sherrando" and the "Second fork of Sherundo" were the South Fork of the Shenandoah River; many of the constables assigned to the upper and lower precincts of the "Second fork of Sherundo" (Augusta VII and Augusta VIII) owned property in Beverley Manor. The James River was the location of one of the most southern precincts in Augusta County (Augusta XVII). The "Cow Pasture" is the Cowpasture River, a tributary of the James River (Augusta XVIII). The "Calf Pasture" is the Calfpasture River, a tributary of the Maury or North River (Augusta XIX). Barbara Vines Little correctly identified the precinct "on Linwell's Creek" as Linnville Creek, a tributary of the North Fork of the Shenandoah River (Augusta V).[218] "Christee's Creek" was Christians Creek, a tributary of the Middle River, which flows through the former Beverley Manor. Between 1753 and 1764, the Augusta County court ordered work on a road from the courthouse at Staunton to Christians Creek; in two of these orders, Christians Creek was called "Christys Creek."[219]

Beverley Manor, sometimes called the Irish Tract, was William Beverley's 118,490 acre 1736 patent between the Middle River and the South River, which covered much of the western half of today's Augusta County. Eight precincts (Augusta VII–XIV) were located in Beverley Manor.[220] Borden's Tract, Benjamin Borden's 92,100 acre 1739 grant, was south of Beverley Manor and covered much of today's Rockbridge County (Augusta XV and Augusta XVI).[221]

In 1745, the constable precincts in Augusta County reached from the border dividing Frederick and Augusta Counties south to the New River (in today's Pulaksi County) and from the Blue Ridge Mountains west to the Cowpasture River (in today's Bath County). These precincts covered a very small part of the immense county of Augusta.

No lists of tobacco planters survive for Augusta County, and the Orange County court did not credit any of the constables of Augusta County for viewing tobacco fields (see p. 22).

AUGUSTA I–VI

These six precincts were the most northern precincts in Augusta County. With the exception of Augusta V, the location of these precincts in the area of today's Rockingham County is based on the residences of the constables appointed to the precincts.

AUGUSTA I (1736–1742)

This precinct was described as "the north River of Gerundo" in 1736 and "at Sherundo County" in 1738. The constables appointed to this precinct lived in the north of today's Rockingham County, which would make this the most northern precinct in Augusta County. Many of the constables appointed to this precinct were ordered to work on roads in Frederick County and have been described as residents of that county. But since several of them were appointed after Frederick County assumed responsibility for its own affairs in 1743, this precinct must have been considered part of Augusta County.[222]

1736   Ordered that James Gill be appointed Constable at the north River of Gerundo and be sworn into the s^d Office accordingly – 21 September 1736 (OCOB 1:108; Little, 153)

1737   James Gill

1738   Daniel Holdman is hereby appointed Constable in the room of James Gill at Sherundo County to be sworn into the said Office accordingly and its further ordered that the said Gills Serve in the said Office till the said Holdman be Sworn into it – 23 November 1738 (OCOB 1:407; Little, 158)

1739   Daniel Holdman

1740   Wm White is hereby appointed Constable in the room of Daniel Holman & its ordered that he be Sumoned by the Sheriff to appear at ye next Court to be Sworn in the said Office accordingly – 27 March 1740 (OCOB 2:133; Little, 161)

Wm White having taken the oaths pre∫cribed by Act of Parliament & Sub∫cribed the Test took ye oaths appointed by a late Act of A∫sembly & was sworn Constable accordingly – 28 August 1740 (OCOB 2:237; Little, 162)

1741   Charles Robinson is hereby appointed Constable in the room of Wm White & its ordered that he be Summoned to appear to the next Court to be ∫worn into the s^d Office accordingly

– 28 May 1741 (OCOB 2:358; Little, 164)

Charles Robinſon being last Court appointed Constable & ordered to be ſummoned to be Sworn in the said Office the Sheriff having returned on the order not executed for want of time its ordered that he be ſummoned to appear at the next Court to be ſworn into yᵉ sᵈ Office – 26 June 1741 (OCOB 2:408)

The order for Summoning Charles Robinſon Constable to be ſworn into the said office being returned not executed because the sᵈ Robinſon is gone to Carolina Its ordered that he be again Summoned agᵗ next Court – 23 July 1741 (OCOB 2:429; Little, 164)

Charles Robinſon having taken the oaths preſcribed by Acts of Parliament & Subscribed the Test took the oaths appointed to be taken by late Acts of Aſsembly was Sworn Conſtable accordingly – 27 August 1741 (OCOB 2:468)

1742   Charles Robinson

AUGUSTA I-A AND AUGUSTA I-B (1743–1745)

In 1743, Augusta I was divided when two constables replaced Charles Robinson.

AUGUSTA I-A (1743–1745)

1743   Ordered that Reily Moor & Wᵐ Flintham serve as Constable in the Precincts that Charles Robinson ſerved they being first sworn into the sᵈ Office before a Justice of the Peace for this County and that [illegible] divide said Precincts between the sᵈ Moor & [Flintham?] – probably 25 August 1743 (OCOB 4:1; Little, 168)

1744   The Order to Sumons Reuben Allen to be Sworn Constable in the Room of Reily Moore and it's Continued until the next Court to be returned – 23 August 1744 (OCOB 4:198; Little, 171)

1745   Ordered that Joſeph Dunham who is appointed a Constable in this County in the Room of Reiley Moore who is discharged from that Office be summoned to appear at the next Court to be sworn into his said Office – 28 February 1744/45 (OCOB 4:270; Little, 172)

Joseph Durham is hereby appointed Constable in the Room of Reily Moore It's Ordered that the Sherif Sumon him to appear at Next Court to Swear into his said Office – 28 June 1745 (OCOB 4:367; Little, 173)

Joseph Denham who is Appointed a Constable in this County having first Taken the Oaths to his Majesties Person and Government and Subscribed the Abjuration Oath and the Test and took the Oath appointed by the Tobacco Law was Sworn into his said office – 25 July 1745 (OCOB 4:393; Little, 173)

The Augusta County court was constituted on 9 December 1745.

AUGUSTA I-B (1743–1745)

1743   Ordered that Reily Moor & Wᵐ Flintham serve as Constable in the Precincts that Charles Robinson ſerved they being first sworn into the sᵈ Office before a Justice of the Peace for this County and that [illegible] divide said Precincts between the s^d Moor & [Flintham?] – probably 25 August 1743 (OCOB 4:1; Little, 168)

1744   Wm Clerk is hereby appointed Conftable in the room of [blank] ffluetham and its ordered that he be *f*ummoned to ye next Court to be Sworn in ye s^d Office accordingly – 26 May 1744 (OCOB 4:133; Little, 170)

The Order for Wm Clark to be summoned to be sworn Constable Cont^d to be ret^d – 26 July 1744 (OCOB 4:190; Little, 170)

1745   William Carrell is hereby appointed Constable in the Room of William Clark who is discharged from that Office and it is ordered that he be sworn into his said Office at the next Court – 27 June 1745 (OCOB 4:356; Little, 173)

John Hodge is hereby appointed Constable in this County in the Room of William Clark who is Discharged from that office and it is Ordered that the said Hodge be Sworn into his said office at the next Court – 22 August 1745 (OCOB 4:411; Little, 173)

The Augusta County court was constituted on 9 December 1745.

AUGUSTA II (1738–1741)

Although the court did not describe this precinct, it may have been in the east of today's Rockingham County since four of the constables appointed to this precinct lived in that area.

1738   On the information of John Tilly that William Frazer hath dangerously wounded one Samuel Rofe [or Ro*f*e] its ordered that the said Tilly who is hereby appointed Constable take the said Fraser into Custody and deliver him unto the Sheriff who is hereby ordered to carry the said Fraser before some one of his Ma[jesties] Justices of ye Peace for this County there to be dealt with as ye Law directs[223] – 27 April 1738 (OCOB 1:295; Little, 156)

John Tilly Sworn Constable & Subscribed the test – 27 April 1738 (OCOB 1:295)

Wm Frazier being brought before the Court for grieviously Wounding & Shooting Samuel Rofer [or Ro*f*er] was Examined vouching the Same he confe*f*seth the facts whereupon its Considered by the Court that the said Frazier enter into Recognizance unto our Sovereign Lord the King for forty pounds Sterling with two Securities for twenty pounds each for the said Frazier keeping his Ma[jesties] peace towards all his Ma[jesties] [illegible] people but more especially toward ye s^d Samuel Rofer – 25 May 1738 (OCOB 1:314)

Ordered on the Motion of Wm Frazier that John Tilly take Samuel Rofe [or Ro*f*e] in Custody till he enter into Recognizance to our Sovereign Lord the King for forty pounds Sterling with two Sufficient Securities each in twenty pounds Sterling for his Good behavior to all his Ma[jestys] people but more Especially to Wm Frazier [illegible] during a twelve month and a day – 23 June 1738 (OCOB 1:344)

A List of Delinquents for the year 1738 – John Tilly – 1 who was constable (Little, 11)

On the motion of John Tilly Constable that he and James Tilly be added to the List of tithables its ordered that they be added accordingly – 28 September 1738 (OCOB 1:378; Little, 157)

1739 Samuel Scott is hereby appointed Constable in the room of John Tilly and its ordered that the Sheriff Summon the said Samuel Scott to appear at the next Court to be Sworn into the s^d Office according to Law[224] – 28 June 1739 (OCOB 2:2; Little, 159)

Samuel Scott having taken the oaths appointed by Law & thofe of a late act of Afsembly Subscribed the Test & was Sworn Constable accordingly – 28 June 1739 (OCOB 2:9; Little, 159)

1740 Wm Williams is hereby appointed Constable in ye room of Saml Scott & its ordered that ye Sheriff Sumon him to appear at ye next Court to be Sworn into ye s^d Office accordingly[225] – 24 July 1740 (OCOB 2:214; Little, 162)

Wm Williams having taken the oaths appointed by Act of Parliament & Subscribed the Test took the oaths appointed by a late act of Afsembly & was Sworn Constable accordingly – 25 September 1740 (OCOB 2:247)

1741 Henry Dowley having taken the oaths prescribed by Act of Parliament & Subscribed the Test took the oaths appointed by late Acts of General Afsembly & was Sworn Constable in room of William Williams accordingly[226] – 27 August 1741 (OCOB 2:469)

The order to take Henry Dowley & James McDowel in Custody is dismisd[227] – 24 September 1742 (OCOB 3:247)

Augusta III (1743–1744)
This precinct was described as "that part of Orange County called Augusta" in 1743. Road orders and deeds place the constables appointed to this precinct in today's Rockingham County.[228]

1743 Adam Miller [and two others] are hereby appointed conftable in that part of Orange County Called Augusta & its ordered that they be fworn into the said office before James Patton Gent or any other Justice in that place who are desired to appoint them their precincts – 24 February 1742/43 (OCOB 3:348; Little, 167)

Richard Mauldin is hereby appointed Conftable in the room of Adam Miller and its ordered that he be fummoned to appear at the next Court to be fworn into ye s^d Office accordingly – 26 May 1743 (OCOB 3:430; Little, 168)

John Davis [and four others] are hereby appointed Conftables and its ordered that the Sheriff fummon them to appear before James Patton Gent to be fworn into ye s^d Office accordingly and the s^d James Patton is hereby desired to lay out for each of them his precinct – 23 June 1743 (OCOB 3:462; Little, 168)

1744 Ordered that Adam Miller Serve as Constable in the Room of Jno Davis and that he be summoned to appear at next Court to swear accordingly and its Continued untill then to make [illegible] – 23 August 1744 (OCOB 4:198; Little, 171)

Augusta III-A and Augusta III-B (1745)
In 1745, this precinct was divided when two constables replaced John Davis.

1745 William Lamb and Ludowick Francisco are appointed Constables in this County in the Room of John Davis who is Discharged from that office and it is Ordered that they be Sworn into their said office at the Next Court – 22 August 1745 (OCOB 4:411; Little, 173)

The Augusta County court was constituted on 9 December 1745.

AUGUSTA IV (1743–1745)
The two constables appointed to this precinct lived in today's Rockingham County.[229]

1743   Edward Erwins [and four others] are hereby appointed Conſtables and its ordered that the Sheriff ſummon them to appear before James Patton Gent to be ſworn into ye s^d Office accordingly and the s^d James Patton is hereby desired to lay out for each of them his precinct – 23 June 1743 (OCOB 3:462; Little, 168)

1744   Edward Erwins

1745   Alexander Blare is appointed Constable in this County in the Room of Edward Irwin who is discharged from that Office and it is Ordered that the said Alexander be sworn into his said Office at the next Court – 28 February 1744/45 (OCOB 4:270; Little, 172)

Alexander Blair is hereby appointed Constable in the Room of Edward Irwin and it's Ordered that the Sherrif Summon him to appear at the next Court to Swear into said Office – 28 June 1745 (OCOB 4:366; Little, 173)

The Augusta County court was constituted on 9 December 1745.

AUGUSTA V (1745)
This precinct was described as "on Linwell's Creek" in 1745.

1745   Samuel Stewart is hereby appointed Constable in this County on Linwell's Creek and it is Ordered that the said Samuel be Sworn into his said Office at the Next Court – 27 June 1745 (OCOB 4:356; Little, 173)

Jeremiah Harriſon is appointed Constable in the Room of Thomas [Samuel] Stewart who is Discharged from that office and he having taken the usual Oaths to his Majesties Person and Government, taken and Subscribed the Abjuration Oath and the Test, was Sworn into his said office and then took the Oath appointed by the Tobacco Law[230] – 22 August 1745 (OCOB 4:412; Little, 173)

The Augusta County court was constituted on 9 December 1745.

AUGUSTA VI (1745)
This precinct was described as "on the South River [South Fork] of Sharrando River." This river flows through today's Warren and Page Counties, in the former Frederick County, and Rockingham County, in the former Augusta County. Since this appointment was made two years after the Frederick County court started handling its own affairs, this precinct must have been considered part of Augusta County.

1745   George Leitch [Little has Seitch] is hereby appointed Constable on the South River of Sharrando River in this County and it is Ordered that he be sworn into his said Office at the

Next Court – 27 June 1745 (OCOB 4:356; Little, 173)

The Augusta County court was constituted on 9 December 1745.

AUGUSTA VII – AUGUSTA XIV

The constables appointed to these eight precincts lived in Beverley Manor. But only two of these eight precincts— Augusta VIII, "at Christee's Creek" and Augusta XII "Beverly Manor District"— describe the precincts as being in the Beverley Manor.

AUGUSTA VII (1738–1741)

This precinct, described as the "Lower precinct of ye Second ffork of Sherundo" in 1738, was in Beverley Manor.[231]

1738   Alex^r Thompson is hereby appointed Constable of ye Lower precinct of ye Second ffork of Sherundo & its ordered that he go before Some one of his Ma[jesties] Justices of ye Peace for this County to be Sworn into ye s^d Office accordingly – 27 April 1738 (OCOB 1:293; Little, 156)

1739   John Carr is hereby appointed Constable in the room of Alex^r Thompson and its ordered that the Sheriff Sumon ye s^d Carr to appear at next Court to be Sworn into ye s^d Office according to Law – 24 May 1739 (OCOB 1:463; Little, 158)

John Carr having taken the oaths appointed by Act of Parliament & Subscribed the Test Took the oath of a Constable and the oaths appointed by a late Act of Aſsembly to be taken was Sworn into the said Office accordingly – 26 July 1739 (OCOB 2:29; Little, 159)

1740   Wm Brown having taken ye oaths appointed by Act of Parliament & by a late Act of Aſsembly & Subscribed the test is hereby appointed Constable in ye room of John Carr – 28 August 1740 (OCOB 2:237; Little, 162)

1741   Robert Patterſon is hereby appointed Conſtable in the room of Wm Brown & its ordered that he be ſumoned to appear at the next Court to be Sworn into the said Office accordingly – 27 August 1741 (OCOB 2:460; Little, 164)

Robert Patterſon having taken the oaths preſcribed by Act of Parliament and Subscribed the Test took the oaths preſcribed by the late Acts of Aſsembly & was Sworn Constable accordingly – 25 September 1741 (OCOB 3:7; Little, 165)

AUGUSTA VIII (1738–1741)

This precinct, described as the "Upper precinct of the Second fork of Sherundo" in 1738, was in Beverley Manor.[232]

1738   Joseph Teaze [Little has Goazd] is hereby appointed Constable of ye Upper precinct of the Second fork of Sherundo & its ordered that he go before some one of his Ma[jesties] Justices of ye Peace for this County to be Sworn into the said Office accordingly[233] – 27 April 1738 (OCOB 1:294; Little, 156)

1739   John Wilson is hereby appointed Constable in the room of Joseph Teaze [Little has Goaze] and its ordered that the Sheriff Sumon him to appear at the next Court to be Sworn into ye s^d Office according to Law – 24 May 1739 (OCOB 1:463; Little, 158)

John Christian having taken the Oaths appointed by Law and Subscribed the Test was Sworn Constable accordingly – 28 June 1739 (OCOB 2:3; Little, 159)

1740 John Wilson is hereby appointed Constable in ye room of John Christian and its ordered that he be Sumoned by ye Sheriff to appear at ye next Court to be Sworn in ye s^d Office accordingly – 27 March 1740 (OCOB 2:133; Little, 161)

Ordered that John Wilson who last Court was appointed Constable in ye room of John Christian be Summoned to appear at ye next Court to Swear into the said Office – 23 May 1740 (OCOB 2:176; Little, 161)

1741 Patrick Cook is hereby appointed Constable in the room of John Wilson who having taken the oaths appointed by Law & Subscribed the Test was Sworn in the s^d office accordingly – 28 May 1741 (OCOB 2:358; Little, 164)

AUGUSTA VIII? (1741)
William Smith, appointed to "Christee's Creek" might have replaced Patrick Cook of Augusta VIII, the precinct where John Christian, who lived on Christians Creek, was constable in 1739.

1741 Wm Smith is hereby appointed Constable at Christee's Creek & its ordered that he be ſummoned by the Sheriff to appear at the next Court to be Sworn in the said Office – 25 September 1741 (OCOB 3:7; Little, 165)

AUGUSTA IX (1743–1745)
This precinct, described as "in Sherandoe" and "in Augusta" in 1745, was assigned to constables living in Beverley Manor.[234]

1742 Thos Turk [Little has Firk] [and five others] are Severally hereby appointed Conſtables & its ordered that the Sherriff Summon them to appear on ye fifteenth of next Month at the house of Patrick Campbell, there to be ſworn into ye s^d Office by W^m Ruſsell James Patton John Lewis & John Buchannan Gents or any one of them & to appear at next Court to take the oaths appointed by a late Act of Parliament – 24 June 1742 (OCOB 3:161; Little, 166)

1743 Ordered That Thomas Turk be sworn in ye office of Constable for this present year and that James Patton Gent lay off his Precinct – 25 August 1743 (OCOB 4:3; Little, 168)

1744 Thomas Turk

This precinct might have been divided when the Orange County court appointed—or tried to appoint—three men to replace Thomas Turk between February and June of 1745.

1745 Robert Moody is appointed Constable in this County in the Room of Thomas Turk who is discharged from that Office and It is Ordered that the said Robert be sworn into his said Office at the next Court – 28 February 1744/45 (OCOB 4:268; Little, 172)

Robert Moodey is hereby appointed Constable in the room of Thomas Turk and It's Ordered that the Sherif Summon him to appear at the next Court to Swear into his said Office – 28 June 1745 (OCOB 4:370; Little, 173)

William Wright is appointed Constable in Sherandoe in this County in the Room of Thomas Turk who is discharged from that Office and It is Ordered that the said William be sworn into his s^d Office at the next Court – 28 March 1745 (OCOB 4:289; Little, 172)

William Wright is appointed a Constable of this County in the Room of Thos Turk who is discharged from that Office and its Ordered that the said Wright be sworn into his Office at the next Court – 28 June 1745 (OCOB 4:371; Little, 173)

David Edmondson is appointed Constable in this County in the Room of Thomas Turk who is Discharged from that office and it is Ordered that he be sworn into his s^d office at the next Court – 23 May 1745 (OCOB 4:326; Little, 172)

James Gilasby is appointed Constable in Augusta in the Room of David Edminston who is Discharged from that office – 27 September 1745 (OCOB 4:427; Little, 174)

The Augusta County court was constituted on 9 December 1745.

AUGUSTA X (1742)

All the constables appointed to this precinct lived in Beverley Manor.[235]

1742 Patrick Martin [and five others] are Severally hereby appointed Conſtables & its ordered that the Sherriff Summon them to appear on ye fifteenth of next Month at the house of Patrick Campbell, there to be ſworn into ye s^d Office by W^m Ruſsell James Patton John Lewis & John Buchannan Gents or any one of them & to appear at next Court to take the oaths appointed by a late Act of Parliament – 24 June 1742 (OCOB 3:161; Little, 166)

AUGUSTA X-A AND AUGUSTA X-B (1743–1745)

In 1743, Augusta X was divided when two constables replaced Patrick Martin.

AUGUSTA X-A (1743–1745)

1743 Robt Poage and John McCutchin are hereby appointed Conſtables in the room of Patrick Martin and its ordered that ye s^d Martin ſummons them to appear before James Patton Gent to be ſworn into ye s^d Offices & ye s^d James Patton is desired to lay out for them their precincts – 30 July 1743 (OCOB 3:515; Little, 168)

1744 Robert Poage

1745 William Baskins is hereby appointed Constable in the Room of Robt Poage and its Ordered that he be summoned to appear here at the Next Court to Swear into his said Office – 24 January 1744/45 (OCOB 4:244; Little, 172)

Ordered that William Baskins who is appointed Constable in the Room of Poge be summoned to appear at the next Court to Swear into the s^d office of Constable – 24 May 1745 (OCOB 4:335; Little, 172)

The Augusta County court was constituted on 9 December 1745.

AUGUSTA X-B (1743–1745)

1743   Robt Poage and <u>John McCutchin</u> are hereby appointed Conſtables in the room of Patrick Martin and its ordered that ye s^d Martin ſummons them to appear before James Patton Gent to be ſworn into ye s^d Offices & ye s^d James Patton is desired to lay out for them their precincts – 30 July 1743 (OCOB 3:515; Little, 168)

1744   <u>John McCutchen</u>

1745   <u>Andrew Picken</u> is appointed Constable in this County in the Room of John McCutchen who is discharged from that Office and It is Ordered that the said Andrew be sworn into his said Office at the next Court – 28 February 1744/45 (OCOB 4:268; Little, 172)

Andrew Pickens is hereby appointed Constable in the Room of John McCutchen and its Ordered that the Sherif Summon him to appear at the Next Court to Swear into his said Office – 28 June 1745 (OCOB 4:367; Little, 173)

The Augusta County court was constituted on 9 December 1745.

AUGUSTA XI (1743–1745)

This precinct, described as "Augusta" in 1743 and "in Sherandoe" in 1745, was assigned to constables living in Beverley Manor.[236]

1743   <u>James Caldwall</u> [and two others] are hereby appointed conſtable in that part of Orange County Called Augusta & its ordered that they be ſworn into the said office before James Patton Gent or any other Justice in that place who are desired to appoint them their precincts – 24 February 1742/43 (OCOB 3:348; Little, 167)

James Caldwell *and James Allen, constables, executed an attachment against the estate of James Rutledge*[237] – 24 September 1743 (OCOB 4:21)

1744   James Caldwele Constable having served one year & Petitioning to be Dischg^d from ye office Its Ordered that Roger Douglaſs do serve in his stead being first sworn into said office before James Patton or John Lewis Gent – 23 February 1743/44 (OCOB 4:50; Little, 169)

On the Petition of James Caldwell to be dischgd from the Office of Constable the ſame is granted – 22 March 1743/44 (OCOB 4:58; Little, 169)

Ordered that <u>Wm Hutchinson</u> be ſummoned to appear next Court to take the Oaths of a Constable & to be sworn into the Office in the Room of James Caldwell – 22 March 1743/44 (OCOB 4:58; Little, 169)

The Order for Wm Hutchinson ſummoned to be sworn Constable Cont^d to be ret^d – 26 July 1744 (OCOB 4:190; Little, 171)

1745   <u>George Caldwell</u> is appointed Constable in Sherandoe in this County in the Room of William Hutcheson who is discharged from that Office and It is Ordered that the said George be sworn into his said Office at the next Court – 28 March 1745 (OCOB 4:289; Little, 172)

George Caldwell is appointed a Constable of this County in the Room of William Hutcheson who is discharged from that Office and it's Ordered that the said Caldwell be sworn into his Office at the next Court – 28 June 1745 (OCOB 4:370; Little, 173)

The Augusta County court was constituted on 9 December 1745.

AUGUSTA XII (1744–1745)
This precinct was described as the "Beverly Mannor District" in 1745.

1744   The Order to Summon's <u>David Mitchell</u> [and four others] of Augusta to Swear as Constables for the said County and it's Continued untill the next Court to be ret^d – 23 August 1744 (OCOB 4:198; Little, 171)

1745   <u>David Mitchell</u> is appointed constable of Beverly Mannor District and it is Ordered that he be sworn into his said Office at the Next Court – 23 May 1745 (OCOB 4:326; Little, 172)

The Augusta County court was constituted on 9 December 1745.

AUGUSTA XIII (1744–1745)
Both constables appointed to this new precinct lived in the Beverley Manor.[238]

1744   Ordered that <u>John Carr</u> [and eight others] be ſworn be ſworn Constables before James Patton John Lewis John Buchanan Geo Robinson Gent or any of them who are to lay off their Precincts – 23 February 1743/44 (OCOB 4:50; Little, 169)

1745   <u>Robert Young</u> is appointed Constable in this County in the Room of John Carr who is discharged from that Office and It is Ordered that the said Robert be sworn into his said Office at the next Court – 28 February 1744/45 (OCOB 4:268; Little, 172)

Robert Young is hereby appointed Constable in the Room of John Carr and It's Ordered that the Sherif Summon him to appear at the next Court to Swear into his said Office – 28 June 1745 (OCOB 4:367; Little, 173)

Robert Young is hereby appointed Constable in this County in the room of John Carr who is Discharged from that office and Ordered that the said Young be Sworn into his said office at the Next Court – 22 August 1745 (OCOB 4:411; Little, 173)

The Augusta County court was constituted on 9 December 1745.

AUGUSTA XIV (1742)
On 24 June 1742, the Orange County court appointed six men constables in one order; two of the six were appointed to precincts in the Beverley Manor (Augusta IX, X). Since all the appointees were ordered to be sworn at the house of Patrick Campbell, who lived in Beverley Manor, it is very likely that the other four appointees also lived in Beverley Manor.

1742   <u>John Steavenſon</u> [and five others] are Severally hereby appointed Conſtables & its ordered that the Sherriff Summon them to appear on ye fifteenth of next Month at the house of Patrick Campbell, there to be ſworn into ye s^d Office by W^m Ruſsell James Patton John Lewis & John Buchannan Gents or any one of them & to appear at next Court to take the oaths appointed by a late Act of Parliament – 24 June 1742 (OCOB 3:161; Little, 166)

1742 James Allen [and five others] are Severally hereby appointed Conſtables & its ordered that the Sherriff Summon them to appear on ye fifteenth of next Month at the house of Patrick Campbell, there to be ſworn into ye s^d Office by W^m Ruſsell James Patton John Lewis & John Buchannan Gents or any one of them & to appear at next Court to take the oaths appointed by a late Act of Parliament – 24 June 1742 (OCOB 3:161; Little, 166)

James Allen *and James Caldwell, constables, executed an attachment against the estate of James Rutledge*[239] – 24 September 1743 (OCOB 4:21)

1742 John Gay [and five others] are Severally hereby appointed Conſtables & its ordered that the Sherriff Summon them to appear on ye fifteenth of next Month at the house of Patrick Campbell, there to be ſworn into ye s^d Office by W^m Ruſsell James Patton John Lewis & John Buchannan Gents or any one of them & to appear at next Court to take the oaths appointed by a late Act of Parliament – 24 June 1742 (OCOB 3:161; Little, 166)

1742 James Cole [and five others] are Severally hereby appointed Conſtables & its ordered that the Sherriff Summon them to appear on ye fifteenth of next Month at the house of Patrick Campbell, there to be ſworn into ye s^d Office by W^m Ruſsell James Patton John Lewis & John Buchannan Gents or any one of them & to appear at next Court to take the oaths appointed by a late Act of Parliament – 24 June 1742 (OCOB 3:161; Little, 166)

AUGUSTA XV (1740–1742)
This precinct was described as "at Borden's Tract" in 1740.

1740 Wm Sawyer is hereby appointed Constable at Bordens Tract & its ordered that he be Summoned by ye Sheriff to appear at ye next Court to be Sworn into the s^d Office accordingly – 23 May 1740 (OCOB 2:176; Little, 161)

Wm Sawyers having taken the oaths appointed by Act of Parliament & Subscribed the Test took ye Oaths appointed by a late Act of Aſsembly was Sworn Constable accordingly – 26 June 1740 (OCOB 2:187; Little, 161)

1741 Gilbert Campbell is hereby appointed Constable in the room of Wm Sevier and its ordered that he be ſummoned to the next Court to be Sworn into the said Office accordingly – 28 May 1741 (OCOB 2:358; Little, 164)

Gilbert Campbell being last Court appointed Constable & ordered that he be Summoned to be Sworn in this Office the Sheriff having returned on the order not executed for want of time its ordered that he be Summoned to appear at the next Court to be sworn in ye s^d Office – 26 June 1741 (OCOB 2:408; Little, 164)

Gilbert Campbell appearing on Last Courts order put in his petition and deſired to be freed from being Constable Setting forth that he was Sick and ailing Wherefore on Consideration of the Court he is dismissed from being Constable – 23 July 1741 (OCOB 2:425; Little, 164)

James McDowell is hereby appointed Constable in the room of Wm Sayers & its ordered that the Sheriff Summon him to appear at the next Court to be Sworn into the said Office accordingly – 23 July 1741 (OCOB 2:425; Little, 164)

James McDowell having taken the oaths appointed by Act of Parliament & Subscribed the Test took the oaths pre∫cribed by late Acts of A∫sembly & was Sworn Con∫table accordingly – 27 August 1741 (OCOB 2:468)

1742   James McDowell

The order to take Henry Dowley & James McDowel in Custody is dismisd[240] – 24 September 1742 (OCOB 3:247)

In 1742 and 1743, this precinct seems to have been divided into two or three subprecincts when the court appointed—or tried to appoint—one, then two, then three men to replace John McDowell.[241]

1742   Gilbert Campbell is hereby appointed Con∫table in the Room of James McDowell and its ordered that the said McDowell ∫ummon him before a Justice of ye Peace to be Sworn into the said Office accordingly – 24 September 1742 (OCOB 3:247; Little, 167)

1743   Gilbert Campbell is hereby appointed Con∫table in the room of James McDowell & its ordered that the Sheriff Summon him to appear at ye next Court to be Sworn in the said Office accordingly – 26 May 1743 (OCOB 3:428; Little, 168)

Andrew Hays and John Mitchell are hereby appointed Con∫tables in ye room of James McDowell & its ordered that they be ∫ummoned to appear before a Justice of ye Peace to be Sworn into ye s^d Offices accordingly – 30 July 1743 (OCOB 3:520; Little, 168)

Ordered that <u>John Mitchale</u> & <u>William Moor</u> & <u>James Anderson</u> be sworn into the office of Constable & that they serve in the Room of James McDowele late Constable and that John Buchannan Gent lay off their Precincts – probably 25 August 1743 (OCOB 4:1; Little, 168)

1744   Ordered that <u>John [James?] Anderson</u> be ∫ummoned to appear at Next Court to swear into the office of Constable for the ensuing Year – 22 March 1743/44 (OCOB 4:58; Little, 170)

The order to ∫ummons John [James?] Ander∫on to be Sworn Constable is continued untill ye next Court to be returned – 26 May 1744 (OCOB 4:138; Little, 170)

The Order to Summons <u>William Mitchell</u> [and four others] of Augusta to Swear as Constables for the said County and it's Continued untill the next Court to be ret^d – 23 August 1744 (OCOB 4:198; Little, 171)

<u>William Moore</u>

1745   <u>John Trimble</u> is appointed Constable in this County in the Room of James Anderson who is discharged from that Office And It is Ordered that the said Trimble be sworn into his said Office at the next Court – 28 February 1744/45 (OCOB 4:268; Little, 172)

James Trimble is hereby appointed Constable in the Room of James Anderson and its Ordered that the Sherif Sumon him to appear at the next Court to Swear into his said Office – 28 June 1745 (OCOB 4:367; Little, 173)

James Greenlay is appointed Constable in this County in the Room of William Moore who is discharged from that Office and It is Ordered that the said James be sworn into his said Office at the next Court – 28 February 1744/45 (OCOB 4:268; Little, 172)

James Greenlay is hereby appointed Constable in the Room of William Moore and its Ordered that the Sherif Summon him to appear at the next Court to Swear into his said Office – 28 June 1745 (OCOB 4:367; Little, 173)

William Mitchell is hereby appointed Constable in the Room of William Moore who is Discharged from that office and it is Ordered that he be Sworn into his said office at the Next Court – 25 July 1745 (OCOB 4:390; Little, 173)

The Augusta County court was constituted on 9 December 1745.

AUGUSTA XVI (1741–1743)

The constables appointed to this precinct lived in the Borden's Tract.[242]

- 1741 Hugh Cuningham having taken the oaths appointed by Acts of Parliament & Subscribed the Test took the oaths prefcribed by a late Act of Afsembly & was Sworn Conftable accordingly – 28 August 1741 (OCOB 2:478)

- 1742 Hugh Cunningham

- 1743 Joseph Lapsley is hereby made Conftable in the room of Hugh Cunningham & its ordered that the said Cunningham caufe him to be fummoned before a Justice of the Peace of this County to be Sworn into the said office accordingly – 26 February 1742/43 (OCOB 3:375)

    Jofeph Lapsley is hereby appointed Conftable in the room of Hugh Cunningham and its ordered that he be fummoned to appear at ye next Court to be fworn into ye s^d Office accordingly – 26 May 1743 (OCOB 3:430; Little, 168)

AUGUSTA XVII (1743, 1745)

This precinct was described as "on the fouth fide James River" in 1743.

- 1743 Tasker Tosh (or Tash) and John Mason are hereby appointed Constables and its ordered that they appear before James Patton Gent to be fworn Conftables for that part of Orange County called Augusta on the fouth fide James River & the said James Patton is defired to lay of their precincts – 30 July 1743 (OCOB 3:517)

- 1745 Robert Mountgomory John Sloen and James Hughes are hereby appointed constables for James River in this County and it is Ordered that their Respective Precints be Divided and laid of by John Bohnannon and George Robinson Gent It is ordered that the said Montgomory Sloen and Hughes be Sworn into their said office at the Next Court – 23 August 1745 (OCOB 4:414; Little, 173)

The Augusta County court was constituted on 9 December 1745.

AUGUSTA XVIII (1745)
This precinct was described as "in the Cow Pasture" in 1745.

1745   James Marye [Little has Maze] is hereby appointed Constable in the Cow Pasture and It is Ordered that he be sworn into his said Office at the next Court – 28 February 1744/45 (OCOB 4:268; Little, 172)

On the Motion of James Patton Gent its Ordered that James Marye Swear as Constable in the Cow Pasture and that the Sheriff Summon him to appear at the Next Court to take the Oath of a Constable – 28 June 1745 (OCOB 4:367)

The Augusta County court was constituted on 9 December 1745.

AUGUSTA XIX (1745)
This precinct was described as "in the Calf Pasture" in 1745.

1745   Robert Grimes and William Hoge are appointed Constables in the Calf Pasture and It is Ordered that they be sworn into their said Office at the next Court – 28 February 1744/45 (OCOB 4:268; Little, 172)

On the Motion of James Patton Gent It's Ordered that Robert Grymes and William Hodge to Serve as Constables in the Calf pasture and it's Ordered that the Sherif Summon them to appear at Next Court to take the Oaths of Constables – 28 June 1745 (OCOB 4:366; Little, 173)

The Augusta County court was constituted on 9 December 1745.

AUGUSTA XX (1744–1745)
The four men appointed constables of this precinct lived in the vicinity of New River in today's Pulaski County at the time of their appointment. This was the most southern precinct in Augusta County.[243]

1744   Ordered that Hamberston Lyon [and eight others] be ſworn be ſworn Constables before James Patton John Lewis John Buchanan Geo Robinson Gent or any of them who are to lay off their Precincts – 23 February 1743/44 (OCOB 4:50; Little, 169)

1744   The Order to Summons Adam Harmon [and four others] of Augusta to Swear as Constables for the said County and it's Continued untill the next Court to be ret^d – 23 August 1744 (OCOB 4:198; Little, 171)

1744   The Order to Summons Jacob Harmon [and four others] of Augusta to Swear as Constables for the said County and it's Continued untill the next Court to be ret^d – 23 August 1744 (OCOB 4:198; Little, 171)

1745   John Castle is appointed Constable in this County in the room of John Davidson who is discharged from that Office and it is ordered that he be sworn into his said office at the next Court – 23 May 1745 (OCOB 4:326; Little, 172)

The Augusta County court was constituted on 9 December 1745.

AUGUSTA UNIDENTIFIED PRECINCTS

Except for a few assignments to "that part of Orange County Called Augusta" or "Augusta," the following constables were not assigned to any specific location in Augusta County. However, they can be identified as constables of Augusta County because they lived in the county at the time of their appointment. Some of these constables may have been assigned to Augusta precincts described above and some were probably assigned to new precincts.

AUGUSTA UNIDENTIFIED PRECINCTS (1743)

In 1743, the Orange County court appointed seventeen constables to Augusta County. Four of these constables were appointed to precincts which were to be laid off by a justice of the peace living in Augusta County, but no other information is available about the location of their precincts.

1743 Cornelius Bryne [and two others] are hereby appointed conſtable in that part of Orange County Called Augusta & its ordered that they be ſworn into the said office before James Patton Gent or any other Justice in that place who are desired to appoint them their precincts – 24 February 1742/43 (OCOB 3:348; Little, 167)

1743 James Hoggshead [and four others] are hereby appointed Conſtables and its ordered that the Sheriff ſummon them to appear before James Patton Gent to be ſworn into ye s^d Office accordingly and the s^d James Patton is hereby desired to lay out for each of them his precinct – 23 June 1743 (OCOB 3:462; Little, 168)

1743 George ffrankling [and four others] are hereby appointed Conſtables and its ordered that the Sheriff ſummon them to appear before James Patton Gent to be ſworn into ye s^d Office accordingly and the s^d James Patton is hereby desired to lay out for each of them his precinct – 23 June 1743 (OCOB 3:462; Little, 168)

1743 John Bryant [and four others] are hereby appointed Conſtables and its ordered that the Sheriff ſummon them to appear before James Patton Gent to be ſworn into ye s^d Office accordingly and the s^d James Patton is hereby desired to lay out for each of them his precinct – 23 June 1743 (OCOB 3:462; Little, 168)

1744 John Bryant

1745 Jacob Day is appointed Constable in this County in the Room of John Bryan who is discharged from that Office and It is Ordered that the said Jacob be sworn into his said Office at the next Court – 28 February 1744/45 (OCOB 4:268; Little, 172)

Jacob Day is hereby appointed Constable in the Room of John Bryne and Its Ordered that the Sherif Sumon him to appear at the next court to swear into his said Office – 28 June 1745 (OCOB 4:367; Little, 173)

AUGUSTA UNIDENTIFIED PRECINCTS (1744)

In 1744, the Orange County court appointed seventeen constables to Augusta County. Seven of these constables were appointed to precincts which were to be laid off by a justice of the peace living in Augusta County, one was appointed to "Augusta" and one lived in Augusta County at the time of his appointment, but no other information is available about the location of their precincts.[244]

1744	Ordered that Simon Acres [and eight others] be ſworn be ſworn Constables before James Patton John Lewis John Buchanan Geo Robinson Gent or any of them who are to lay off their Precincts – 23 February 1743/44 (OCOB 4:50; Little, 169)
1744	Ordered that James Been [and eight others] be ſworn be ſworn Constables before James Patton John Lewis John Buchanan Geo Robinson Gent or any of them who are to lay off their Precincts – 23 February 1743/44 (OCOB 4:50; Little, 169)
1744	Ordered that John Archer [and eight others] be ſworn be ſworn Constables before James Patton John Lewis John Buchanan Geo Robinson Gent or any of them who are to lay off their Precincts – 23 February 1743/44 (OCOB 4:50; Little, 169)
1744	Ordered that Hugh Corruthers [and eight others] be ſworn be ſworn Constables before James Patton John Lewis John Buchanan Geo Robinson Gent or any of them who are to lay off their Precincts – 23 February 1743/44 (OCOB 4:50; Little, 169)
1744	Ordered that Robert Voland [and eight others] be ſworn be ſworn Constables before James Patton John Lewis John Buchanan Geo Robinson Gent or any of them who are to lay off their Precincts – 23 February 1743/44 (OCOB 4:50; Little, 169)
1744	Ordered that W^m McFeeters [and eight others] be ſworn be ſworn Constables before James Patton John Lewis John Buchanan Geo Robinson Gent or any of them who are to lay off their Precincts – 23 February 1743/44 (OCOB 4:50; Little, 169)
1744	Ordered that John Young [and eight others] be ſworn be ſworn Constables before James Patton John Lewis John Buchanan Geo Robinson Gent or any of them who are to lay off their Precincts – 23 February 1743/44 (OCOB 4:50; Little, 169)
1744	The order to be ſummons Wm Anderſon to be ſworn Constable is continued untill ye next Court to be returned – 26 May 1744 (OCOB 4:138; Little, 170)
1744	The Order to Summons Robt Daviſson [and four others] of Augusta to Swear as Constables for the said County and it's Continued untill the next Court to be ret^d – 23 August 1744 (OCOB 4:198; Little, 171)

AUGUSTA UNIDENTIFIED PRECINCTS (1745)
In 1745, the Orange County court appointed thirty-two constables to Augusta County. Three of these constables were appointed to precincts some place in "that part of this County called Augusta."

1745	John King [and two others] are appointed Constables in that part of this County called Augusta and Ordered that they be Sworn into their said Office at the Next Court – 22 August 1745 (OCOB 4:413; Little, 173)
	John King is by the Court appointed Constable in that Part of this County called Augusta & he having taken the Usual Oaths to his Majesties Person and Government and took and subscribed the Abjuration Oath and test was Sworn into his said office accordingly – 26 September 1745 (OCOB 4:423; Little, 173)
1745	John Seewright [and two others] are appointed Constables in that part of this County called

Augusta and Ordered that they be Sworn into their said Office at the Next Court – 22 August 1745 (OCOB 4:413; Little, 173)

1745 David Logan [and two others] are appointed Constables in that part of this County called Augusta and Ordered that they be Sworn into their said Office at the Next Court – 22 August 1745 (OCOB 4:413; Little, 173)

APPENDIX:
ORANGE COUNTY, VIRGINIA, TITHABLE PRECINCTS, 1735–1757

The counties of colonial Virginia were divided into three different types of precincts: processioning, tithable and constable. In 1662, the Virginia Assembly passed the first act directing the parish vestries to procession the property—go around to mark the boundaries—of all landowners in the colony every four years.[245] From 1735 and every four years thereafter, the following order appeared in the Orange County court order books:

> Pursuant to the Act of Assembly for settling the title and bounds of lands and for preventing unlawfull hunting and ranging, this Court doth order and direct that the Vestry of Saint Thomas Parish do divide the same into so many Precincts as to them shall seem convenient for Processioning every particular person's land with the same, that they do appoint the particular times between the last day of September and the last day of March next coming when it shall be made in every such Precinct and that they do appoint at least two honest intelligent Freeholders of every respective Precinct to see such processioning performed and to take and return to the Vestry an account of every person's land they shall procession and of the persons present at the same and of what lands in their respective Precincts they shall fail to procession and the particular reason of such failure.[246]

The vestry presented a record of their processioning to the county clerk, who filed the report in the county records.[247] Of the three parishes responsible for Orange County: St. George's from 1721, St. Mark's from 1731 and St. Thomas' after 1740, reference to this processioning appears only in the vestry books of St. George's Parish. (The vestry books of St. Mark's Parish have survived; those of St. Thomas' Parish have not.) On 30 August 1731, the St. George's vestry divided the parish into six precincts and ordered three men (or any two of them) to "procession all the Lands . . . and that they begin their procession the first Munday in October next and make their return by the Last day of March next Ensueing." Eight months later, on 19 April 1738, the result of the processioning was recorded in the vestry book. Robert Stubblefield and Robert Goodloe, who were ordered to procession all the land from the Spotsylvania County line between the Pamunkey River and the River Ta as high as Duglas Run, reported that from January 13 to March 24, they "processioned the Line Between Samuel Ham and Nath^a Sanders In the presence of Samuel Ham and Charles Filks Pigg overseer . . . the Line Between Jno Warren and Nath^a Sanders In presence of Jno Warrin and Samuel Filks Pigg . . . the Line Between John Warrin and Samuel Ham" and so on, identifying thirty property lines they had walked and recorded, as well as the names of eight landowners who were absent or "Refused by Reason there was no body to shew the Line" or "Refused by Reason his Land was in Dispute." Processioners rarely described the physical boundaries of property; when they did, they used transitory geographical markers, like "beginning at a Red oak and then to two white oaks."[248]

In 1661, the Virginia Assembly passed the first acts directing counties to collect lists of all their tithables—all males sixteen and older and all slave or free female Negros, mulattos and Indians sixteen and older. Over subsequent years, the Assembly made minor changes to the way this was to be done and the definition of who was and who was not a tithable. County courts were to divide the county into four precincts (later, "convenient" precincts) and appoint a commissioner (later, a justice) every year before 10 June "to take the List of tithables" in a prescribed geographical precinct. (Justices in Orange County were usually appointed to take the lists of tithables in May.)[249] The justice was supposed to post a notice at a church or chapel—where attendance was compulsory—in his precinct before the 10th of June informing the householders where they were to turn in their lists on the 10th or 11th of June.

Heads of households listed the names of all tithables in a specific order: the head of the household, sons listed oldest to youngest, male relatives, white servants and apprentices and non-white male and female slaves. (The constables' tobacco planter lists noted the name of only the tobacco planter and the number—not the names—of tithables in his or her household.) To ensure that every tithable in Virginia was counted, masters or mistresses of households had to inform the parish of the names of all free and slave children born in their household within one year of their birth. All slaves who were purchased were to be presented at court so their ages could be determined and recorded. The Orange County court order books are full of registrations like, "Tenner a Negro Girl belonging to Charles Fushee is by the Court Adjudged to be Twelve years old."[250] The only people in Virginia not counted as tithables were the governor or commander-in-chief of the colony and his domestic servants; the president, masters, scholars and domestic servants of the College of William and Mary; ministers; constables in office and mariners.[251]

After the justice received the lists from the householders in his precinct, he composed a master list of the tithables and then delivered each householder's list and his master list to the county clerk. The clerk compiled a list of all tithables in the county from the justices' lists and posted his list at the courthouse to ensure "that if any concealment [of tithables] have been made, the person liveing neare them may discover them to the court."[252] Then, in September, the clerk delivered his list to the Virginia Assembly.

Unfortunately, no Orange County tithable lists have been found.[253] However, there is a good body of supplementary information about these lists. Delinquent lists—heads of households who failed to turn in their lists of tithables—were compiled annually for the court by the sheriff or deputy sheriff. Barbara Vines Little published ten of these delinquent lists with the tobacco planter lists.[254] Some of these lists note the number of tithables in the delinquent's household, and some explain the delinquency. Most delinquents were runaways, but sometimes the householder had no estate, could not be found, was dead or, like Zachary Fleshman, had enough of frontier living and returned to Germany.[255] The court order books contain a complete record of the justices who were appointed to collect these lists of tithables and a description of their precincts. The court also recorded the names of heads of households who failed to turn in their tithable lists (delinquents) or who petitioned to have their lists added to a justices' list (and so identifies where they were living) or who petitioned to be exempted (William Lucas petitioned for his blind son, Moses, to be "considered as an act of Charity and be set Levy free").[256] The total number of tithables living in the county was recorded at the end of the year in the annual county levy, and the county's annual expenses were divided by this total to determine how much each tithable in the county was to be taxed.

When the Orange County court appointed justices to collect the lists of tithables, it usually described the boundaries of their tithable precincts.[257] These descriptions, like the court's descriptions of the constable precincts, are often a challenge for a twenty-first century reader to understand. Geographical markers like the Rapidan River, the Blue Run and the Southwest Mountains are obvious; however, locations like "the road that comes from the Mouth of the Robinson River" or "Seayres old houses" or "where Francis Wisdom formerly lived" are not so obvious.[258] Although precinct boundaries did change over the years, sometimes the boundaries only appeared to change when the court used different markers to describe the same boundaries; for instance, the southern boundary of the tithable precinct in southwest "Culpeper" County was called Raccoon Ford in 1744 and 1745, but it was called the Courthouse—which was near Raccoon Ford—in 1746 and 1747.[259] And the precinct covering "Orange" and "Greene" Counties was described as "on the south side the Rappadan" from 1735 to 1738; but in 1739, the same precinct was described as "at the Southwest Mountains." It is interesting that in 1733, when the Spotsylvania County court appointed two justices to collect the lists of the scattered and few tithables living in today's Orange, Culpeper, Madison, Rappahannock and Greene Counties, they ordered one justice "to take the List of Tithables at the South West Mountains and all the rest of the South side the Rappadan" and the other justice "on the North side of Rappadan . . . excluding the South West Mountains & the South side of the Rappadan."[260]

Appendix

There were fewer tithable precincts than constable precincts. Between 1735 and 1749, when Culpeper (today's Culpeper, Madison, Rappahannock) County was formed, Orange County—excluding Augusta and Frederick—was divided into two to six tithable precincts compared with nine to twelve constable precincts; after 1749, there were four to five tithable precincts compared with five to six constable precincts.[261] Occasionally—less often than one might expect—tithable and constable precincts had the same, or almost the same, boundaries; for instance, the two tithable precincts in today's Culpeper County and the constable precincts Culpeper I and Culpeper II were on the south and the north sides of Mountain Run. Sometimes the court used the same wording to describe both precincts: the 1746 and 1747 tithable precinct in southeast "Culpeper" and the 1748 Culpeper I constable precinct were both from "Muddy Run to the upper end of Mount Poney and from thence to the Courthouse."[262]

Following are the tithable precinct appointments made by the Orange County court from 1735 to 1757 and my identification of the general location of each precinct. After 1757, the boundaries of these precincts were fixed, and the court simply ordered judges to collect the lists of tithables where they or another justice had collected them the previous year.

1735, June 17

Tithable Precincts in "Orange" and "Greene" Counties
　Thomas Chew is appointed to take the lists of tithables on the south side the Rappadan (Little, 152; OCOB 1:18)
　and
　Francis Slaughter Gent is appointed to take the Lists of Tithables in the Great fork of Rappahannock on the North side the Robinson River (Little, 152; OCOB 1:18)
Tithable Precinct in "Madison" County
　James Barber Gent is appointed to take the lists of tithables between the Rappadan & the Robinson (Little, 152; OCOB 1:18)
1,111 tithables were recorded in the 1735 Orange County levy (OCOB 1:41 [18 November 1735])

1736, May 18

Tithable Precinct in "Orange" and "Greene" Counties
　Thos Chew Gent is appointed to take the List of tithables on the Southside the Rappidan this present Year (Little, 153; OCOB 1:76)
Tithable Precincts in north "Culpeper" County and south "Culpeper" County
　Goodrich Lightfoot Gent and Robert Eastham Gent are appointed to take the List of tithables in the Great ffork this present Year (Little, 153; OCOB 1:76)
Tithable Precinct in "Madison" County
　James Barbour Gent is appointed to take the List of tithables in the fork of the Rappidan this present Year (Little, 153; OCOB 1:76)
1,316 tithables were recorded in the 1736 Orange County levy (OCOB 1:123 [19 October 1736])

1737, May 26

Tithable Precinct in "Orange" and "Greene" Counties
　Thomas Chew Gent is appointed to take the List of tithables on ye South side the Rappidan this present Year (Little, 155; OCOB 1:171)
Tithable Precinct in north "Culpeper" County
　Robt Green Gent is appointed to take the List of tithables between the mountain run North River and great mountains this present Year (Little, 155; OCOB 1:171)
Tithable Precinct in south "Culpeper" County
　W^m Ru∫sell Gent is appointed to take List of tithables from the point of ye fork up ye southside of ye mountian run to ye Great Mountains this present Year (Little, 155; OCOB 1:171)

Appendix

Tithable Precinct in "Madison" County
    James Barbour Gent is ordered to take the List of tithables this present year in ye said precinct that was allotted to him Last Year (Little, 155; OCOB 1:171)

1,538 tithables were recorded in the 1737 Orange County levy (OCOB 1:233 [27 October 1737])

1738, May 25

Tithable Precinct in "Orange" and "Greene" Counties
    Ordered that Richard Winslow Gent take the List of tithables this present year in the precinct which Thomas Chew Gent had last year (Little, 156; OCOB 1:312)

Tithable Precinct in north "Culpeper" County
    Francis Slaughter Gent is hereby appointed to take the List of tithables in ye precinct that Robt Green Gent had last year (Little, 156; OCOB 1:312)

Tithable Precinct in south "Culpeper" County
    Wm Rufsell Gent is hereby appointed to take the list of tithables in the same precinct he had last Year (Little, 156; OCOB 1:312)

Tithable Precinct in "Madison" County
    Benjamin Cave Gent is hereby appointed to take the List of tithables in ye same precinct that James Barbour Gent had last year (Little, 156; OCOB 1:312)

Tithable Precinct in Augusta (and Frederick?) County
    Ordered that ye Sheriff of Sharrendo gives publick Notice to all that have not given in their Lists of tithables at Sherendo & the Irish Tract do give 'em in by next Court or delivir 'ems to Wm Rufsell Gent (Little, 157; OCOB 1:378 [28 September 1738])

2,507 tithables were recorded in the 1738 Orange County levy[263] (OCOB 1:399 [26 October 1738])

1739, May 24

Tithable Precinct in "Orange" and "Greene" Counties
    Richard Winslow Gent is hereby appointed to take the List of tithables at the Southwest Mountains this present Year (Little, 158; OCOB 1:460)

Tithable Precinct in north "Culpeper" County
    Abraham ffields Gent is appointed to take the List of tithables this prefent Year between the Mountain run & North river (Little, 158; OCOB 1:460)

Tithable Precinct in south "Culpeper" County
    John Finlafson Gent is appointed to take the List of tithables between the Rappadan & Mountain run this present Year (Little, 158; OCOB 1:460)

Tithable Precinct in "Madison" County
    Benj^a Cave Gent is hereby appointed to take the List of tithables in the Little fork this prefent year (Little, 158; OCOB 1:460)

1,904 tithables were recorded in the 1739 Orange County levy (OCOB 2:86 [22 November 1739])

1740, May 22

Tithable Precinct in "Orange" County
    Zachary Taylor Gent is hereby appointed to take the list of tithables below ye blue run on ye South side ye Rappidan as low as the Wildernefs Bridge this prefent year (Little, 161; OCOB 2:165)

Tithable Precinct in west "Orange" and "Greene" and "Madison" Counties
    Richard Winslow Gent is hereby appointed to take the List of tithables in ye little fork & above blue run on ye South side of rapidan (Little, 161; OCOB 2:165)

Tithable Precinct in north "Culpeper" County
    John Cattlot is hereby appointed to take the List of tithables between the Mountain run & ye north river for

Appendix

this preſent year (Little, 161; OCOB 2:165)

Tithable Precinct in south "Culpeper" County

James pallard is hereby appointed to take the List of tithables between ye Mountain run & ye rapidan for this preſent Year (Little, 161; OCOB 2:165)

2,107 tithables were recorded in the 1740 Orange County levy (OCOB 2:281 [27 November 1740])

1741, May 27

Tithable Precinct in north "Orange" County

Zachary Taylor Gent is hereby appointed to take the List of tithables in St Thomas parish below blue run to the road that comes from the Robinſon River this preſent year (Little, 164; OCOB 2:357)

Tithable Precinct in south "Orange" County

Edward Spencer Gent is hereby appointed to take the List of all tithables in St Thomas parish below the road that comes from the Mouth of the Robinson River this preſent Year (Little, 164; OCOB 2:357)

Tithable Precinct in west "Orange" and "Greene" and "Madison" Counties

George Taylor Gent is hereby appointed to take the List of All the tithables in St Thomas's Parish above the blue run & in the Little fork this preſent year (Little, 164; OCOB 2:357)

Tithable Precincts in north "Culpeper" County and south "Culpeper" County

Henry ffiold & John Cattlet Gent are hereby appointed to take the List of tithables in St Marks Parish this present Year (Little, 164; OCOB 2:357)

2,192 tithables were recorded in the 1741 Orange County levy (OCOB 3:58 [27 November 1741])

1741/42, February 25

Tithable Precinct in north "Orange" County

Thomas Chew Gent is hereby appointed to take the List of tithables in St Thomas's Parish below the blue run to the road that comes from the Robinson river this preſent Year (Little, 165; OCOB 3:147)

Tithable Precinct in south "Orange" County

Edward Spencer Gent is hereby appointed to take the List of tithables in St Thomas's Parish below the road that comes from the Mouth of ye Robinſon River this preſent Year (Little, 165; OCOB 3:147)

Tithable Precinct in west "Orange" and "Greene" and "Madison" Counties

George Taylor Gent is hereby appointed to take the List of tithables in St Thomas's Parish above the blue run and in the little fork this preſent year (Little, 165; OCOB 3:147)

Tithable Precinct in north "Culpeper" County

Robert Eastham Gent is hereby appointed to take the List of tithables on the Northſide of ye Mountain run in St Marks parish for this preſent Year (Little, 165; OCOB 3:147)

Tithable Precinct in south "Culpeper" County

W^m Ruſsell Gent is hereby appointed to take the List of tithables on the Southſide the Mountain run in St Marks Parish for this Preſent Year (Little, 165; OCOB 3:147)

2,286 tithables were recorded in the 1742 Orange County levy (OCOB 3:295 [26 November 1742])

1743, May 26

Tithable Precincts in "Orange" County and in west "Orange" and "Greene" Counties

Thomas Chew and Edward Spencer Gent are hereby appointed to take the List of tithables in St Thomas's parish this preſent Year (Little, 168; OCOB 3:431)

Tithable Precincts in north "Culpeper" County and southeast "Culpeper" County and southwest "Culpeper" County

Robert Eaſtham Goury ffield and James Pendleton Gent are hereby appointed to take the list of tithables in St Marks Parish this preſent Year (Little, 168; OCOB 3:431)

2,373 tithables were recorded in the 1743 Orange County levy (OCOB 4:29 [25 November 1743])

The Frederick County court was constituted on 11 November 1743.

Appendix

1744, May 24
Tithable Precinct in north "Orange" County
    Thos Chew Gent is hereby appointed to take the list of tithables this pre*f*ent Year below the blue run down to ye mouth of ye Robinson and above the road that goes thence to ye Offied thence to ye Rappidan & to the Lower part of ye county (Little, 170; OCOB 4:108)

Tithable Precinct in south "Orange" County
    Captn Edward Spencer is hereby appointed to take the List of tithables this pre*f*ent year from ye Robbi*f*son below the Offied road to Col^o Thos Chews pre*f*ent (Little, 170; OCOB 4:108)

Tithable Precinct in west "Orange" and "Greene" Counties
    George Taylor Gent is hereby appointed to take the list of all the tithables above blue run this pre*f*ent Year (Little, 170; OCOB 4:108)

Tithable Precinct in north "Culpeper" County
    Robert Ea*f*tham Gent is hereby appointed to take the List of tithables in the Little fork this pre*f*ent Year (Little, 170; OCOB 4:108)

Tithable Precinct in southeast "Culpeper" County
    John ffinlafson Gent is hereby appointed to take the list of tithables in the Lower part of ye Great fork this pre*f*ent Year (Little, 170; OCOB 4:108)

Tithable Precinct in southwest "Culpeper" County
    James Pendleton Gentleman is hereby appointed to take the List of tithables from the mouth of little fork to Mountponey & thence to the raccoon ford this pre*f*ent Year (Little, 170; OCOB 4:108)

Tithable Precincts in Augusta County
    Peter Scholl Gent is hereby appointed to take the List of tithables this pre*f*ent year in ye lower part of Augusta County as far as John Shinson & round ye Peeked Mountains thence to ye Gapp of ye north Mountain at Peter Cravens (Little, 170; OCOB 4:108)
    and
    John Lewis Gent is hereby appointed to take the List of tithables this pre*f*ent year from Linwell's Creek and Cravens upwards to Col^o Pattons Mill and John Buchannan Gent is hereby appointed to take the List of tithables in the remainder part of Augusta County (Little, 170; OCOB 4:108)

2,535 tithables were recorded in the 1744 Orange County levy (OCOB 4:229 [23 November 1744])

1745, May 23
Tithable Precinct in north "Orange" County
    Pursuant to Law the Court doth appoint George Taylor Gent to Take the List of Tithables above the road from the Wilderne*f*s run Bridge to the fork of the Robinson River in St Thomas's Parish for the Ensuing Year (Little, 172; OCOB 4:327)

Tithable Precinct in south "Orange" County
    Pursuant to Law the Court doth appoint Edward Spencer Gent to take a List of the Tithables below the road from the wilderne*f*s Run Bridge in St Thomas's Parish for the Ensuing year (Little, 172; OCOB 4:327)

Tithable Precinct in north "Culpeper" County
    Pursuant to Law the Court doth appoint Robert Green Gent to Take a List of the Tithables in the little fork for the ensuing year (Little, 172; OCOB 4:327)

Tithable Precinct in southeast "Culpeper" County
    Pursuant to Law the Court doth appoint Francis Slaughter Gent to take a List of the Tithables in the Lower Part of the Great fork for the Insuing year (Little, 172; OCOB 4:327)

Tithable Precinct in southwest "Culpeper" County
    Pursuant to Law the Court doth appoint Philip Clayton Gent to take a list of the Tithables from the mouth of the Little fork to Mount Pony & from thence to the Rackoon Ford for the Ensuing year (Little, 172; OCOB 4:328)

Appendix

Tithable Precincts in Augusta County
> Pursuant to Law the Court doth appoint Peter Schull Gent to Take a list of the Tithables from Frederick County Line to Thompson's Ford on the Middle River and Cro/s from the blue Ridge to the north Mountain for the Ensuing Year (Little, 172; OCOB 4:328)
> and
> Pursuant to Law the Court doth appoint John Lewis Gent to take a list of Tythables from the north Mountain to the upper Part of Beverlys Patent Line in Beverly Manor Cro/sing from the blue Ridge to the north Mountain including all the Inhabitants of the Cow and Calf Pastures and the Setlers back of the same for the Ensuing Year (Little, 172; OCOB 4:328)

2,557 tithables were recorded in the 1745 Orange County levy (OCOB 4:449 [29 November 1745])

The Augusta County court was constituted on 9 December 1745.

1746, May 22

Tithable Precinct in north "Orange" and "Greene" Counties
> Ordered that George Taylor Gent do Take the List of Tithables in that Part of St Thomas's Parish above his House and above Pamunky Road up to the Great Mountains for the Ensuing year (Little, 174; OCOB 4:470)

Tithable Precinct in south "Orange" County
> Ordered that Edward Spencer Gent Do take the List of Tithables in that Part of St Thomas's Parish in this County below George Taylors House for the Ensuing year (Little, 174; OCOB 4:471)

Tithable Precinct in north "Culpeper" County
> Ordered that James Pendleton Gent do take the List of Tithables in the North Little Fork in this County for the Ensuing year (Little, 174; OCOB 4:471)

Tithable Precinct in southeast "Culpeper" County
> Ordered that Robert Slaughter Gent do take the List of Tithables in the Lower Part of St Marks Parish from the Mouth of Muddy Run to the upper End of Mountpony and from thence to the Court House for the Ensuing Year (Little, 174; OCOB 4:471)

Tithable Precinct in southwest "Culpeper" County
> Ordered that Philip Clayton Gent Do take a list of Tithables in the upper Part of St Marks Parish for the Ensuing year (Little, 174; OCOB 4:471)

2,594 tithables were recorded in the 1746 Orange County levy (OCOB 4A:103 [27 November 1746])

1747, May 28

Tithable Precinct in north "Orange" County
> Ordered that George Taylor Gent take the Lists of Tithables in that part of St Thomas's Parish which lies above his house & Above the Pamunky road for this year (Little, 176; OCOB 4A:152)

Tithable Precinct in south "Orange" County
> Ordered that Edward Spencer Gent take the lists of Tithables in that Part of St Thomas's Parish which lies below the Plantation of George Taylor Gent & below the Pamunky road for this year (Little, 176; OCOB 4A:152)

Tithable Precinct in north "Culpeper" County
> Ordered that Robert Eastham Gent take the lists of Tithables in the north Little fork in St Marks Parish for this year (Little, 176; OCOB 4A:152)

Tithable Precinct in southeast "Culpeper" County
> Ordered that Abraham Field Gent take the Lists of Tithables in the lower end of St Marks Parish from the mouth of Muddy run to the upper end of Mount Poney & from thence to the Court House for the Present year (Little, 176; OCOB 4A:152)

Tithable Precinct in southwest "Culpeper" County

Appendix

Ordered that Goodrich Lightfoot Gent take the list of Tithables in the upper end of St Marks Parish for the Present year (Little, 176; OCOB 4A:153)

2,679 tithables were recorded in the 1747 Orange County levy (OCOB 5:82 [27 November 1747])

1748, May 27

Tithable Precinct in north "Orange" County

Ordered that Thomas Chew Gent take the List of Tithables in the upper End of Saint Thomas's Parish where George Taylor Gent took them last Year (Little, 177; OCOB 5:117)

Tithable Precinct in south "Orange" County

Ordered that Benjamin Cave Gent take the List of Tithables in the lower End of St Thomas's Parish where Edward Spencer Gent took them last year (Little, 177; OCOB 5:117)

Tithable Precinct in north "Culpeper" County

Ordered that James Pendleton Gent take the List of Tithables in the North little fork (Little, 177; OCOB 5:117)

Tithable Precinct in southeast "Culpeper" County

Ordered that Robert Slaughter Gent take the List of Tithables in the lower End of the Great Fork (Little, 177; OCOB 5:117)

Tithable Precinct in southwest "Culpeper" County

Ordered that Philip Clayton Gent take the List of Tithables in the upper End of the Great Fork (Little, 177; OCOB 5:117)

2,788 tithables were recorded in the 1748 Orange County levy (OCOB 5:158 [24 November 1748])

The Culpeper County court was constituted on 18 May 1749.

1749, June 22

Tithable Precinct in north "Orange" County

Ordered that William Taliaferro Gent do take a List of the Tithables in the County on the North Side of the main Road up to Seayres's old Houses acrofs to the Mouth of the Robinson River (Little, 178; OCOB 5:180)

Tithable Precinct in south "Orange" County

Ordered that Benjamin Cave do take a List of the Tithables in the County on the South Side of the Road he lives on up to the Pamunky Road by the middle Church (Little, 178; OCOB 5:180)

Tithable Precinct in northwest(?) "Orange" County

Ordered that George Taylor Gent do take a List of the Tithables in this County from the Mouth of the Robinson River and Seayrer's old House up to blue Run (Little, 178; OCOB 5:180)

Tithable Precinct in west "Orange" and "Greene" Counties

Ordered that Henry Down, Gent., do take a List of Tithables in this County above the Blue Run (OCOB 5:181)

1,277 tithables were recorded in the 1749 Orange County levy (OCOB 5:233 [24 November 1749])

1750, May 24

Tithable Precinct in north "Orange" County

Francis Moor Gent is appointed to take the list of tithables this year in the precincts where William Taliaferro Gent took them last year (Little, 179; OCOB 5:249)

Tithable Precinct in south "Orange" County

William Taliaferro Gent is appointed to take the list of tithables this year in the Precincts where Benjamin Cave took them last year (Little, 179; OCOB 5:249)

Tithable Precinct in northwest(?) "Orange" County

Joseph Thomas Gent is appointed to take the list of tithables this year in the precinct where Geo Taylor took them last year (Little, 179; OCOB 5:249)

Tithable Precinct in west "Orange" and "Greene" Counties

Appendix

Henry Downs is appointed to take the list of Tithables in the same Precinct he took in the Last year (Little, 179; OCOB 5:249)

1,363 tithables were recorded in the 1750 Orange County levy (OCOB 5:285 [22 November 1750])

1751, May 22
Tithable Precinct in north "Orange" County
  Edward Spencer Gent is appointed to take the list of Tithables in this County from the Mouth of the Robinson between the River & main Road to Fredericksburg to the Lower end of the County (Little, 180; OCOB 5:294)

Tithable Precinct in south "Orange" County
  Alexander Waugh Gent is appointed to take the List of Tithables in this County on the South side of the Road that leads from the mouth of the Robinson to Fredericksberg & aCrofs to the Pamunky road & all below the said Pamunkey Road to Spotsylvania line (Little, 180; OCOB 5:294)

Tithable Precinct in northwest(?) "Orange" County
  Thomas Chew Gent is appointed to take the List of Tithables in this County below Blue Run as low as the Pamunky road below the Middle Church & aCrofs to the mouth of the Robinson (Little, 180; OCOB 5:294)

Tithable Precinct in west "Orange" and "Greene" Counties
  Richard Winslow Gent is appointed to take the list of all the Tithables in this County above Blue Run (Little, 180; OCOB 5:294)

1,443 tithables were recorded in the 1751 Orange County levy (OCOB 5:338 [29 November 1751])

1752, May 28
Tithable Precincts in "Orange" County
  Thomas Chew Gent is appointed to take the list of Tithables in this County above Blue Run & above the Court House up to Mr James Colemans (Little, 181; OCOB 5:371)
  and
  Charles Curtis, Joseph Thomas, William Taliaferro & Francis Moore Gent are appointed to take a List of all the Tithables in this County below the Court house Up to Mr. James Colemans (Little, 181; OCOB 5:371)

1,441 tithables were recorded in the 1752 Orange County levy (OCOB 5:395 [24 November 1752])

1753, April 28
Tithable Precinct in north "Orange" County
  Alex^r Waugh Gent is appointed to take the list of Tith^s in this County from the head of Mountain Run & mouth of Robinson Run Between the River & the Main Road by Capt Caves down to the lower end of the County (Little, 183; OCOB 5:438)

Tithable Precinct in southeast "Orange" County
  Benjamin Cave Gent is Appointed to take the list of Tithables in this County on the South side of the Mountain Mountain Road up to the Road to Terrys Run (Little, 183; OCOB 5:438)

Tithable Precinct in southwest "Orange" County
  Charles Curtis Gent is Appointed to take the List of Tith^s in this County on Pamunkey above the Road to Terry Run (Little, 182; OCOB 5:438)

Tithable Precinct in northwest(?) "Orange" County
  Thomas Chew Gent is appointed to take the list of Tithables in this County from the Blue Run down to the head of the Mountain Run & the mouth of the Robinson River (Little, 182; OCOB 5:438)

Tithable Precinct in west "Orange" and "Greene" Counties
  James Madison Gent is appointed to take the List of Tith^s in this county above b [torn] Run (Little, 182; OCOB 5:437)

Appendix

1,551 tithables were recorded in the 1753 Orange County levy (OCOB 5:512 [23 November 1753])

1754, April 25
Tithable Precinct in north "Orange" County
    Thomas Jameson Gent is appointed to take the list of Tithables in this County Between the River & the Mountain Road that goes by Capt Caves from the head of the Mountain Run aCrofs to the Mouth of the Robinson down to the lower end of the County (Little, 184; OCOB 6:3)
Tithable Precinct in southeast "Orange" County
    Benjamin Cave Gent is Appointed to take list of Tithables in this County on the South side the Main Road from the Pamunky Road that leads to Terrys Run Bridge down to Wildernefs Bridge (Little, 184; OCOB 6:3)
Tithable Precinct in southwest "Orange" County
    Tavener Beale Gent is appointed to take the list of Tithables in this County from Terrys Run bridge up the Road to the Main Road below the Church & all on the South Side the said main Road up to the Blue Run to the plant^n where Francis Wisdom lives (Little, 184; OCOB 6:2)
Tithable Precinct in northwest(?) "Orange" County
    James Madison Gent is appointed to take the list of Tith^s in this County from the Blue Run down to the mouth of the Robinson & aCrofs to the head of the Mountain Run Between the River & the Road from below the Church up to where Francis Wisdom formerly lived (Little, 184; OCOB 6:3)
Tithable Precinct in west "Orange" and "Greene" Counties
    William Bell Gent is appointed to take the list of Tithables in this County above the blue Run (Little, 184; OCOB 6:2)
1,643 tithables were recorded in the 1754 Orange County levy (OCOB 6:56 [28 November 1754])

1755, April 25
Tithable Precinct in north "Orange" County
    Thomas Jameson Gent is appointed to take the List of Tith^s in this County Between the River & the Mountain Road that go's by Capt Caves from the head of the Mountain Run acrofs to the Mouth of the Robinson River & down to the Lower end of the County (Little, 186; OCOB 6:106)
Tithable Precinct in southeast "Orange" County
    Jeremiah Morton Gent is Appointed to take the list of Tith^s in this County on the South Side of the Main Road from Pamunky road that leads to Terrys run down to the Wildernefs Run Bridge (Little, 186; OCOB 6:106)
Tithable Precinct in southwest "Orange" County
    Taverner Beale Gent is Appointed to take the list of Tith^s in the County from Terrys Run Bridge up the Road to the Church Hall on the South side the Main Road up to the Blue Run to the plantation where Francis Wisdom formerly Lived (Little, 185; OCOB 6:105)
Tithable Precinct in northwest(?) "Orange" County
    James Madison Gent is Appointed to take the list of Tith^s in this County from the blue Run down to the Mouth of the Robinson & aCrofs to the head of Mountain Run between the Rappadan & Main Road up to the Plantation where Fran^s Wisdom formerly lived (Little, 186; OCOB 6:106)
Tithable Precinct in west "Orange" and "Greene" Counties
    William Bell is Appointed to take the list of Tith^s in this County above Blue Run (Little, 185; OCOB 6:105)
1,665 tithables were recorded in the 1755 Orange County levy (OCOB 6:184 [27 November 1755])

1756, May 27
Tithable Precinct in north "Orange" County
    Francis Moore Gent is appointed to take the list of Tith^s in this County in the precinct where Thomas Jameson Gent took them the Last Year (Little, 187; OCOB 6:236)
Tithable Precincts in south(?) "Orange" County

Appendix

Thomas Jameson & Jeremiah Morton Gent are Appointed to take the list of Tithables in the Other part of this County (Little, 187; OCOB 6:237)

Tithable Precinct in central(?) "Orange" County

Thomas Chew Gent is Appointed to take the list of Tith^s from the Blue Run down to the Mouth of the Robinson & a Cro*f*s to Terrys Run Bridge (Little, 187; OCOB 6:236)

Tithable Precinct in west "Orange" and "Greene" Counties

William Bell Gent is Appointed to take the list of Tith^s in County above Blue Run (Little, 187; OCOB 6:236)

1,595 tithables were recorded in the 1756 Orange County levy (OCOB 6:300 [25 November 1756])

1757, March 25

Tithable Precinct in north "Orange" County

Thomas Jameson Gent is Appointed to take the list of tithables in this County between the Mountain Road by Seayre's old house to the mouth of the Robinson down to the Lower end of the County (Little, 188; OCOB 6:336)

Tithable Precinct in south "Orange" County

Richard Thomas Gent is appointed to take the list of Tithables in this County on the South Side of the Mountain Road that leads from Mr Colemans down to Frederceksburg (Little, 187; OCOB 6:336)

Tithable Precinct in northwest(?) "Orange" County

Rowland Thomas Gent is Appointed to take the list of Tithables in this County below blue Run down to the mouth of the Robinson aCro*f*s to the Mountain Road by Seayres old houses between the s^d Road & the Rappadan River (Little, 188; OCOB 6:336)

Tithable Precinct in west "Orange" and "Greene" Counties

William Bell Gent is appointed to take the list of tithables in this County above blue Run (Little, 187; OCOB 6:336)

1,632 tithables were recorded in the 1757 Orange County levy (OCOB 6:358 [24 November 1757])

TABLE 1. Tobacco planter lists: concordance

Little Page	Precinct	See Page	Little Page	Precinct	See Page	Little Page	Precinct	See Page
1	Orange I (1735)	24	41	Delinquent (1756)		82	Orange I (1766)	31
2	Orange I (1735)	24	42	Orange I (1756)	29	83	Orange I (1766)	31
3	Madison I (1736)	75	43	Orange I (1756)	29	84	Orange V (1766)	59
4	Orange IV (1736)	50	44	Orange V (1756)	59	85	Orange V (1766)	59
5	Madison I (1737)	75	45	Orange IV (1756)	53	86	Orange II (1766)	40
6	Culpeper I (1737)	63	46	Orange I (1757)	29	87	Orange II (1766)	40
7	Orange I (1737)	26	47	Orange I (1757)	29	88	Orange II & III (1767)	41
8	Orange I (1737)	26	48	Delinquent (1757)		89	Orange II & III (1767)	41
9	Orange II (1737)	33	49	Orange II (1757)	38	90	Orange V (1767)	60
10	Delinquent (1737)		50	Orange II (1757)	38	91	Orange V (1767)	60
11	Delinquent (1738)		51	Orange III (1757)	46	92	Orange I (1767)	31
12	Delinquent (1738)		52	Orange I (1758)	30	93	Orange I (1767)	31
13	Orange I (1738)	26	53	Orange I (1758)	30	94	Orange II (1768)	41
14	Orange III (1738)	43	54	Orange II (1758)	38	95	Orange II (1768)	41
15	Orange V (1739)	56	55	Orange II (1758)	38	96	Orange I (1768)	31
16	Madison I (1739)	76	56	Orange III (1758)	46	97	Orange I (1768)	31
17	Madison I (1739)	76	57	Orange II (1759)	38	98	Orange V (1768)	60
18	Orange I (1739)	26	58	Orange II (1759)	38	99	Orange V (1768)	60
19	Orange III (1739)	43	58	Orange I (1759)	30	100	Orange I (1769)	31
20	Madison II (1739)	80	59	Orange I (1759)	30	101	Orange I (1769)	31
21	Orange II (1739)	33	60	Orange II-B (1760)	39	102	Orange V (1769)	60
22	Delinquent (1749)		61	Orange II-A (1760)	38	103	Orange V (1769)	60
23	Delinquent (1747)		62	Orange I (1761)	30	104	Orange V (1769)	60
23	Delinquent (1748)		63	Orange I (1761)	30	105	Orange V (1769)	60
24	Delinquent (1748)		64	Orange I (1762)	30	106	Orange III (1769)	48
25	Orange II (1749)	35	65	Orange I (1762)	30	107	Orange IV (1768)	55
26	Orange IV (1749)	51	66	Orange III (1762)	47	108	Orange IV (1768, 1769)	55
27	Delinquent (1751)		67	Orange IV (1763)	54	109	duplicate p. 74	
28	Orange I (1752)	28	68	Orange II-B (1763)	40	110	duplicate p. 75	
29	Delinquent (1753)		69	Orange II-A (1763)	39			
30	Orange I (1753)	29	70	Orange III (1764)	47			
31	Orange III (1753)	45	71	Orange IV (1764)	54			
31	Orange II-A (1753)	36	72	Orange II (1764)	40			
32	Orange II-A (1754)	36	73	Orange II (1764)	40			
33	Orange II-B (1754)	37	74	Orange I (1764)	30			
34	Orange IV (1751)	51	75	Orange I (1764)	30			
35	Orange II-A (1755)	36	76	Orange I (1765)	31			
36	Orange I (1755)	29	77	Orange I (1765)	31			
37	Orange I (1755)	29	78	Orange III (1765)	47			
38	Orange III (1755)	46	79	Orange II (1765)	40			
39	Orange III (1756)	46	80	Orange II (1765)	40			
40	Orange II (1756)	37	81	Orange III (1766)	47			

TABLE 2. Tobacco planter lists: statistics

Page	Precinct	Year	Constable	Tiths Credited	Tiths Reported	Actual Count	Tith Range	Aver. Tiths	Planters
	Orange I	1735	Ambrose Jones						
	Orange I	1735	Edmund Manion						
1–2	Orange I	1736	Edmund Manion	190	190	190	1–13	3.0	62
7–8	Orange I	1737	Samuel Pound	162	162	242[a]	1–15	3.3	72
13	Orange I	1738	Samuel Pound	216	216	257[b]	1–26	3.6	70
18	Orange I	1739	Samuel Pound	192	275	279[c]	1–14	3.5	79
	Orange I	1740	Samuel Pound	175					
	Orange I	1741	Samuel Pound	130 ½					
	Orange I	1742	James Whiting						
	Orange I	1742	Thomas Wharton	189					
	Orange I	1743	Thomas Wharton	199					
	Orange I	1744	James Minor	295					
	Orange I	1745	James Minor	224					
	Orange I	1746	James Minor						
	Orange I	1747	John Smith, Jr.						
	Orange I	1747	John Wooten ?						
	Orange I	1748	Elijah Morton	258					
	Orange I	1749	Elijah Morton						
	Orange I	1750	Alex. McDaniel	303					
	Orange I	1751	Alex. McDaniel	320					
28	Orange I	1752	Alex. McDaniel	325	325	330	1–14	3.5	95
30	Orange I	1753	Alex. McDaniel	347	347	319[d]	1–18	3.5	90
	Orange I	1754	John Morten						
36–37	Orange I	1755	John Williams	415	420	419[e]	1–20	3.4	125
42–43	Orange I	1756	John Williams	418	418	418	1–19	3.8	110
46–47	Orange I	1757	John Williams	417	417	413	1–18	3.7	112
52–53	Orange I	1758	John Williams	380	380	385	1–13	3.6	108
58–59	Orange I	1759	John Williams	410	415	411[f]	1–16	3.5	116
	Orange I	1760	John Williams	400					
62–63	Orange I	1761	John Williams	417	417	419	1–24	3.5	118
64–65	Orange I	1762	John Williams	423	423	423	1–21	3.4	125
	Orange I	1763	John Williams	443					
74–75	Orange I	1764	John Williams	491	491	480[g]	1–30	3.4	140
	Orange I	1764	Arjalon Price, Jr.						
76–77	Orange I	1765	William Price	427	427	445[h]	1–20	3.3	134
82–83	Orange I	1766	William Price	501	501	454[i]	1–20	3.3	151
92–93	Orange I	1767	William Price	568	568	578	1–36	3.8	148
96–97	Orange I	1768	William Price	524	524	538	1–45	4.4	119

Table 2 (*continued*)

Page	Precinct	Year	Constable	Tiths Credited	Tiths Reported	Actual Count	Tith Range	Aver. Tiths	Planters
100–101	Orange I	1769	William Price	552	552	529[j]	1–26	4.0	139
	Orange II	1735	John Henderson						
	Orange II	1736	George Smith						
9	Orange II	1737	George Smith	102	102	121[k]	1–8	2.7	44
	Orange II	1738	George Smith						
21	Orange II	1739	Henry Rice	117	117	167[l]	1–7	2.5	66
	Orange II	1740	John Mallory	125					
	Orange II	1741	John Mallory						
	Orange II	1742	Malachi Chiles	135					
	Orange II	1743	Robert Bickers	139					
	Orange II	1744	Robert Bickers	201					
	Orange II	1745	John Mallory	208					
	Orange II	1746	John Mallory	99					
	Orange II	1747	Thomas Gahagan	133					
	Orange II	1748	John Henderson						
	Orange II	1748	John Chapman	241					
	Orange II	1749	Steph. Smith Noblet						
25	Orange II	1749	James Mitchel	312	312	310	1–16	3.3	94
	Orange II	1750	James Cox	318					
	Orange II	1751	James Cox	232					
	Orange II	1752	Joseph Chandler						
31	Orange II-A	1753	Roger Bell	197	197	197	1–14	3.8	52
	Orange II-B	1753	John Gollorthun						
32	Orange II-A	1754	Thomas Graves	221	221	226	1–12	3.9	57
33	Orange II-B	1754	Charles Harrison	203	203	205	1–16	3.3	63
35	Orange II-A	1755	Thomas Graves	236	236	237	1–12	3.7	63
	Orange II-B	1755	Joseph Reynolds						
40	Orange II	1756	Benjamin Cave	332	332	339[m]	1–14	4.0	85
49–50	Orange II	1757	Benjamin Cave	382	382	381	1–17	3.8	90
54–55	Orange II	1758	William Cook	436	437	436	1–17	4.0	107
57–58	Orange II	1759	William Cook	396	430	432[n]	1–13	4.2	102
61	Orange II-A	1760	William Cook	172	172	172	1–17	3.7	47
60	Orange II-B	1760	Samuel Faulkner	150	150	150	1–12	2.7	54
	Orange II	1761	Benjamin Cave	396					
	Orange II	1762	Benjamin Cave	411					
69	Orange II-A	1763	Benjamin Cave	257	257	260	1–11	3.1	82
68	Orange II-B	1763	Manoah Singleton	141	141	151	1–13	3.0	52

Table 2 (*continued*)

Page	Precinct	Year	Constable	Tiths Credited	Tiths Reported	Actual Count	Tith Range	Aver. Tiths	Planters
	Orange II-B	1763	John Conner, Jr.						
72–73	Orange II	1764	Manoah Singleton	432	432	386[o]	1–15	3.4	114
79–80	Orange II	1765	John Oakes	361	361	371	1–17	3.1	117
86–87	Orange II	1766	John Oaks	402	402	402	1–17	3.3	123
88–89	Orange II & III	1767	Edmund Burrus	743	743	743	1–43	4.6	162
94–95	Orange II	1768	Edmund Burrus	453	453	457	1–17	3.5	131
	Orange II	1769	Edmund Burrus	476					
	Orange II	1770	Edmund Burrus	498					
14	Orange III	1738	William Bell	170	242/170	242[p]	1–18	5.0	48
19	Orange III	1739	Elijah Daniel	196	250	249[q]	1–18	5.7	44
	Orange III	1740	Robert Bickers	193					
	Orange III	1741	Robert Bickers ?						
	Orange III	1742	Solomon Ryon	217					
	Orange III	1743	Solomon Ryon	237					
	Orange III	1744	Solomon Ryon						
	Orange III	1745	Solomon Ryon						
	Orange III	1746	Peter Rucker	416					
	Orange III	1747	Peter Rucker						
	Orange III	1748	Zachary Gibbs						
	Orange III	1749	Dunkin Bohannon ?						
	Orange III	1750	Wm. McDonaugh	253						
	Orange III	1751	Wm. McDonaugh	239						
	Orange III	1752	Wm. McDonaugh						
31	Orange III	1753	John Bohannon	245	245	245	3–20	9.0	27
	Orange III	1754	Thomas White						
38	Orange III	1755	Thomas White	441	441	432	1–53	7.6	58
39	Orange III	1756	Thomas White	397	397	421	1–56	6.6	62
51	Orange III	1757	Thomas White	233	233	253[r]	1–33	7.0	36
56	Orange III	1758	Thomas White	405	405	405	1–32	6.7	61
	Orange III	1759	Thomas White						
	Orange III	1760	Timothy Burgess						
	Orange III	1761	Joseph Rogers						
66	Orange III	1762	Elijah Finnel	207	207	286[s]	1–19	7.0	61
	Orange III	1763	Elijah Finnel						
70	Orange III	1764	Robert Bickers	342	379	380[t]	1–20	7.1	53
78	Orange III	1765	William Leek	471	471	490[u]	1–44	7.3	66
81	Orange III	1766	William Leek	588	588	440[v]	1–44	7.6	58

Table 2 (*continued*)

Page	Precinct	Year	Constable	Tiths Credited	Tiths Reported	Actual Count	Tith Range	Aver. Tiths	Planters
	Orange III	1767	*See Orange II*						
	Orange III	1768	William Finnell						
106	Orange III	1769	William Finnell	263	263	263	1–41	9.4	28
	Orange III	1770	William Finnell	285					
	Orange IV	1735	Henry Downs	147					
4	Orange IV	1736	Henry Downs	233	233	227	1–17	3.2	71
	Orange IV	1737	Abraham Bletsoe, Jr.						
	Orange IV	1738	John Cleaveland	79					
	Orange IV	1739	John Cleaveland	38					
	Orange IV	1740	John Cleaveland	41					
	Orange IV	1741	John Cleaveland						
	Orange IV	1742	John Cleaveland	84					
	Orange IV	1743	John Cleaveland						
	Orange IV	1744	John Cleaveland						
	Orange IV	1745	John Cleaveland						
	Orange IV	1746	John Cleaveland						
	Orange IV	1747	John Cleaveland						
	Orange IV	1748	John Askew						
26	Orange IV	1749	Philip Bush	187	187	187	1–20	4.2	47
	Orange IV	1750	Robert Dearing	201					
34	Orange IV	1751	Robert Dearing	244	244	243	1–22	4.3	56
	Orange IV	1752	John Eubank						
	Orange IV	1753	John Eubank						
	Orange IV	1754	William Lukas, Jr.						
	Orange IV	1755	William Cleaveland						
45	Orange IV	1756	John Bryant	120	153	162[w]	1–12	3.2	48
	Orange IV	1757	John Bryant						
	Orange IV	1758	Joshua Furguson						
	Orange IV	1759	William Ham						
	Orange IV	1760	William Coursey						
	Orange IV	1761	Joseph Smith						
	Orange IV	1761	Thomas Shackleford						
	Orange IV	1762	William Grant	344					
67	Orange IV	1763	Thomas Price	358	360	348	1–16	4.0	87
71	Orange IV	1764	John Tilly	414	414	403	1–25	4.3	96
	Orange IV	1765	Thomas Price ?						
	Orange IV	1766	Mereman Marshall						

Table 2 (*continued*)

Page	Precinct	Year	Constable	Tiths Credited	Tiths Reported	Actual Count	Tith Range	Aver. Tiths	Planters
	Orange IV	1767	Joseph Martin						
107–108	Orange IV	1768	John Griffin	no credit	314	310	1–13	3.8	82
108	Orange IV	1769	John Griffin	490	336	336^x	1–21	4.3	79
	Orange IV	1770	John Griffin	339					
15	Orange V	1739	Thomas Calloway	46	66	67^y	1–8	2.0	33
	Orange V	1740	Thomas Calloway	64					
	Orange V	1741	Honorios Powell	58					
	Orange V	1742	Honorios Powell						
	Orange V	1743	Honorios Powell	65					
	Orange V	1744	Honorios Powell	103					
	Orange V	1745	Honorios Powell						
	Orange V	1746	Honorios Powell						
	Orange V	1747	Honorios Powell						
	Orange V	1748	David Zachary						
	Orange V	1749	David Zachary						
	Orange V	1750	John Goodall						
	Orange V	1751	John Goodall						
	Orange V	1752	John Goodall						
	Orange V	1753	John Goodall						
	Orange V	1754	John Goodall						
	Orange V	1755	John Goodall						
44	Orange V	1756	John Goodall	214	214	214	1–12	2.9	73
	Orange V	1757	Unknown						
	Orange V	1758	Unknown						
	Orange V	1759	Unknown						
	Orange V	1760	Unknown						
	Orange V	1761	Unknown						
	Orange V	1762	James Coursey						
	Orange V	1763	Robert Cave						
	Orange V	1764	Robert Cave						
	Orange V	1765	Richard Bruce						
84–85	Orange V	1766	Richard Bruce	286	286	287	1–15	2.6	109
90–91	Orange V	1767	Jeremiah Bryant	312	312	313	1–15	2.6	118
98–99	Orange V	1768	Jeremiah Bryant	346	346	345	1–14	3.1	112
102–105	Orange V	1769	Anthony Golding	293	295	315	1–15	3.0	99
	Culpeper I	1735	Peter Russell	119					

Table 2 (*continued*)

Page	Precinct	Year	Constable	Tiths Credited	Tiths Reported	Actual Count	Tith Range	Aver. Tiths	Planters
	Culpeper I	1736	James Kirk						
	Culpeper I	1737	William Taylor						
6	Culpeper I	1737	Isaac Haddock	143	143	209^z	1–11	3.0	66
	Culpeper I	1738	Isaac Haddock						
	Culpeper I	1739	William Rumsey						
	Culpeper I-A	1740	James Conner						
	Culpeper I-B	1740	Simon Miller						
	Culpeper I-A	1741	William Nash	100					
	Culpeper I-B	1741	Thomas Parks, Jr						
	Culpeper I-A	1742	George Underwood						
	Culpeper I-B	1742	Gerhard Banks	39					
	Culpeper I-A	1743	John Coleman						
	Culpeper I-A	1743	Roger Topp						
	Culpeper I-B	1743	Joseph Kirk						
	Culpeper I-A	1744	Roger Topp						
	Culpeper I-B	1744	William Nash						
	Culpeper I-A	1745	Roger Topp						
	Culpeper I-B	1745	William Nash						
	Culpeper I	1746	James Abbet	276					
	Culpeper I	1747	Daniel Carter						
	Culpeper I	1748	Daniel Carter						
	Culpeper I	1749	George Roberts						
	Culpeper II	1735	John Roberts	110					
	Culpeper II	1736	Wm. Wilson Holmes						
	Culpeper II	1737	Nathaniel Hillon	152					
	Culpeper II	1738	Nathaniel Hillon	181					
	Culpeper II	1739	Thomas Dillard						
	Culpeper II	1740	Thomas Dillard	213 ½					
	Culpeper II-A	1741	Joseph Norman						
	Culpeper II-B	1741	John Chissum	93 ½					
	Culpeper II-A	1742	Samuel Parks	196					
	Culpeper II-B	1742	John Chissum	85					
	Culpeper II-A	1743	Alex. McQueen	191					
	Culpeper II-B	1743	William White	112					
	Culpeper II-A	1744	Isaac Norman						
	Culpeper II-B	1744	William White	185					
	Culpeper II-A	1745	Isaac Norman	202					

Table 2 (*continued*)

Page	Precinct	Year	Constable	Tiths Credited	Tiths Reported	Actual Count	Tith Range	Aver. Tiths	Planters
	Culpeper II-B	1745	Samuel Scott	180					
	Culpeper II-A	1746	John Favour	197					
	Culpeper II-B	1746	Samuel Scott	260					
	Culpeper II-A	1747	John Reynolds	200					
	Culpeper II-B	1747	William White	281					
	Culpeper II-A	1748	James Graves	302					
	Culpeper II-B	1748	William White	151					
	Culpeper II-A	1749	John Field						
	Culpeper II-B	1749	Rowland Cornelius						
	Culpeper II-B	1749	James Graves						
	Rappahannock	1735	Francis Brown						
	Rappahannock	1736	Francis Brown						
	Rappahannock	1737	Francis Brown						
	Rappahannock	1738	Thomas Kennerley						
	Rappahannock	1739	Daniel Brown, Jr.						
	Madison I	1735	David Philips	99					
3	Madison I	1736	David Philips	no credit	237 ½	165[aa]	1–13	2.5	67
5	Madison I	1737	David Philips	237 ½	172	172	1–17	2.5	70
	Madison I	1738	William Crawford	153					
16–17	Madison I	1739	James Picket	204	294	283[bb]	1–15	2.2	127
	Madison I	1740	William Jackson						
	Madison I	1741	Thomas Rucker						
	Madison I	1742	John Howard						
	Madison I	1743	James Picket	119					
	Madison I	1744	Tully Choice						
	Madison I	1744	William Henderson						
	Madison I	1745	William Henderson	351					
	Madison I	1746	William Henderson	193					
	Madison I	1747	William Henderson	366					
	Madison I-A	1748	William Henderson						
	Madison I-B	1748	William Rice						
	Madison II	1735	William Rush						
	Madison II	1736	John Michael						
	Madison II	1737	John Michael	51 ½					
	Madison II	1738	John Michael						

Table 2 (*continued*)

Page	Precinct	Year	Constable	Tiths Credited	Tiths Reported	Actual Count	Tith Range	Aver. Tiths	Planters
20	Madison II	1739	John Michael	70	100	90[cc]	1–10	1.7	53
	Madison II-A	1740	Thomas Garrel						
	Madison II-B	1740	Timothy Terril						
	Madison II-A	1741	Mathew Stanton	22 ½					
	Madison II-B	1741	Richard Burdine						
	Madison II-A	1742	Richard Yarborough	89					
	Madison II-B	1742	Richard Burdine						
	Madison II-A	1743	Richard Yarborough						
	Madison II-B	1743	Richard Burdine						
	Madison II-A	1744	Richard Yarborough						
	Madison II-B	1744	Richard Burdine						
	Madison II-A	1745	Richard Yarborough						
	Madison II-B	1745	Richard Burdine						
	Madison II-A	1746	Richard Yarborough						
	Madison II-B	1746	Zach. Blankenbaker						
	Madison II-A	1747	Daniel Brown						
	Madison II-B	1747	Zach. Blankenbaker	99					
	Madison II-A	1748	Russell Hill						
	Madison II-B	1748	Zach. Blankenbaker	102					
	Madison II-A	1749	Beaumont Sutton						
	Madison II-B	1749	Robert Hutcheson ?						

[a] Pound's incorrect tithable total was 228, from which he inexplicably subtracted 66: 228-66=162.

[b] Pound's correct tithable total was 257, from which he inexplicably subtracted a series of numbers and reported 216.

[c] It is not known why the court credited Pound 192 tithables, when he reported 275.

[d] McDaniel's tithable total was 319, to which he added 35 for summoning a jury and inexplicably subtracted 7: 319+35-7=347.

[e] Williams inexplicably subtracted 5 from his 420 tithable total.

[f] Williams noted a tithable total of 410, but wrote "In all 415."

[g] Williams' correct tithable total was 480, to which he added 11 for an overpaid levy.

[h] Price's correct tithable total was 445, from which he inexplicably subtracted 18: 445-18=427.

[i] This is an example of a constable's especially careless addition.

[j] This is an example of a constable's especially careless addition.

[k] Smith's incorrect tithable total was 120, from which he inexplicably subtracted $17^{1/2}$: $120-17^{1/2}$=102.

[l] Rice's correct tithable total was 167, from which he inexplicably subtracted 50: 167-50=117.

[m] Cave a tithable total of 339, from which he inexplicably subtracted 6.

[n] It is not known why the court credited Cook 396 tithables, when he reported 430.

[o] Singleton's tithable total was 386, to which he added 11 for his levy and 35 for summoning a jury: 386+11+35=432.

Table 2 (*continued*)

[p] Bell's correct tithable total was 242, from which he inexplicably subtracted 72: 242-72=170.

[q] It is not known why the court credited Daniel 196 tithables, when he reported 250.

[r] White correctly totaled 253 tithables, but for some reason reported 233.

[s] Finnel counted 279 tithables, but wrote "The Whole 207."

[t] It is not known why the court credited Bickers 342 tithables, when he reported 379.

[u] This is an example of a constable's especially careless addition.

[v] Leek totaled 440 tithables, added 195 for three duties and inexplicably subtracted 47: 440+195-47=588.

[w] Bryant wrote on his list "In all 153" and for some reason deducted 32: "152-32 ded^t."

[x] In 1768, Griffin was not credited for the 314 tithables he noted on his list. In 1769, he reported 336 tithables, but the court credited him 490 tithables—160 less than the two year total. Was he fined for not submitting his 1768 list on time?

[y] Calloway reported 66 tithables, but the court credited him 46. Is this a clerk or a transcription error?

[z] Haddock totaled 205 tithables, from which he inexplicably subtracted 62: 205-62=143.

[aa] In 1736, Philips was not credited with the 165 tithables he noted on his list. In 1737, he reported 172 tithables, but the court credited him 237 tithables—100 less than the two year total. Was he fined for not submitting his 1736 list on time?

[bb] Picket reported 294 tithables, but the court credited him 204. Is this a clerk or a transcription error, or the court's deduction?

[cc] It is not known why the court credited Michael 70 tithables, when he reported 100.

NOTES

Works frequently cited in the notes have been identified by the following abbreviations:

ACRO	*Augusta County Road Orders 1745–1769*, Nathaniel Mason Pawlett, et al. (Charlottesville, VA, 2003)
CCDB A–B	*Culpeper County, Virginia, Deeds (1749–1762)* (Deed Books A–C), comp. John Frederick Dorman, 2 vols. (Washington, DC, 1975–76)
FCRO	*Frederick County Road Orders 1734–1772*, Gene Luckman and Ann Brush Miller (Charlottesville, VA, 2005)
Hening	William Waller Hening, ed., *The Statutes at Large: Being a Collection of all the Laws of Virginia from the First Session of the Legislature, in the year 1619*, 13 vols. (Charlottesville, VA, 1969)
Little	Barbara Vines Little, *Orange County, Virginia, Tithables 1734–1782*, 2 vols. (Orange, VA, 1988)
OCDB 1–8	*Orange County, Virginia: Deed Books 1–8, 1735–1743*, comp. John Frederick Dorman, 3 vols. (Washington, DC, 1961–71)
OCDB 9–20	*Deed Abstracts of Orange County, Virginia, 1743–1779 (Deed Books 9–20)*, comp. Ruth and Sam Sparacio, 5 vols. (McClean, VA, 1985–88)
OCOB 1	*Orange County, Virginia, Order Book One, 1734–1739*, comp. Barbara Vines Little (Orange, VA, 1990)
OCOB 1–4, 4A	Orange County, Virginia, Order Books 1–4, 4A (1734–1747), Rolls 30 and 31, Library of Virginia microfilms
OCOB 5–7	*Orange County, Virginia, Order Books 1747–1763 (Order Books 5–7)*, comp. Ruth and Sam Sparacio, 6 vols. (McClean, VA, 1997–2000)
OCOB 7–8	Orange County, Virginia Order Books 7–8 (1763–1777), Roll 33, Library of Virginia microfilm
OCRO 1734–	*Orange County Road Orders 1734–1749*, Ann Brush Miller (Charlottesville, VA, 2004)
OCRO 1750–	*Orange County Road Orders 1750–1800*, Ann Brush Miller (Charlottesville, VA, 2004)
SCOB	*Order Book Abstracts of Spotsylvania County, Virginia, 1732–1735*, ed. Ruth and Sam Sparacio, 2 vols. (McLean, VA, ca. 1990)
SCRO	*Spotsylvania County Road Orders 1722–1734*, Nathaniel Mason Pawlett (Charlottesville, VA, 2004)
VLP	*Virginia Land Office Patents and Grants*, Online database and digital images, Library of Virginia

Notes

1. These lists were found in the Orange County Loose Papers at the Virginia State Archives (Little, Preface). Orange County is one of the few counties where these lists have been found (Unsigned, Review of *Orange County, Virginia, Tithables, 1734–1782*, by Barbara Vines Little, *Virginia Genealogical Society Newsletter* 15 [Jan.–Feb. 1989]: 6). Little also identified a list of tobacco planters found in some loose Goochland County papers and tentatively dated it 1735 (Barbara Vines Little, "Goochland County Tithables, c 1735," *Magazine of Virginia Genealogy* 46 [August 2008]: 235–236).

2. Gene Borio, "Tobacco Timeline," article, 1993–2007, *Tobacco News and Information* (http://www.tobacco.org/History/Tobacco_History.html : accessed 12 April 2009).

3. Edmund S. Morgan, *American Slavery, American Freedom* (New York: W. W. Norton, 1975), 90–91; *Virginia Records Timeline: 1553–1743*, Library of Congress, *The Thomas Jefferson Papers* (http://lcweb2.loc.gov/ammem/collections/jefferson_papers/mtjvatm.html : accessed 20 April 2009).

4. Marie Jenkins Schwartz, *Born in Bondage, Growing Up Enslaved in the Antebellum South* (Cambridge, MA: Harvard University Press, 2000), 117–118.

5. Hogsheads: OCOB 2:439 (24 July 1741), 3:242 (24 September 1742); rolling roads: Hening, 4:91 (1720); OCOB 1:11 (18 March 1734/35), 5:457 (28 June 1753), 6:548 (28 November 1760); tobacco warehouses: OCOB 3:242 (24 September 1742), 5:13 (24 July 1747), 5:80 (27 November 1747), 6:55 (28 November 1754), 6:310 (27 November 1756), 6:344 (25 August 1757), 6:418 (24 August 1758).

6. The earliest tobacco warehouse certified by the Virginia Assembly in the far west was established in 1788 at Mecklenberg in Berkeley County—formerly Shepherdstown of Frederick County (Hening 12:717 [1788]).

7. Hening 4:251 (1730). For eighteenth century tobacco production in Virginia see T. H. Breen, *Tobacco Culture, The Mentality of the Great Tidewater Planters on the Eve of Revolution* (Princeton, NJ: Princeton University Press, 1985); Eugene M. Scheel, *Culpeper, A Virginia County's History Through 1920* (Orange, VA: Green Publishers, 1982), 34–35; Leo S. Mason, "To Have Lived Then – the 1700s," in *An 18th Century Perspective: Culpeper County*, compiled and edited by Mary Stevens Jones (Culpeper, VA: Culpeper Historical Society, 1976), 123.

8. Albert Ogden Porter, *County Government in Virginia: A Legislative History, 1607–1904* (New York: AMS Press, 1966), 86–87; debt paid with crop note: OCOB 5:394 (24 November 1752); witness paid with tobacco: OCOB 6:677 (23 September 1762); alcohol: OCOB 1:58 (16 March 1735/36); debts: OCOB 5:144 (24 June 1748); David Bruce: OCOB 1:54 (17 February 1735/36), see also OCOB 5:284 (22 November 1750); civil suit: OCOB 1:59 (16 March 1735/36).

9. Hening 1:478 (1658).

10. Hening 1:164 (1632), 1:224–229 (1640), 1:399 (1656), 4:87 (1720), 6:51 (1748); "Acts of the General Assembly, January 6, 1639–40," *William and Mary Quarterly*, Second Series, 4 (January 1924), 16–31.

11. Stacy L. Lorenz, "Policy and Patronage, Governor William Gooch and Anglo-Virginia Politics, 1727–1749," in *English Atlantics Revisited: Essays Honouring Professor Ian K. Steele*, ed. Nancy Lee Rhoden (Ithaca, NY: McGill-Queen's University Press, 2007), 81–106; A. G. Roeber, *Faithful Magistrates and Republican Lawyers: Creators of Virginia Legal Culture, 1680–1810* (Chapel Hill, NC: University of North Carolina Press, 1981), 96–100.

12. Hening 4:242–243 (21 May 1730).

13. Hening 4:507–509 (1736), 6:51–53 (1748).

14. Hening 8:325 (1769).

15. Roeber, 96–98; Alan Kulikoff, *Tobacco and Slaves: The Development of Southern Culture in the Chesapeake, 1680–1800* (Chapel Hill, NC: University of North Carolina Press, 1986), 110–114; OCOB 1:404 (26 October 1738), see also OCOB 1:92 (20 July 1736) and 2:154 (12 May 1740).

Notes

16. SCOB 1732–1734:147 (5 September 1732), 163–164 (3 October 1732), 261 (2 October 1733), 351 (1 October 1734); Ann K. Blomquist, *Goochland County, Virginia, Court Order Books 1 & 2, 1728–1731* (Westminster, MD: Heritage Books, 2007), 394 (GCOB 2:175 [3 August 1731]), 409 (GCOB 2:191a [3 September 1731]); Ann K. Blomquist, *Goochland County, Virginia, Court Order Book 3, 1731–1735* (Westminster, MD: Heritage Books, 2006), 23 (GCOB 3:19 [17 November 1731]).

17. Hening 1:246 (1643), 344 (1645), 419 (1656); John Grenier, *The First Way of War: American War Making on the Frontier, 1607–1814* (Cambridge: Cambridge University Press, 2005), 24.

18. Mary Gwaltney Vaz's, *Local Government in the Virginia Piedmont, 1720–1759* (Ann Arbor, MI: UMI Dissertation Services, 1997) is an excellent analysis of colonial Virginia public officials based on documentary evidence from Orange and Goochland Counties.

19. Oliver Perry Chitwood, *Justice in Colonial Virginia* (1905; reprint, Union, NJ: Lawbook Exchange, 2001), 113; Porter, 34; Hening 1:246 (1643).

20. Hening 3:410 (1705), 2:352 (1676), 5:238 (1744); OCOB 6:315 (24 February 1757).

21. Vaz, 74; the spelling of names on some tobacco planter lists is almost incomprehensible (Little, 7, 45).

22. OCOB 5:260 (28 June 1750); Charles Herbert Huffmann, ed., *The Germanna Record*, No. 6 (Culpeper, VA: Memorial Foundation of the Germanna Colonies, June 1965), 18, 19, 79.

23. Percy Scott Flippin, *The Royal Government in Virginia, 1624–1775*, Studies in History, Economics and Public Law 84 (New York: Columbia University, 1919), 319; OCOB 2:84 (22 November 1739), 3:362 (25 February 1742/43).

24. Vaz, 55.

25. Constables Henry Downs became a vestryman, a burgess and a justice; William Bell became a militia officer and a vestryman; John McDowell became a militia officer and a justice; Elijah Morton became a justice; Richard Morgan, John Roberts, Peter Russell and Samuel Scott became militia officers (Ulysses P. Joyner, Jr., *The First Settlers of Orange County, Virginia 1700–1776*, 2nd ed. [Baltimore: Gateway Press, 2003], A-14, 15, 17).

26. In 1734, the Spotsylvania County court granted a constable's request to divide his precinct because it was too large (SCOB 1734–1735:297 [2 April 1734]).

27. Spotsylvania County constables Ambrose Jones, Henry Downs, Peter Russell and William Rush continued as constables of Orange County (SCOB 1734–35: 350 [1 October 1734]); OCOB 1:3 [21 January 1734/35], 4 [18 February 1734/35]).

28. Oaths taken by an attorney: OCOB 7:423 (23 April 1767), by a Presbyterian minister: OCOB 1:213 (22 September 1737), by German Protestants seeking to be naturalized (one of these German Protestants, Zacharias Blankenbaker, became a constable of Madison II in 1747): OCOB 3:313 (28 January 1742/43), 3:346 (24 February 1742/43).

29. OCOB 1:437 (22 March 1737/38).

30. Sir Frederick Pollock, "The Oath of Allegiance," article, The Online Library of Liberty (http://oll.libertyfund.org/index.php?option=com_content&task=view&id=1422&Itemid=284 : accessed 12 August 2009); full oath of office: OCOB 1:89–90 (20 June 1736), 6:593 (24 February 1763); William Williams: OCOB 1:213 (22 September 1737).

31. Hening 4: 243 (1730).

32. Deer: Hening 5:60–63 (1738); Constables John Smith, Jr., Orange I (1747); Roger Bell, Orange II-A (1753); John Bohannon, Orange III (1753); John Eubank, Orange IV (1753); uninspected tobacco: Hening 5:151 (1742).

33. Joyner, *Settlers*, 118–124; OCOB 4:481 (23 May 1746).

Notes

34. Constables Samuel Pound, Orange I (1737, 1739); John Gollorthun, Orange II-B (1753); John Michael, Madison II (1736–1739); and Zachary Blankenbaker, Madison II-B (1746, 1747).

35. William Waters: OCOB 4:448 (29 November 1745); Samuel Drake: OCOB 4A:100 (23 October 1746), OCDB 10:75, Ulysses P. Joyner, Jr., *Orange County Land Patents*, 2nd ed. (Orange, VA: Orange County Historical Society, 1999), 143, no. 53.

36. OCOB 5:338 (29 November 1751). It is possible that James Isbell was constable of Orange III in 1751, since a James Isbell appears on the 1753 Orange III tobacco planter list and there is no record of a constable appointed to this precinct in 1751.

37. Also Constables Honorias Powell, Orange V, was appointed 28 August and Samuel Scott, Culpeper II, was appointed 22 August.

38. See Charles Robinson, Augusta I (1741); OCOB 2:336 (27 March 1741); 1738 Constables Lewis Stevens, Frederick I; Thomas Low, Frederick II and James Gill, Augusta I.

39. The first regulation concerning constables in the statutes of the Virginia Assembly ordered constables to assist sheriffs in notifying all residents of their county to pay the levy on tithables (Hening 1:281 [1643]).

40. From 1721 to 1731, St. George's Parish was responsible for parishioners living in the newly formed Spotsylvania County, which included the vast territory of what would become Orange County (John Frederick Dorman, transcr. and ed., *Saint George's Parish, Spotsylvania County, Virginia, Vestry Books, 1726–1817* [Fredericksburg, VA: The Transcriber, 1998]). In 1731, St. Mark's Parish was formed from St. George's Parish and encompassed all of Orange County (Rosalie Edith Davis, transcr. and ed., *Saint Mark Parish Vestry Book and Levies 1730–1785: Spotsylvania, Orange and Culpeper Counties, Virginia* [Manchester, MO: Privately Printed, 1983]). In 1740, St. Thomas' Parish was formed from St. Mark's Parish and was responsible for today's Orange, Greene, and a small strip of Madison Counties. No vestry books for this parish have been found.

41. Vaz, 9–22.

42. Chitwood, 114; Vaz, 18; apprehending slaves: OCOB 4A:151 (28 May 1747); Alexander McDaniel: OCOB 5:326, 335, 337 (27 September, 28 and 29 November 1751); slave found guilty of theft: OCOB 6:416 (24 August 1758).

43. Sometimes they were constables, but were not so identified; see OCOB 2:274–275 (23 October 1740) and 7:61 (22 October 1763).

44. Escaped prisoners: Hening 4:488 (1736), 5:520 (1748); seamen: Hening 6:24 (1748); deserters: Hening 6:563 (1755), 7:91 (1757), 7:506 (1762).

45. Hening 2:481 (1680), 3:459 (1705), 4:130 (1723), 4:203 (1727), 5:50 (1738), 5:553–56 (1748), 6:109 (1748), 6:363 (1753), 8:135 (1765); OCOB 1:91 (20 July 1736).

46. Hening 5:95 (1740), 6:420 (1754), 7:16 (1756), 7:96 (1757); Susan Chiarello, transcr., "Militia Fines, Insolvents, and Removals King and Queen County," *Magazine of Virginia Genealogy* 46 (August 2008): 173.

47. Hening 5:337 [1745], 5:340 [1746]; Vaz, 53; Constables Samuel Pound, Orange I (1741, 1742); Alexander McDaniel, Orange I (1752, 1753); Manoah Singleton, Orange II (1764) and William Leek, Orange III (1766). The Orange County levies note payment "To ffrancis Slaughter as Coroner & to ye Constable – 183 [pounds of tobacco]" (OCOB 1:122 [19 October 1736]) and "To the Constables for Summoning of Jury on ye Same [Talom] – 50 [pounds of tobacco]" (OCOB 3:48 [22 October 1741]). James Isbell—never identified as a constable—was paid thirty pounds of tobacco for summoning a coroner's jury (OCOB 5:338 [29 November 1751]).

48. Tobacco: Hening 4:392 (1734), 5:152 (1742), 6:183 (1748), 8:75 (1765), 8:318 (1769); spirits: Hening 4:471 (1736), 5:313 (1745), 7:269 (1759); cattle: 5:177 (1742), 6:125 (1748), 8:247 (1766); skins:

Notes

Hening 4:431 (1734), 6:92 (1748); deer skins: 5:62 (1738), see also here p. 9.

49. Hening 7:36–38 (1756); Morgan, 3; OCOB 3:445 (27 May 1743).

50. Dorman, *Saint George's Parish,* 7; Davis, *Saint Mark Parish,* 61; vagrants: Porter, 94; Hening 5:340 (1745), 6:30 (1748), 6:476 (1755); the insane: Hening 5:225 (1744), 8:379 (1769).

51. Attachments executed by identified constables appear in the description of the precincts; attachments executed by "the Constable": OCOB 2:76 (27 September 1739); 3:92 (28 November 1741); 3:168, 169, 174 (22 July 1742); 3:255 (24 September 1742); 3:270, 271 (25 September 1742); 3:305 (27 November 1742); 3:332, 343 (29 January 1742/43); 3:459 (28 May 1743); 3:519, 520, 521 (30 July 1743).

52. OCOB 3:170 (22 July 1742).

53. Hening 4:301 (1730), see also 4:97 (1722), 5:358 (1745), 6:145 (1748), 8:363 (1769); OCOB 7:528 (27 October 1768). "Western frontier settlers used a winter-rotting process to separate fibers from stalks [of flax and hemp]; the harvested plants were spread out in the fields to allow the fall and winter rains and ground frost to leach out the gum substance binding the lint to the main stalk, a process which could take up to three months. After the hemp had been [thus] winter-rotted . . . an additional procedure, involving the scraping of the hemp so that only the fiber remained (scutching), resulted in a more finely processed 'neat' hemp." (Barbara Crawford and Royster Lyle, Jr., *Rockbridge County Artists and Artisans* [Charlottesville, VA: University Press of Virginia, 1995], 233n. 16); see also G. Melvin Herndon, "Hemp in Colonial Virginia," *Agricultural History* 37 (1963): 86.

54. OCOB 7:425 (28 May 1767), 7:439 (25 June 1767), 7:445 (28 July 1767), 7:457 (22 October 1767), 7:482 (28 April 1768), 7:490 (26 May 1768), 7:528 (27 October 1768).

55. OCOB 2:83 (22 November 1739), 5:76 (26 November 1747).

56. Hening 6:489 (1755).

57. Hening 4:73 (1718), 4:350 (1732), 4:419 (1734), 5:50 (1738), 5:340 (1745).

58. Little, 28, 30, 73, 81.

59. Mathew Stanton of Madison II was paid 22 pounds of tobacco, Edmund Burrus of Orange II was paid 743 pounds of tobacco. The court recorded 145 tobacco-viewing lists submitted by constables. The total of tithables on these 145 lists was 36,578 with an average of 252 tithables.

60. Vaz, 50, 51; Hening 2:242 [1730].

61. Robert L. Mears, "Cost of Some Items in Colonial Virginia," article, *Eastern Shore Public Library: Tales from the Eastern Shore* (http://www.espl.org/genealogy/tales/tobacco.htm : accessed 8 August 2009).

62. Exempted from levies: Hening 4:170 (1726), 6:41 (1748); from militia: Hening 3:336 (1705); from grand juries: Hening 5:523 (1748), OCOB 6:366 (27 April 1758); Orange I constables reimbursed: Edmund Manion (1736), Samuel Pound (1738) and Alexander McDaniel (1753); Orange IV Constables Henry Downs (1736) and John Cleveland (1744); Peter Russell, Culpeper I (1735); John Roberts, Culpeper II (1735).

63. Vaz (38) noted that 48 percent of the 326 constables appointed in Orange and Goochland Counties between 1728 and 1759 were paid for viewing tobacco.

64. Orange IV Constables William Lucas, Jr. (1754) and Mereman Marshall (1766), Culpeper I-A Constables James Conner (1740) and Roger Topp (1744), Culpeper I Constable Daniel Carter (1748), Madison I Constables Thomas Rucker (1741) and John Howard (1742).

65. Hening 4:243 (1730); SCOB 1732–1734:170 (7 November 1732), 184 (6 February 1732/33), 268 (6 November 1733); SCOB 1734–1735 (7 February 1733/34); 1736 Constables Edmund Manion of Orange I, James Kirk of Culpeper I, David Phillips of Madison I and Colvert Anderson of Frederick II.

66. Hening 4:242 (1730).

Notes

67. Dorman, *Saint George's Parish*, 4, 5, 9, 10, 19, 20; Lorenz, 99n. 20; James D. Watkinson, Barbara Vines Little, Neil McDonald, Online discussion about "sucker hunting," 17–19 June 2003, Library of Virginia, *VA-Hist Archives Listserv 15.5* (http://listlva.lib.va.us/cgi-bin/wa.exe?A2=va-hist;X3GsmA; 20030619153427-0500 : accessed 3 July 2007).

68. Unsigned tobacco planter lists: Little, 28, 33, 35, 56, 67, 74–75, 76–77.

69. Hening 4:242 (1730); Little, 5, 45, 84, see also 26, 33, 76.

70. Little, 4, 34, 35, 46, 68, 98, 49, 76.

71. A 1633 Virginia law directed "gunsmiths and naylers, brickmakers, carpenters, joyners, sawyers and turners, be compelled to worke at their trades and not suffered to plant tobacco or corne or doe any other work^e in the ground" (Hening 1:208 [1633]).

72. Reverends: Lizabeth Ward Papageorgiou, *The Colonial Churches of St. Thomas' Parish, Orange County, Virginia* (Baltimore: Clearfield Company, 2008), 47, 50, 51; Timothy Crosthwait and Charles Curtis: Joyner, *Settlers*, 123–27.

73. Little, 43, 32, 54–55.

74. Alphabetized lists: Little, 36–37, 42–43, 46–47, 62–63, 84–85.

75. Reverend.: Little, 66, 70, 78, 81, 88; Madam: Little, 30, 38, 51, 65, 66; old: Little, 8, 106; deceased: Little, 56, 78, 80, 84, 89.

76. Quarter: Little, 70; estate: Little, 76; Mine Run: Little, 21.

77. Little, 45 and 30, 72–73, 74–75, 81; see also table 2, notes a, b, e, h, k, l, m, p, z.

78. Little, 21 (Rice), 19 (Daniel), 69 (Cave), 67 (Price), 68 (Singleton).

79. Little, 69, 9, 75, see also 4 and 44.

80. SCOB 1732–1734:258 (5 September 1733).

81. Tending charges brought by constables: Samuel Pound (1737, 1738) and Alexander McDaniel (1750) of Orange I; Philip Bush (1749) and William Lucas, Jr. (1754) of Orange IV; Honorias Powell, Orange V (1741); Nathaniel Hillon (1737), Samuel Parks (1742) and Samuel Scott (1746) of Culpeper II; David Phillips, Madison I (1737); John Michael, Madison II (1737); see also Nathaniel Hedgman, Xn. 172).

82. Hening 4:242 (1730) and see previous note 81.

83. Hening 8:325 (1769), OCOB 8:80 (23 August 1770), 8:93 (25 October 1770).

84. Of the forty-seven Orange County justices who served between 1734 and 1743, ten lived in Frederick County: Andrew Campbell, Thomas Chester, Jost Hite, George Hobson, Morgan Morgan, James Pollard, Richard Thomas, David Vaunce, James Wood and possibly John Smith. Ten Orange County justices, who served between 1735 and 1745, were residents of Augusta County: Benjamin Borden, John Buchanan, Samuel Givens, John Lewis, John McDowell, James Patton, George Robinson, William Russell, Peter Schull and Richard Woods (Joyner, *Settlers*, A-14).

85. See, for example, Augusta Unidentified Precincts (1744).

86. OCOB 1:378 (28 September 1738), 4:449 (29 November 1745); 1738: "A List of the Delinquents Over Sharandore for ye year 1738" (Little, 12); 1739: "Shurando sheriff" paid 299 pounds of tobacco "for delinquents" (OCOB 2:80 [25 October 1739]); 1740: "To Thos Postgates account for delinquents 1802½" (OCOB 2:275 [26 September 1740]). A strange appointment was that of "Richard Winslow Gent Sworn Undersheriff for that part of this County called the Irish Tract [Beverley Manor]" (OCOB 3:24 [25 September 1741]). Not only was it unusual for a gentleman to assume the office of deputy sheriff, but this gentleman, who was appointed a justice of the Orange County Court in 1736, appeared on nine Orange III tobacco planter lists between 1738 and 1767. So why was a resident of the Orange III constable precinct appointed deputy

sheriff in Augusta County?

87. Readers will notice two different syles of the entries quoted from the Orange County order books: entries with the eighteenth century orthography, abbreviations, punctuation (and lack of) faithfully copied from the Library of Virginia's microfilmed Orange County Order Books 1–4, 4A, 7 and 8 (1734–1747, 1763–1772) and entries with modernized spelling and punctuation copied from Ruth and Sam Sparacio's transcriptions of Orange County Order Books 5 and 6 (1747–1763) (*Orange County, Virginia, Order Books, 1743–1763* [McLean, VA: Antient Press, 1997–2000]).

88. For James Taylor's 1722 land patent, see Joyner, *Patents*, section 5, no. 10; for the location of the Southwest Mountain Chapel, see Papageorgiou, 20.

89. Papageorgiou, 114n. 4.

90. I found nothing further in the court orders about Samuel Pound's charge against Elizabeth Roser for tending succors. It is possible that the case appeared as a summary dismissal, and I missed it.

91. See p. Xn. X. (O3n4).

92. There is nothing in the court orders about James Minor replacing Thomas Wharton. James Minor was probably the son of William Minor (or Miner), who appears on the 1739 and 1752 Orange I tobacco planter lists. In 1743, William and James Minor worked on a road in the area of the Pine Stake with twenty-eight other men, most of whom appear on the 1739 and 1752 Orange I lists (OCRO 1734, 85 [26 May 1743]).

93. There is nothing in the court orders about John Smith, Jr. replacing James Minor, but a John Smith appears on all Orange I tobacco planter lists. The last word of this order is difficult to read, but it could be "Neck." Several Orange County road orders mention a "Road from Raccoon ford to the Old Trap Called the Neck road," which was in the Orange I precinct (OCRO 1750, 18 [28 May 1752], 129 [28 November 1771], 204 [28 April 1795]).

94. Who did the court appoint on 27 August 1747? The Sparacios transcribed the name in OCOB 5:39 and 5:84 as "Morton" and "Booton," but Little transcribed the name as "Wooton" and "Boston [?Wooten]" (Little, 176, 177). A John Boston appears on almost all Orange I tobacco planter lists. No Wooton or Wooten appears on any of the tobacco planter lists; however, a John Wooton was involved in two Orange County court cases in 1744 and 1745 (OCOB 4:141, 256), and on 28 March 1740, the court ordered a George Wooton (and Samuel Pound, a former Orange I constable) to work on a road from the Mine Run Bridge to Wilderness Run—landmarks in the Orange I precinct (OCRO 1734, 44). A Wooten Family site documents a George Wooten living in Orange County at this time with a son, John (Forrest Hale, "Wooten Family," article, 1999, *Rootsweb* [http://archiver.rootsweb.ancestry.com/th/read/WOOTEN/1999-07/0932661541 : accessed 9 May 2009]).

95. There is nothing in the court orders about John Morton replacing John Harvey or Elijah Morton; however, William Morton and his sons John and Elijah appear on Orange I tobacco planter lists from 1735, and John Morton served as constable of Orange I in 1754.

96. The Sparacios transcribed this order "extending from the mouth of the Robinson down the River as low as the Old Trap" (OCOB 5:272).

97. Concerning Margaret Bruce, see p. 11.

98. This Sparacio transcription does not make sense; it seems to be missing some words.

99. Arjalon Price, Jr. appears on the 1764 and 1765 Orange I tobacco planter lists, but Manoah Singleton appears on the 1763 to 1768 Orange II lists. This erroneous order was corrected on 28 March and 23 May 1765 when the court ordered John Oakes to replace Arjalon Price, Jr. as constable of Orange II and ordered William Price to replace Arjalon Price, Jr. as constable of Orange I. The tobacco planters on William Price's 1765 list and John William's 1764 Orange I list are the same.

100. On 26 May 1757, a surveyor was charged for not maintaining "the Road from the Tomb Stone above

Capt. Caves up to Pamunky road" (OCRO 1750, 48). The Tombstone was below the Southwest Mountain Road and today's Rhoadesville (Papageorgiou, 95–96).

101. Papageorgiou, 22–23.

102. James Coleman's large holdings lay along the border of Orange and Louisa Counties (VLP 29:356).

103. Papageorgiou, 36–37.

104. "Robert" Smith was a court error: Henry Rice replaced George, not Robert, Smith.

105. See p. Xn. X. (Or III n2?)

106. Since Thomas Gahagan viewed tobacco fields in 1747, the "1748" in this order, issued by the court three years after Thomas Gahagan was constable, must be a court error.

107. There is nothing in the court orders about John Henderson replacing Thomas Gahagan. One month after Henderson was sworn into office, John Chapman was sworn constable in place of Thomas Gahagan—not John Henderson. Whatever the explanation for this confusing appointment, John Henderson appears on all Orange II tobacco planter lists from 1737 to 1768, he served as Orange II constable in 1735, and he was appointed a third time—but did not serve—in 1755.

108. There is no other mention of Stephen Smith Noblet in the Orange County court orders. A 22 September 1743 Orange County deed records a "George Smith, alias Noblet" and "Charles Smith, alias Noblet," who were out-of-wedlock sons of Samuel Smith. A Stephen I. K. Smith is also mentioned in this deed, but his relationship to Samuel Smith is not clear (OCDB 9:1–2). A Stephen Smith and a Stephen I. K. Smith appear on eight Orange II tobacco planter lists from 1749 to 1768. A George Smith was an Orange II constable in 1736, 1737 and 1738 and appears on Orange II tobacco planter lists up to 1763. In the case of George, Charles and probably Stephen Smith, the alias "Noblet" was used to denote an illegitimate birth. For a discussion of aliases in English historical documents, see Mike Brown; "Some Devon Surname Aliases," article, 2000(?), *GENUKI* (http://genuki.cs.ncl.ac.uk/DEV/DevonMisc/Aliases.html : accessed 22 January 2009).

109. There is nothing in the court orders about James Mitchell replacing Stephen Smith Noblet or John Chapman. However, the boundaries of the precinct Mitchell was assigned are the boundaries of Orange II, and all constables assigned to Orange II from 1740 to 1748 appear on Mitchell's 1749 list of tobacco planters. This constable signed his name "James Mitchull" (Little, 25), but over a one year period, his name is spelled five different ways in the court orders. Variant spellings of names in the eighteenth century was not unusual (see p. Xn. X, Xn. Xas noted below OrIIn14, OrIIInX and Papageorgiou, 111n 13).

110. Roger Bell appears on all Orange II tobacco planter lists from 1735.

111. About half of the tobacco planters on the 1749 Orange II tobacco planter list appear on the 1753, 1754 and 1755 Orange II-A lists and the other half on the 1754 Orange II-B list.

112. Either Lawrence Harrison's appointment was a court error or he was replaced by Charles Harrison. Lawrence Harrison appears on Charles Harrison's 1754 Orange II-B tobacco planter list.

113. Joseph Reynolds probably did not serve as constable of Orange II-B in 1755. Joseph Reynolds—if that is the correct spelling of his name—appears on almost all Orange II and Orange II-B tobacco planter lists. It is interesting that his name is spelled differently on each list: Ranolds, Raynold, Renels, Rennolds, Renold, Redolds, Ronnold, Runnald, Runolds, Runyolds.

114. Capt. [Reuben] Daniel appears on every Orange II tobacco planter list from 1749 to 1768 (OCOB 6:527, 557). John Conner, Jr. and Sr. appear on Manoah Singleton's 1763 Orange II-B tobacco planter list. Conner later served as constable of Orange II in 1774 (and possibly 1772–1773) and was replaced by Manoah Singleton on 22 December 1774 (Little, 203). Since Conner was sworn into office, did the court appoint two constables to Orange II-B in 1763, or is this a court error?

115. See p. Xn. X. (OI, note 14.

Notes

116. James Taylor's 1722 land patent, see Joyner, *Patents*, section 5, no. 10.

117. Frank S. Walker, Jr., *Remembering: A History of Orange County, Virginia* (Orange, VA: Orange County Historical Society, 2004), 54.

118. Robert Bickers was constable of Orange III and was credited for viewing the tobacco fields in 1740 and 1764. However, a Robert Bickers was also a constable of Orange II in 1743 and 1744, and he appears on nine Orange II tobacco planter lists between 1737 and 1764 as Robert Beger, Bicker, Bickers, Bigers, Bigore and Bigors. In 1754, 1758, 1764 and 1769, Robert and William Bicker (also Bigers, Bigore, Bigors) appear next to each other on the Orange II lists, and on all four lists they appear near the same planters. Therefore these are all variant spellings of the surname Bickers. In 1764, when Robert Bickers was constable of Orange III, Robert and William Bigers appear on the Orange II tobacco planter list. A number of documents place Robert Bickers between Beaverdam Run (Clear Creek) and Berry's Run, branches of the Pamunkey River, from 1728 until his death in 1775 (Joyner, *Patents*, 25, Section 8, nos. 53, 141, 142, 143, 144, 149). This Robert Bickers had sons Robert, Jr., who was dead in 1763, and William, who executed his father's will (Lucyle Bickers Middleton, "Bickers Family Newsletter," 1995, no. 9, *Rootsweb* [http://freepages.genealogy. rootsweb.ancestry.com/~mimsfamily/Documents_Bickers_Newsletters : accessed 18 June 2009]). As explained in the introduction to Orange III, planters on the border of Orange II and Orange III occasionally appeared one year on the Orange II list, one year on the Orange III list, and one year on both tobacco planter lists. However, Robert Bickers did not live near the border of these two precincts. Since there is no evidence that two Robert Bickers lived in Orange County in 1740 and 1764, it is difficult to explain why this Bickers, who lived in Orange II and appeared on nine Orange II lists between 1737 and 1764, was constable—and was credited for viewing tobacco—of Orange III in 1740 and 1764.

119. There is no mention in the court orders about Robert Bickers' replacement. In 1742, the court appointed Thomas Wharton and Solomon Ryon to the eastern ("lower") and western ("upper") parts of James Whiting's Orange I precinct (see p. X (CI intro and CIn. 3 for discussion of "upper" and "lower" in these colonial documents). The wording of this order and the fact that both Wharton and Ryon appear for over three decades only on Orange I tobacco planter lists, makes it appear that the court divided Orange I into two precincts. However, all the constables who succeeded Solomon Ryon appear on Orange III tobacco planter lists or can be documented living inside the boundaries of Orange III, and planters on the 1753 and 1754 Orange III lists are the same as on the earlier 1738 and 1739 lists (no tobacco planter lists survive for any precinct between 1740 and 1748). So, even though Solomon Ryon appears only on Orange I tobacco planter lists, and even though the wording of the court's 1742 order appears to appoint him to the western part of the Orange I precinct, the evidence confirms that Ryon served his three year term as constable of Orange III.

120. Why was William McDonough ordered to replace Peter Rucker, who was constable of this precinct four years earlier and was succeeded by four appointees—at least two of whom served as constables—in 1747, 1748 and 1749? All four appointees lived in the Orange III precinct: McDonough, Zachary Gibbs and Dunkin Bohannan appear on Orange III tobacco planter lists, and John Moran worked on a road from the Island Ford, inside the boundaries of Orange III, in 1742 (OCRO 1734, 76 [24 November 1742]).

121. John Grigsby appears on five Orange III tobacco planter lists between 1753 and 1766.

122. James D. Watkinson mentioned this petition in an online discussion about sucker hunting (Watkinson et al.). In e-mail correspondence, he told me that he had found this petition in the Orange County "loose papers" or "judgements" when he was processing documents for the Circuit Court Records Project (James D. Watkinson, e-mail message to author, 1 September 2009).

123. This list has only 27 tobacco planters with a total of 245 tithables compared with over 50 tobacco planters with 441 tithables on the 1755 Orange III list.

124. More than half of the tobacco planters on this list appear on the 1738 and 1739 Orange III tobacco

planter lists, two appeared previously in Orange I, the remainder did not appear on any earlier lists.

125. A John and Jonathan Finnel appear on the 1755 Orange III tobacco planter list, and William Finnel was reappointed and served as constable of Orange III from 1768 to 1772.

126. A Thomas Burgess appears on the 1756, 1757 and 1758 Orange III tobacco planter lists, but Timothy Burgess appears on the 1759 and 1764 Orange II lists. Was this a court error or was Timothy Burgess living in Orange III in 1760?

127. Joseph Rogers appears on the 1757, 1759 and 1760 Orange II tobacco planter lists. In 1762, he worked on a road from below the Middle Church to the Northanna—within Orange II-A—with three other planters who lived in the Orange II precinct (OCRO 1750, 76 [25 November 1762]).

128. "Although the date is plainly 1760, the list was found with other 1766 papers and Order Book 7, page 402, 27 November 1766, has the following entry: 'To Wm Leek Constable for viewing tobacco fields and ecetera 588' " (Little, 81).

129. See p. Xn. X (Orange V)n 1.

130. Nothing else appears in the court orders about these charges brought against John Eubank. It is possible that the case appeared as a summary dismissal, and I missed it.

131. All Orange IV constables, who served from 1738 to 1749, and a third of the tobacco planters on the 1736 Orange IV tobacco planter list appear on this list, the remaining planters do not appear on any earlier lists.

132. In the petition Robert Deering submitted to the court in 1754, he correctly stated that he had been a constable for two years, and he requested the court to pay him the 244 pounds of tobacco owed him for viewing tobacco in "1750." (His total of 244 is correct.) But since the court credited him 201 pounds of tobacco for viewing tobacco fields in 1750 and 244 pounds of tobacco for viewing tobacco fields in 1751, this was his 1751, not 1750, list of tobacco planters.

133. There are several reasons a person was considered unqualified to be a constable (see p. 6). Bradley Kimbrow (or Kimbrough), who appears on the 1751 Orange IV tobacco planter list, may have been disqualified because he was illiterate (OCDB 13:219 [25 February 1762]).

134. Nothing further appears in the court orders about this case against Darby Haney. It is possible that the case appeared as a summary dismissal, and I missed it.

135. The 1761 and 1762 appointees, Thomas Shackelford and William Grant, appear on the 1763 Orange IV tobacco planter list.

136. Thomas, not John, Price was the 1763 Orange IV constable. A Thomas—but no John—Price appears on three Orange IV tobacco planter lists. Even though Thomas Price's name does not appear on his 1763 list of tobacco planters, either as constable or as a tobacco planter (it was not unusual for a constable to exclude his name and the number of his tithables from his own list), and even though the number of tithables he reported (360) is not the same he was credited by the court (358), this list was, nevertheless, compiled by Thomas Price. This list, like the 1756 Orange IV list of tobacco planters, illustrates the confusion about the borders of this precincts: half of the names of tobacco planters appear on earlier Orange IV lists, but about one quarter appear on earlier Orange II or Orange III lists. In addition, ten tobacco planters appear on both the 1763 Orange IV and the Orange II-A lists, but are crossed off the Orange II-A list.

137. Is this a court error? Why did the court order Mereman Marshall to replace Thomas Price, the 1763 constable, not John Tilly, the 1764 constable?

138. In 1768, John Griffin was not credited for the 314 tithables he recorded on his list of tobacco planters. In 1769, he reported 336 tithables, but the court credited him 490 tithables—160 less than the two year total. Was he fined for not submitting his 1768 list on time?

139. "James River Mountains" appears only a few times in early Orange County documents. Three times

between 1735 and 1741, the court ordered men to work on a road or roads to the James River Mountains (OCRO 1734, 12 [16 September 1735], 22 [23 April 1737], 57 [25 June 1741]). There were also a few orders around the same time which mentioned a James River Mountain Road, which passed east-west through today's Greene and west Orange Counties (SCRO, 89 [6 August 1734], OCRO 1734, 33 [27 July 1738], 81 [26 February 1742/43], 86 [27 May 1743]). All these orders describe roads to the Blue Ridge Mountains, and Little (214) correctly said this "James River Mountain" referred to the Blue Ridge Mountains. The James River originates in Alleghany and Botetourt Counties in western Virginia, flows four hundred miles southeast through counties far south of Greene and Orange Counties and empties into the Chesapeake Bay. So why were the Blue Ridge Mountains called the James River Mountains? Although this question needs more research, the answer might lie in Alexander Spotswood's 1716 expedition from Germanna westward to the Blue Ridge Mountains. John Fontaine, a member of the expedition, wrote in his journal that when the expedition ascended the mountains through a (Swift Run) gap, they "came to the very head spring of James River . . . at the very top of the Appalachian mountains" (W. W. Scott, *A History of Orange County, Virginia: From its Formation in 1734 (O.S.) to the end of Reconstruction in 1870; compiled mainly from Original Records With a Brief Sketch of the Beginnings of Virginia, a Summary of Local Events to 1907, and a Map* [Richmond, VA: Everrett Waddey, 1907], chapter 12). Of course, this was not the headspring of the James River, it was a branch of the South Fork of the Shenandoah. But it is possible that it was this belief that the James River started in this mountain range that led to these mountains being called the James River Mountains. In the first half of the eighteenth century, the Blue Ridge Mountains—so called at least as early as 1731 (VLP Northern Neck Grant C:174 [29 June 1731])—were called the James River Mountains; the "high mountains" (Virginia General Assembly's 1721 act for erecting Spotsylvania County [Hening 4:77]); and the Great Mountains (VLP 13:341 [28 September 1727]).

140. Captain William Bell appears on the four Orange V tobacco planter lists (1766–1769), and Captain John or Johnny Scott appears on the 1763, 1764, 1768 and 1769 Orange IV lists.

141. Thomas Callaway correctly reported 66 tithables, but the court credited him 46. Was this a court error? About one-third of the tobacco planters on this first 1739 Orange V list appear on the 1736 Orange IV list, the remainder did not appear on any earlier list, and one-third of these planters do not appear on any subsequent list.

142. George Douglas appears on the 1739 Orange V tobacco planter list.

143. Although there is no mention in the court orders about Honorias Powell replacing Thomas Callaway, Honorias Powell and the planters he charged with tending suckers, Madam [Elizabeth] Stannard and Thomas Wood, appear on the 1739 Orange V tobacco planter list.

144. Although this list dates seventeen years after the last Orange V list of tobacco planters in 1739, a third of the planters on the 1739 list—including Honorias Powell and several large landowners—appear on this 1756 list.

145. Capt. [William] Bell, see p. Xn. X. OVn2; James Coursey appears on the 1767 and 1768 Orange V tobacco planter lists.

146. Although there is nothing in the court orders about Jeremiah Bryant replacing Richard Bruce, Bryant appears on Bruce's 1766 tobacco planter list and Bruce appears on Bryant's 1767 list.

147. Hazel River (also called Elk, Eastham, Aestham's, South River): "in the Little Fork of Rappahannock River, and on the North side of the South river of Rappahannock now called Elk River" (VLP 11:153 [1722], 11:196 [1723], 13:16 [1726], 15:289 [1734]); Rapidan River: "the falls of Rappa[hannock] River beg. on the south side the South River called Rappidanna" (VLP 10:290 [1716]).

148. Culpeper I-A constables Roger Topp and George Underwood lived near Potato Run (John Blankenbaker, *Germanna History*, Note 1000, *Rootsweb* [http://homepages.rootsweb.com/~george/johns

germnotes/germhs9.html : accessed 12 February 2008]); William Kelly worked on a road "to the place where the Courthouse [at Raccoon Ford] is to be built" (OCRO 1734, 19 [26 November 1736]); James Conner worked on a road from Mount Pony to Germanna (OCRO 1734, 27 [24 November 1737]). Culpeper I-B constables Simon Miller and Thomas Parks worked on a road from Germanna to Wilderness Bridge (OCRO 1734, 15 [18 May 1736]); Joseph Kirk worked on a road from Germanna to the Mountain Run Bridge (OCRO 1734, 116 [23 January 1745/46]); and Peter Russell worked on a road to the [Great] Fork Church (OCRO 1734, 101 [29 June 1744]. William Nash, who lived in the vicinity of Bleu Cowslip Run, a tributary of the Rapidan east of Raccoon Ford, served as a constable of both Culpeper I-A in 1741 and Culpeper I-B in 1744–45 (OCDB 4:360, CCDB C:149–152).

149. The use of "upper" and "lower" for west and east also appears in other descriptions of constable precincts: Orange I in 1742, Orange V in 1739, Culpeper I in 1749, Culpeper II in 1741 and 1744, Augusta VII and Augusta VIII in 1738.

150. Robert Slaughter, the justice assigned to the "Lower Part of St Marks Parish," was ordered to build a bridge at Germanna in today's southeast Culpeper County (OCRO 1734, 72 [23 July 1742]). Philip Clayton, the justice assigned to the "upper Part of St Marks Parish," lived north of the town of Culpeper at Catalpa (see p. 67), and he petitioned for a road from the courthouse near Raccoon Ford to Mount Poney to the Mountain Road, which was between Culpeper I-A and Culpeper I-B (OCRO 1734, 92 [25 November 1743]).

151. "Parks" is written over "Sparks."

152. Alexander McQueen, John Favour, John Reynolds and Isaac Norman, father of Joseph, worked on roads from Norman's Ford, Flat Run, and Stonehouse Mountain (OCRO 1734, 6 [18 February 1734/35], 90 [25 August 1743], 92 [25 November 1743], 98 [24 May 1744]), 120 [26 May 1746]).

153. John Chissum and Samuel Scott worked on roads to and from the Point of the Little Fork, Indian Run and Crooked Run (OCRO 1734, 19 [25 November 1736], 24 [22 May 1737], 26 [22 September 1737], 49 [28 August 1740], 122 [24 July 1746]).

154. See p. X (CI intro).

155. In 1742, the court ordered a road "layd off to Col^o Slaughers Mill into Carters old road that leads to Normans ford" (OCRO 1734, 75 [24 September 1742]). Col. Charles Carter owned extensive acreage near Norman's Ford and between Mount Poney and Mountain Run (Scheel, *Culpeper*, 38, 132). Eugene M. Scheel places Slaughter's Mill near the mouth of Mountain Run (Eugene M. Scheel, *Culpeper County [Map]* [Washington, DC: Williams & Heintz, 1975]).

156. Scheel, *Culpeper*, 169, 340; OCRO 1734, 92 (25 November 1743).

157. OCDB 10:49; CCDB A:140, 489; John Frederick Dorman, comp. *Orange County, Virginia, Will Book 1–2: 1735–1778* (Washington DC: Dorman, 1958–1961), 2:9; Margaret Jeffries, "Virginia W.P.A. Historical Inventory Project. Survey Report: Arlington, 1937 Jan. 27," article, *Library of Virginia, LVA Catalogs* (http://lvaimage.lib.va.us/VHI/html/07/0145.html : accessed 17 May 2009); Margaret Jeffries, "Virginia W.P.A. Historical Inventory Project. Survey Report: Maple Wood, 1937 June 30," article, *Library of Virginia, LVA Catalogs* (http://lvaimage.lib.va.us/VHI/html/07/0311.html : accessed 17 May 2009); Dennis J. Yancey, "Yancey Place Names," *The Yancey Family Surname Resource Center* (http://yanceyfamily genealogy.org/places.htm : accessed 18 May 2009).

158. OCDB 10:223.

159. An Orange County road order offers a hint about the location of this road. In 1740, residents between Indian Run and the North (Hedgman's) River were ordered to work on a road from Davis's Ford to Scott's Road (OCRO 1734, 50 [26 September 1740]). Since this 1748 precinct boundary continued to Indian Run, Scott's Road must have passed northeast from Yancey's Mill to the vicinity of Indian Run in the Little Fork.

Notes

160. Little, 178.

161. Hedgeman's River (also called the Rappahannock or North River) and the Hazel River (also called the Elk, Eastham, Aestham's or South River) form the Little Fork. This North River was so described in Henry Willis' petition to patent land on the "southside of the North River of the little fork of the Rappahannock River in Spotsylvania County" on 12 April 1728 ("Petition of Henry Willis, 1728 Apr. 12," digital image, *Library of Virginia, LVA Catalogs* [http://lva.virginia.gov/whatwehave : accessed 12 March 2009]). Thornton's River was also called the North River, the North Fork of the Gourdvine River and the Firth River. Francis Thornton patented land on the "north side the North River of the Gourd Vine Fork going by the name of the River Firth" (VLP 14:154 [11 July 1731]). The Hughes River, a tributary of the Hazel River, was also called the North River: "in the great fork of the Rappahannock River under the Ragged Mountain . . . on the south side of the North River in the great fork of the Rappahannock at the mouth of Beaverdam Run" (VLP 13:299 [2 September 1728]). See also Scheel, *Culpeper*, 19 and Blankenbaker, Note 224.

162. Although Andrew Glaspee was tried on these charges, I found nothing further in the court orders about the charges brought against Col. Charles Carter. It is possible that the case appeared as a summary dismissal, and I missed it.

163. Thomas, not Edward Dillard, served as constable. Thomas Dillard and his father, Edward, owned land on Muddy Run (VLP 15:445 [27 February 1734/35], OCDB 2:45 [23 November 1737]).

164. I found nothing further in the court orders about Samuel Parks' charge against David Williams for tending tobacco suckers. It is possible that the case appeared as a summary dismissal, and I missed it. It is interesting that the same charges were brought against—the same?—David Williams, overseer of Mrs. Elizabeth Stannard's plantation, by Honorias Powell, constable of Orange V, on 25 September 1741. In this case, Williams was tried and found not guilty.

165. There were two Samuel Scotts living contemporaneously in Orange County (see p. Xn. X). AIV).

166. I found nothing further in the court orders about these charges against Joseph Caves and John Wilson. However, since I was carefully noting all mention of Caves, I am very confident that I did not miss a follow-up to this case in the court orders.

167. John Field was the son of Abraham Field, who owned property on Mountain Run and Flat Run (Eugene Allen Field, "Descendants of Abraham Field, Westmoreland County, Virginia, 1636–1674," article, 2008 [http://www.luciefield.net/abrahamfieldwestmoreland.pdf : accessed 4 April 2009]). In 1739, Abraham Field, Orange County justice, collected the lists of tithables from households "between the Mountain run & North river" (OCOB 1:460).

168. In 1735, Francis Brown, Daniel Brown and Thomas Kennerley were ordered to work on a road from Beaverdam Run to Thornton's Mill (OCRO 1734, 5 [18 February 1734/35]). Thornton's Mill was southeast of Sperryville in today's Rappahannock County (Nancy Meyer, "Take a Hike: Mary's Rock/Shenandoah National Park," article, 2004, *Shenandoah.com Stories* [http://www.shenandoah.com/stories/ ?id=7333 : accessed 9 October 2009]; *Map of Culpeper County with parts of Madison, Rappahannock, and Fauquier counties, Virginia, 1863?*, Map, Washington DC?: U.S. Bureau of Topographical Engineers, 1863?, *American Memory, Map Collections, 1500–2004*, Library of Congress [http://lcweb2.loc.gov/cgi-bin/map_item.pl : accessed 10 February 2009]).

169. Rowland Cornelius purchased 400 acres of Daniel Brown's land grant in Gourdvine Fork on 28 September 1748 (CCDB A:84).

170. William Rice, constable of Madison I-B, lived in the area of White Oak Run, Dark Run and Smith's Run in the center of today's Madison County (OCOB 1:379, VLP 17:120 (20 July 1736), CCDB C:37). For the St. Thomas' Parish boundaries, see Papageorgiou, 28–29.

171. In 1736, David Phillips was not credited for viewing tobacco. On his 1736 list, he tabulated the

Notes

following figures:
165 (the total number of tithables on Philips' 1736 list)
+172 (the total number of tithables on Philips' 1737 list)
337
−100½
237½ (the number of tithables credited Philips in 1737)

Since this 1736 list includes the total number of tithables from his 1737 list of tobacco planters, he could not have turned in the 1736 list until after he had viewed the tobacco fields in 1737. This is probably explained by the charge "for not looking after suckers . . . this present Year" brought against Phillips on 25 November 1736. The charge was dismissed on 25 March 1737, when he presented his 1736 list to the court. The subtracted 100½ pounds of tobacco may have been a penalty imposed by the court for not submitting his 1736 list on time.

172. Nathanael Hedgeman owned a large plantation on Hedgeman's River near Tin Pot Run (in the Culpeper II precinct). It is never stated in the court orders who brought these tending charges against Hedgeman. The case against him was referred to the next court on 24 March, 28 April and 25 May 1738, and he was found not guilty on 22 June 1738 (OCOB 1:287, 305, 319, 333).

173. James Picket reported 294 tithables, and the court credited him 204 tithables. Did the court mistakenly credit him 204 tithables, or was there some reason he received less than he had claimed?

174. Although a William, James and Edward Herndon resided in Orange County at this time (James Herndon appears on the 1749 Orange II tobacco planter list), no Herndon or Herondon appear on the Madison I tobacco planter lists. This is undoubtedly a court error. William Henderson appears on the 1736 and 1739 Madison I tobacco planter lists. William Rice, who was appointed constable of Madison I with William Henderson in 1749, also appears on the Madison I tobacco planter lists.

175. Huffman, 18, 79.

176. Constables of Madison II-A worked on roads along the border of today's Madison and Culpeper Counties. Richard Yarbrough (or Yarborough) worked on a road from Crooked Run to the German Road (OCRO 1734, 77 [26 November 1742]) and Daniel Brown worked on a road from Fox Mountain to Mount Poney (OCRO 1734, 127 [28 February 1746/47]). Russell Hill and five other men who appear on the 1739 Madison II tobacco planter list worked on a road "from the old German road by John Wilhites to the Church at Tennant's old Field" (OCRO 1734, 132 [27 August 1747]). John Wilhite owned land in the Hebron Valley (Huffman, 68–69), and Eugene M. Scheel suggests the Church at Tennant's Old Field was between Crooked Run and Devil's Run on the border of today's Culpeper and Madison Counties (Eugene M. Scheel, *Madison County* [*Map*], [Washington, DC: Williams & Heintz, 1984]).

177. William Rush was a Spotsylvania County constable in 1734 and continued as constable in the newly formed Orange County in 1735 (SCOB 1734–1735, 350 [1 October 1734]).

178. John Layton and Thomas Walker appear on the 1739 Madison II tobacco planter list; however, Henry Kendall appears on the 1739 and 1756 Orange V lists, and in 1738, he was overseer of a road from "the mouth of the South Branch [Conway River] of Rappadan River at the great Mountains to Jacksons Mill," a road which ran along the border of Orange V and Madison I (OCRO 1734, 28 [23 February 1737/38]).

179. This is possibly the same Daniel Brown who was constable of the Rappahannock precinct in 1739. Between 1735 and 1743, Daniel Brown worked on a road in the Gourdvine Fork (see p. 149nn. 168, 169), then in 1747, he was overseer of a road from Fox Mountain (near the border of today's Culpeper and Madison Counties) to Mount Poney (OCRO 1734, 127 [28 February 1746/47]).

180. Leonard Ziegler (or Ziglar) lived on Stoney Run near Mount Pony, in the area of Culpeper I, near his father-in-law, Christopher Zimmerman, who appears on the 1737 Culpeper I tobacco planter list (Blankenbaker, Note 665).

Notes

181. Hening 5:79 (1738).

182. John David Davis, *Frederick County, Virginia, Minutes of Court Records* (Westminster, MD: Heritage Books, 2008) 1:5, 6, 15, 16.

183. The Frederick County court ordered a road to "Robert Harper's at the mouth of the Shanando" on 7 May 1754. Harper's Ferry was first mentioned in a road order on 1 April 1755 (FCRO, 72, 79).

184. The Cacapon River and the Little Cacapon appear as the "Great Caporn" and the "Little Cape Caporn" in the Orange County road orders, as the "Great Cape Capon" and "Cape Cacapon" in the Frederick County road orders (OCRO 1734, 168; FCRO, 233) and as the "Cacapehon River" and "Little Cacapehon" on Giles Robert de Vaugondy's 1755 map of Virginia (*Carte de la Virginie et du Maryland*, Map [Paris: Chez de Vaugondy, 1757–58], *Alabama Maps*, Rucker Agee Map Collection, Birmingham [Alabama] Public Library, [http://alabamamaps.ua.edu/historicalmaps/us_states/Virginia/ index_Before1900.html : accessed 1 February 2009]). See also Little, 214 and Cecil O'Dell, *Pioneers of Old Frederick County, Virginia* (Marceline, MO: Walsworth Publishing, 1995), 536.

185. Opequon Creek is usually spelled "Opecken" or "Opeckon," but it also appears as "Opeken" and "Oppecan" in the Orange County and the Frederick County road orders. It is spelled "Opecken" on Vaugondy's 1755 map of Virginia (OCRO 1734, 169; FCRO, 235; Vaugondy, *Carte*). A 1741 Orange County court order recorded an action of debt between two men "in Opechen Settlement in Orange County & Colony of Virg^a" (OCOB 3:74 [28 November 1741]).

186. Tuscarora Creek is spelled "Taskerora," "Toskorara," "Tuscorora," "Tuscarora" and "Tusegrora" and is described as a branch and a creek in the Orange County and the Frederick County road orders (OCRO 1734, 169; FCRO, 236). There is another Tuscarora Creek in Loudoun County, Virginia, which Little (215) identified as the location of the precinct assigned to the Frederick County constables.

187. This waterway always appears as simply Bullskin, never Bullskin Run, in the Orange County and the Frederick County road orders (OCRO 1734, 168; FCRO, 233).

188. On 25 March 1744, Patrick Daugherty and Thomas Cherry witnessed—as neighbors often did—a sale of land on "warm Spring branch near Putomack River" to Thomas Berwick. In 1746, Thomas Cherry and Thomas Berwick worked on a road from Warm Spring to Sleepy Creek (Amelia C. Gilreath, abstr., *Frederick County, Virginia, Deed Books, 1743–1758 (Deed Books 1–4)*, [Nokesville, VA: Gilreath, 1989], 1:133; FCRO, 21 [5 August 1746]).

189. The only other mention I found of the fourth branch of the Potomac was a 30 April 1788 obituary in the Virginia Gazette and Winchester Advertiser: "Mr. John Clarke, of Winchester, drowned when his wagon was upset while attempting to ford the fourth branch of the Potowmack" ("fourth branch," digital image, *Library of Virginia LVA Catalogs* [http://lva.virginia.gov/whatwehave : accessed 12 March 2009]).

190. On 23 October 1740, the Orange County court paid 300 pounds of tobacco to "Thos Chester for keeping ferry" (OCOB 2:274). Chester's Ferry appears frequently—usually as "Chesters"—in the Orange County and the Frederick County road orders (OCRO 1734, 18, 163; FCRO, 174). See also O'Dell, 364.

191. Scott's Mill, so spelled in the precinct assignments, is usually spelled "Scots" in the Orange County and the Frederick County road orders (OCRO 1734, 166; FCRO, 179); it appears as both "Scots" and "Scotts" on a 10 August 1744 road order (FCRO, 7). Other orders for roads to Scott's (or Johnston's) Mill: FCRO, 5 [8 June 1744], 14 [3 October 1745], 17 [4 March 1745/46], 33 [4 January 1748/49].

192. John Funk's Mill: OCRO 1734, 80 (24 February 1742/43); Robert Scott Brundage, "Maps, Mills, Chapel, Roads, Water Ways, Migration [in Old-Frederick Co]," article, 1998, *Rootsweb* (http://newsfeed.rootsweb.com/th/read/OLD-FREDERICK-CO-VA/1998-03/0889274906 : accessed 12 October 2008); Johan Philip Sonner's 1776 Northern Neck Grant N:53 was on "Funk's Mill Run a Branch of and on the West Side of the North River of Shenandoah" (Louis Moses, "Where is Funk's Mill Run?," article, 2001, *Rootsweb*

[http://archiver.rootsweb.ancestry.com/th/read/VAFREDER/2001-12/1007409709 : accessed 12 October 2008]).

193. Morgan Morgan was granted his patent on 12 November 1735 (VLP 16:388). The earliest mention of this chapel may have been on 22 September 1737 when William Williams (see pp. 152n. 197, 155n. 225), a Presbyterian minister, swore to uphold the tenets of the Church of England "as is required & certified his intentions of holding his meetings at his own plantation & on the plantation of Morgan Morgan" (OCOB 1:213). This chapel was called the "New Chappell" on 26 February 1741/42, it appears as "Morgan Morgans Chapple" on 5 March 1746/47 and thereafter as "Morgans Chapple" (OCRO 1734, 65; FCRO, 25, 177).

194. Brundage; Eric Lewis, "How Did They Get Here?" *The Guardian, Newsletter of the Jefferson County WV Historical Society* 6, no. 3 (2008): 4 (http://jeffersonhistoricalwv.org/newsletter/July08-Guardian.pdf : accessed 9 October 2008); OCRO 1734, 81 [24 February 1742/43], 86 [27 May 1743]; FCRO, 7 [10 August 1744].

195. The Shenandoah (river and region) is spelled sixteen different ways in the Orange County and the Frederick County road orders and is spelled "Shennando" on Vaugondy's 1755 map of Virginia (OCRO 1734, 168; FCRO, 235; Vaugondy, *Carte*). " 'Gerundo' is merely another form of Shenandoah" (John W. Wayland, *A History of Rockingham County* [Harrisonburg, VA: C. J. Carrier, 1980], 40n. 15). Little (215) suggested that the Orange County justices might have been referring to the village of Sherando in today's southeast Augusta County. But this is unlikely, since the court never used a town—if Sherando even existed in the mid-eighteenth century—to describe a precinct.

196. OCOB 1:378 (28 September 1738), 2:15 (29 June 1739).

197. Samuel Hews and a number of men who served as constables in Frederick County—John Tradan, Abraham Yates, Andrew Hampton, Cornelius Newkirk, John Pitts, John Petite and Henry Robinson—were accused of slander by Rev. William Williams, who lived on the Opequon near Martinsburg in today's Berkeley County, West Virginia (OCOB 1:356 [27 July 1738]).

198. There is nothing in the court orders between 27 March 1740 and 23 July 1741 to explain why John McQuin was accused of "being aloofe [a loose] man" or why Niswanger did not assume the position of constable.

199. Joseph Vaunce's assignment was probably to Frederick I: he owned land in the vicinity of Meadow Brook near Middletown in today's Frederick County between 1744 and 1773, and Joseph Vaunce and Peter Stephens petitioned for a road through their land in 1757, and John Niswanger and Joseph McDowell worked on this road (O'Dell, 300; FCRO, 86 [1 March 1757]). Stephens, Niswanger and McDowell were all appointed constables of Frederick I.

200. John Petite, the first constable assigned to the precinct "on Opeakon" in 1735, was granted land in the same year "on the west side of Opechon Creek" (VLP 16:411 [12 November 1735]).

201. Although I found nothing about Providence Williams' residence in 1735, he petitioned for a road "from Frederick Town to the mouth of the South branch of Potomack" in 1750 (FCRO, 43 [15 February 1749/50]). Frederick Town, today's Winchester, is on the west side of Opequon.

202. It is interesting that George Thurston was described and acted as a constable one month before the court appointed him. Abraham Wiseman was the constable of neighboring Frederick I in 1735.

203. I found nothing further in the court orders about this charge against Colvert Anderson. It is possible that the case against him appeared as a summary dismissal, and I missed it.

204. Thomas Postgate may not have served because he was appointed deputy sheriff of Frederick County a month later, on 15 June 1736, and "Sworn Undersheriff for that part of this County called Sherundo" on 29 June 1739 (OCOB 1:85, 2:15). Apparently, the court was not pleased with his performance: on 23 August

Notes

1739, the court "Ordered that Thomas Postgate be Summoned to the next Court to Shew Cause why he doth not his duty in his office." A month later, Postgate answered the court "that he was taken Sick" and the summons was dismissed (OCOB 2:50 [23 August 1739], 65 [27 September 1739]).

205. O'Dell (219, 220) identified the constable who replaced Peter Wolf as Huckle Guilder; see also p. Xn. X concerning the Guilders.

206. Although the court did not appoint anyone to replace John Pitts, several of the constables I have identified as succeeding him lived in the same area as the three constables appointed to this precinct in 1735, 1736 and 1737. On 27 May 1743, Samuel Murris (or Morris) and Isaac Pennington were ordered to survey a road "from Teagues ffery to Bullskin and from thence to Kerseys fferry." Three of the eight constables I have assigned to Frederick IV—John Tradan, Thomas Hart and Robert Worthington—worked on this road and, therefore, lived in the same area as Morris and Pennington. This road passed through "John Tradans old place" and "[John] Pitts Marsh" on Bullskin (OCRO 1734, 86; Gilreath, 1:455; O'Dell, 105–106). Moses Teague's Ferry was on the Potomac River near Shepherdstown in today's Jefferson County, and Kersey's (latter Berry's) Ferry crossed the Shenandoah River near Berry in today's Clarke County (Brundage; FCRO, 1 [9 December 1743]; see also Josiah Look Dickenson, "The Manor of Greenway Court," *Proceedings of the Clarke County Historical Association* 8 (1948): 45–46 (http://www.clarkehistory.org/publications/CCHA_Proceedings_Vol_08(1948).pdf : accessed 12 October 2008).

207. It is possible that the appointments of John Pitts and Thomas Sheppard, recorded one after the other on 26 May 1737, meant the court intended to divide Frederick IV.

208. Although there is nothing in the court orders about Robert Worthington replacing Thomas Hart, as noted above (p. Xn. X), Worthington lived in this precinct, therefore it is likely he was appointed constable of this precinct.

209. This must be a court error because Gilbert, not Huckill, Guilder was the 1741 Frederick V constable. From 1734, the brothers Huckle and Gilbert Guilder lived west of the Shenandoah near today's Berryville in Clarke County (O'Dell, 219, 220). Berryville was between the precincts of Frederick III ("Scott's Mill to Chesters") where Hugh (or Huckle) Guilder was constable in 1738 and Frederick V ("Bull Skin to Scott's Mill") where Gilbert Guilder was constable in 1741.

210. I was unable to find where John Welton, Jr. was living in 1740; however, in 1749 and 1750, he administered the estate of his father, John Welton, Sr., and the estate was appraised by Jesse Pugh and Jeremiah Smith. Appraisers were usually neighbors, and at this time, Pugh and Smith owned land on Back Creek and Hogue Creek, northwest of Winchester between the Cacapon River and Opequon Creek. If John Welton, Jr. was living in this area in 1740, then his appointment to "Cape Cappurn" (the Cacapon River) was near his residence. (Dee Ann Buck, comp., *Abstracts of Frederick County, Virginia: Wills, Inventories & Abstracts, 1743–1816* [Fairfax, VA: The Compiler, ca. 2004] 1:284, 358; Vaz, 50; O'Dell, 200, 202.)

211. It was not unusual for the court to miswrite an appointee's first name: Edward for Edmund Manion, Robert for George Smith, John for James Mitchel, Edward for Edmund Burrus, John for Thomas Price, Robert for William Rumsey, Edward for Thomas Dillard. So it is very likely that the first two orders were directed to Joseph, not John, Edwards. There was a John Edwards who appears on the 1738 and 1739 Orange I tobacco planter lists and worked on a road from the Mine Run Bridge to Wilderness Run—landmarks in Orange I—in 1740 (Little, 13, 18; OCRO 1734, 44 [28 March 1740]). However, on the same day that the court continued the order to summon John Edwards to be sworn constable, Thomas Wharton was appointed and then served as constable of Orange I. So this John Edwards could not have been appointed constable of Frederick County in 1742. Joseph Edwards lived about sixteen miles northwest of Winchester on Cacapon River in today's Hampshire County (O'Dell, 536). Edwards may have been first appointed on 25 September 1741 on one of the first four missing pages of OCOB 3. John Nation was appointed constable of Frederick III

Notes

on 25 September 1741, then on 26 February 1741/42, the summons for both Nation and Edwards to be sworn was continued until the next court (OCOB 3: 7, 106).

212. On 23 June 1743, Mathias Seltzer was ordered to work on a road "from Massanutten to Thornton's Mill," and seven years later, he was granted "150 acres adjoining said Selzer Massanutten Tract" (OCRO 1734, 87; VLP Northern Neck Grant G:431 [10 August 1750]). The Massanutten Mountains are on the west side of the South Fork of the Shenandoah River and run through today's Shenandoah and Rockingham Counties. Since Seltzer was ordered to work on a road to Thornton's Mill (see p. Xn. X (Rapp)), it is likely that he was living in today's Shenandoah County, formerly part of Frederick County.

213. Joseph A. Waddell, *Annals of Augusta County, Virginia, from 1726 to 1871* (Bridgewater, VA: C. J. Carrier, 1958), vi.

214. Lyman Chalkley, *Chronicles of the Scotch-Irish Settlements in Virginia: Extracted from the Original Court Records of Augusta County, 1745–1880* (Baltimore: Genealogical Publishing, 1965), 1:4-133.

215. See Augusta I-A, III, IV, X-A, XI, XIII, XVII, XX, Unidentified 1743 and 1744.

216. See p. Xn. X. (Fred intro re Sherundo)

217. See p. Xn. X. (re "Gerundo.") Two of the constables assigned to Augusta I, Daniel Holdman and Charles Robinson, worked on a road for the "Inhabitants of the North branch of the Sharendo" (OCRO 1734, 51 [27 November 1740]).

218. Little, 214; Samuel Stewart, appointed constable to Augusta V, on "Linwell's Creek," patented 180 acres on the "Middle Branch of Linwells Creek" in Augusta County on 5 September 1749, but he was living in Augusta County from at least 27 September 1745 (VLP 27:377, OCRO 1734, 114).

219. Road from the courthouse to Christians Creek: ACRO 44 (19 May 1753), 45 (21 May 1753), 51 (27 November 1753), 77 (24 November 1760), 79 (20 February 1761), 102 (22 June 1764); from the courthouse to "Christys Creek": ACRO 46 (22 May 1753), 91 (22 May 1762). William Smith, assigned to Augusta VIII, "at Christee's Creek," owned land on Christians Creek (James Raymond Hildebrand, *The Beverley Patent, 1736, including original grantees, 1738–1815, in Orange & Augusta Counties, VA.* Map, 1954, *Rootsweb* [http://www.rootsweb.ancestry.com/~vaaugust/bevswmap.html : accessed 20 October 2008]).

220. William Beverley's 1736 patent: VLP 17:154 (6 September 1736); the Irish Tract, see OCOB 1:378 (28 September 1738) and 3:24 (25 September 1741).

221. Benjamin Borden's 1739 patent: VLP 18:360 (6 November 1739).

222. Five Augusta I constables owned land or worked on roads to or from Smith's Creek, a tributary of the North River (North Fork of the Shenandoah), which flows through today's southern Shenandoah and northern Rockingham Counties: William Carrol (VLP Northern Neck Grant G:235 [21 July 1749]), John Hodge on a "branch of North River of Shanando called Smith's Creek" (VLP 25:295 [12 January 1746]), James Gill (OCRO 1734, 56 [29 May 1741]), Daniel Holdman and Charles Robinson (OCRO 1734, 50 [27 November 1740]). The other constables owned land on the "North River of Shannandoah," which runs through the length of today's Shenandoah County and has its headwaters in the north of Rockingham County: Reuben Allen (VLP Northern Neck Grant G:263 [9 August 1749]), Reily Moore (VLP Northern Neck Grant G:272 [15 August 1749]), William Clark (VLP Northern Neck Grant G:269 [12 August 1749]) and William White (VLP 18:295 [29 June 1739]).

223. John Tilly and William Frazier lived in Augusta County. Between 26 April 1738 and 10 September 1740, John Tilly owned land someplace "on Sherundo Riv . . . part of 5000 acres taken up by Jacob Stover" (OCDB 2:300, 4:240). This land might have been in the area of one of Jacob Stover's 5000 acre grants "on the second fork of Sherrando River . . . above the mouth of Hawks Bill Creek" in southeast "Rockingham" County close to Swift Run Gap and the "Greene" County border (VLP 15:129 [15 December 1733]). In 1738, John Tilly, constable, petitioned the Orange County court to add his and James Tilly's names to the list of

Notes

tithables; and, in 1739, James Tilly appeared on the Orange V ("Greene" County) tobacco planter list. In 1764, a John Tilly (the same?) was constable of Orange IV. William Frazier and Samuel Ro*f*er do not appear on any of the tobacco planter lists. On 28 March 1745, William Frazier and Adam Miller (a constable of Augusta III) were ordered to work on a road from Jackson's Mill (in the south of today's Madison County) to the "Top of the [Blue] Ridge" and into Augusta County at "Frazier's little Island," and on 19 May 1749, William Frazier was ordered to work on a road in Augusta County (OCRO 1734, 106; ACRO, 16).

224. There were two Samuel Scotts living contemporaneously in Orange County: one was a constable of Culpeper II-B in 1745 and 1746, the other was recorded on 14 December 1739 in James Wood's Survey Notebook of the original settlers of Rockingham County as living on 400 acres "On end of Peeked Mtn. on br. of So. R. called Cub Run Adj. Jacob Stover" (O'Dell, 268, 274). Scott was later granted this land on 30 August 1744 (VLP 23:746).

225. There were two William Williams living at the same time in Orange County. Cecil O'Dell said that the William Williams who replaced Samuel Scott as constable in 1740 was a preacher living on Opequon Creek (near Martinsburg), but that cannot be correct because Martinsburg is almost one hundred miles from Cub Run where Samuel Scott lived (O'Dell, 128–132 and see p. 152n. 197). Another William Williams bought 200 acres on Mill Creek, a branch of the South River of the Shenandoah a little south of Cub Run, on 26 August 1741 and was granted an additional 350 acres in the same place in 1743 (OCDB 5:62; VLP 21:286 [30 June 1743]). Like Samuel Scott, Williams probably resided on this land before 1741.

226. On 16 August 1741, Jacob Stover sold land "on w. side Blue Ridge Mts & e. side of South branch of Shenandoah River joining Henry Dowley" (OCDB 6:64), and on 23 November 1744, Henry Dowley worked on a a road "to Saml Scotts on the Peeked Mountain" (OCRO 1734, 105).

227. I found no earlier order describing these charges against Henry Dowley and James McDowell, the 1741 constable of Augusta XV.

228. Richard Mauldin, Jr. patented 2000 acres on the south side of Peeked Mountain and the south side of the South River of "Shanado" on 30 June 1743 (VLP 20:510); John Davies was recorded living on Smith Creek on 17 December 1739 in James Wood's Survey Notebook of original Rockingham County settlers and patented this land on 10 July 1745 (O'Dell, 274; VLP 23:896); Adam Miller, Ludowick Francisco and Samuel Scott were ordered to work on a road from Swift Run Gap in southeast "Rockingham" County on 11 February 1745/46 and 21 November 1746 (ACRO 1, 6).

229. Edward Erwin settled on Long Glade Run, a tributary of the North Fork of the Shenandoah, which flows through south "Rockingham" and north "Augusta" Counties; Alexander Blair was granted land on the "North River of Shanando called the Long Glade" on 24 March 1740 (Lou Hudson Pellican, "CORRECTING the family of Edwin Erwin, Jr.," article, 2006, *Rootsweb* [http://www.rootsweb.ancestry.com/~ vaaugust/ erwin.htm : accessed 12 March 2009]; VLP 19:938). Edward Erwine and Alexander Blair served in Capt. John Smith's 1742 Augusta Militia Company (Chalkley, 2:508).

230. Jeremiah Harrison was granted land on "Linwell's Creek" on 10 February 1748/49; on 17 February 1761, Harrison sold some of this land, which adjoined Samuel Stewart's land (VLP 27:108; Chalkley, 3:129).

231. James D. Small ("The Beverly Patent," map and index, 2000, *Rootsweb* [http://www.rootsweb. ancestry.com/vaaugust/BeverlyPatent.htm : accessed 14 October 2008]) notes the following Beverley Manor land owners: James, father of John, Carr (I-3, 1739), Robert Patterson (G-2, 1740), Alexander Thompson (H-6).

232. Beverley Manor land owners: Joseph Teaze (Small, I-6, 1739), John Wilson (Small, A-6, 1738 and B-6, 1739), John Christian (Small, E-7, 1739), Patrick Cook (Small, B-6, 1740).

233. A Tease (or Teas, Tees) family appears in Augusta County court records (Chalkley, 1:614), and Joseph Tees worked on roads in Augusta County (ACRO, 17 [22 May 1749], 36 [17 June 1752]).

234. Four constables assigned to this precinct owned land in the northeast section of Beverley Manor

north of Tinkling Spring: William Wright (Small, H-4, 1749), David Ediston [Edmondson] (Small, I-5, 1740), James Gillespie [Gilasby] (Small, I-4, 1740), Robert Turk, father of Thomas (Small, J-3, 1739; Chalkley, 3:125), James Moodey (Small, D-6, 1740).

235. Beverley Manor land owners: Patrick Martin (Small, B-5, 1740), Robert Poage (Small, F-3, 1739 and B-9, 1740), John Baskins (Small, H-4, nd), John McCutchin (Small, B-7, 1741), John Pickens (Small, G-3, 1740).

236. The three constables assigned to this precinct owned land in Beverley Manor near Tinkling Spring and were members of the Tinkling Spring Church: John Caldwell (Small, G-6, 1738), George Caldwell (Small, E-6, 1740), William Hutchinson (Small, G-4, 1741); see also Carmen J. Finley, "Tinkling Spring Church Photo Album," article, 2008, *Rootsweb*, (http://www.rootsweb.ancestry.com/~vaaugust/ photo.html : accessed 12 November 2008).

237. James Allen was appointed to an unidentified Augusta precinct in 1742.

238. John Carr, see p. Xn. X; Robert Young (Small, B-4 and C-4, 1749).

239. James Caldwell was constable of Augusta XI in 1743 and 1744.

240. I found no earlier order about charges against James McDowell and Henry Dowley, the 1741 Augusta II constable.

241. Whatever the personal names of Mitchell (John or William), Anderson (James or John) or Trimble (John or James), these orders clearly describe appointments to subprecincts of Augusta XV.

242. Oren F. Morten (*A History of Rockbridge County, Virginia* [Staunton, VA: McClure Co., 1920], 299, 346) identified Joseph Lapsley and Gilbert Campbell as constables assigned to Borden's Tract and said Joseph Lapsley purchased land in the Borden Tract in 1742.

243. In 1746, Jacob Harmon, Jacob Castle (father of John) and Humberston Lyon were ordered to work on a road from Adam Harmon's (who lived on the New or Woods River) "to the River and North branch of Roan Oak" (OCRO 1734, 109 [24 May 1745]; ACRO, 6 [19 November 1746]). Adam Harmon was one of the first settlers near Inglis' Ferry near the confluence of the New River and Little River in today's Pulaski County (Lewis Preston Summers, *History of Southwest Virginia, 1746–1786, Washington County, 1777–1870* [1903; reprint, Johnson City, TN: Overmountain Press, 1989], 51).

244. William Anderson was granted 400 acres in Augusta County on both sides of the "Middle River of Shanando" on 10 June 1740 (VLP 19:632).

245. Hening 2:102 (1661/62), 3:325–329 (1705), 3:530–535 (1710), 5:426–430 (1748).

246. OCOB 6:122 (26 June 1755).

247. Porter, 96–97.

248. Dorman, *Saint George's Parish*, 19–20, 25–28; Davis, *Saint Mark Parish*.

249. Justices were infrequently appointed in February, March, April; they were appointed after the 10th of June on 17 June 1735 (OCOB 1:18) and 22 June 1749 (OCOB 5: 180, 181).

250. OCOB 5:408 (22 February 1753).

251. Hening 2:19 (1661), 2:83–84 (1662), 2:170 (1662), 2:280 (1670), 2:296 (1672), 2:479 (1680), 3:258–59 (1705), 4:133 (1723), 6:40–44 (1748).

252. Hening 2:280 (1670).

253. Little (111–149) published eleven 1782 Orange County, property tax lists with the tobacco planter lists. They are the closest to a tithable list to survive for Orange County.

254. Little, 10, 11, 12, 22, 23, 24, 27, 29, 41, 48.

255. Little, 24.

Notes

256. Little, 163; OCOB 2:356 (27 May 1741).

257. After 1757, the court appointed justices "in the same precinct [he] took them last year" or "in the precincts that [the former justice] took them in last year" (OCOB 6:257 [25 April 1760]).

258. OCOB 2:357 (27 May 1741), 5:3 (25 April 1754), 6:336 (25 March 1757).

259. OCOB 4:108 (24 May 1744), 4:328 (23 May 1745), 4:471 (22 May 1746), 4A:152 (28 May 1747).

260. OCOB 1:18 (17 June 1735), 1:76 (18 May 1736), 1:171 (26 May 1737), 1:312 (25 May 1738), 1:460 (24 May 1739); SCOB 1732–1734:202 (1 May 1733).

261. See p. 21–22 concerning tithable precincts in Frederick County and Augusta County.

262. OCOB 4:471 (22 May 1746), 4A:152 (28 May 1747), 5:85 (28 November 1747).

263. The count of 2,507 tithables is correct. But why were there 1,538 tithables in 1737, then 2,507 tithables in 1738, then 1,904 tithables in 1739? Were the Augusta (and possibly Frederick) County tithables included in the 1738 total this year?

BIBLIOGRAPHY

"Acts of the General Assembly, Jan. 6, 1639–40." *William and Mary Quarterly*, 2d ser., 4 (January 1924): 16-31.

Blankenbaker, John. *Germanna History*. Articles. 2009. *Ancestry.com*. http://homepages.rootsweb.ancestry.com/~george/johnsgermnotes/germhist.html : accessed 12 February 2010.

Blomquist, Ann K. *Goochland County, Virginia, Court Order Books 1 & 2, 1728–1731*. Westminster, MD: Heritage Books, 2007.

_____. *Goochland County, Virginia, Court Order Book 3, 1731–1735*. Westminster, MD: Heritage Books, 2006.

Borio, Gene. "Tobacco Timeline." Article. 1993–2007. *Tobacco News and Information*. http://www.tobacco.org/resources/history/Tobacco_History.html : accessed 12 April 2009.

Böÿe, Herman. *A Map of the state of Virginia, constructed in conformity to law from the late surveys authorized by the legislature and other original and authentic documents, by Herman Böÿe, 1825*. Map. Washington, DC: Selmar Siebert and Co., 1859. Library of Congress, *Map Collections: 1500–2004*. http://lcweb.2.loc.gov/cgi-bin/query/D?gmd:3:./temp/~ammem_5i2f : accessed 2 January 2009.

Breen, T. H. *Tobacco Culture, The Mentality of the Great Tidewater Planters on the Eve of Revolution*. Princeton, NJ: Princeton University Press, 1985.

Brown, Mike. "Some Devon Surname Aliases." Article. 2000? *Genuki*. http://genuki.cs.ncl.ac.uk/DEV/DevonMisc/Aliases.html : accessed 22 January 2009.

Brundage, Robert Scott. "Maps, Mills, Chapel, Roads, Water Ways, Migration [in Old-Frederick Co]." Article. 1998. *Rootsweb*. http://listsearches.rootsweb.com/th/read/OLD-FREDERICK-CO-VA/1998-03/0889274906 : accessed 12 October 2008.

Buck, Dee Ann, comp. *Abstracts of Frederick County, Virginia: Wills, Inventories & Accounts, 1743–1816*. Fairfax, VA: The Compiler, ca. 2004.

Chalkley, Lyman. *Chronicles of the Scotch-Irish Settlement in Virginia: Extracted from the Original Court Records of Augusta County, 1745–1800*. 3 vols. Baltimore: Genealogical Publishing, 1965.

Chiarello, Susan, transcr. "Militia Fines, Insolvents, and Removals King and Queen County." *Magazine of Virginia Genealogy* 46 (August 2008): 173–180.

Chitwood, Oliver Perry. *Justice in Colonial Virginia*. 1905. Reprint. Union, NJ: Lawbook Exchange, 2001.

Crawford, Barbara and Royster Lyle, Jr. *Rockbridge County Artists and Artisans*. Charlottesville, VA: University Press of Virginia, 1995.

Crozier, William Armstrong, ed. *Spotsylvania County Records, 1721–1800*. Baltimore: Genealogical Publ., 1971.

Davis, John David. *Frederick County, Virginia, Minutes of Court Records*. Westminster, MD: Heritage Books, 2008.

Davis, Rosalie Edith, transcr. and ed. *Saint Mark Parish Vestry Book and Levies 1730–1785: Spotsylvania, Orange and Culpeper Counties, Virginia*. Manchester, MO: Privately Printed, 1983.

Dickenson, Josiah Look. "The Manor of Greenway Court." *Proceedings of the Clarke County Historical Association* 8 (1948): 45–46. http://www.clarkehistory.org/publications/CCHA_Proceedings_Vol_08(1948).pdf : accessed 12 October 2008.

Bibliography

Dorman, John Frederick, comp. *Culpeper County, Virginia, Deeds (1749–1762)*. 2 vols. Washington, DC: Dorman, 1975–1976.

_____, comp. *Culpeper County, Virginia, Will Book A, 1749–1770*. Washington, DC: Dorman, 1956.

_____, comp. *Orange County, Virginia: Deed Books 1–8, 1735–1743*. 3 vols. Washington, DC: Dorman, 1961–1971.

_____, comp. *Orange County, Virginia, Will Books 1–2: 1735–1778*. Washington, DC: Dorman, 1958–1961.

_____, transcr. and ed. *Saint George's Parish, Spotsylvania County, Virginia, Vestry Books, 1726–1817*. Fredericksburg, VA: The Transcriber, 1998.

Field, Eugene Allen. "Descendants of Abraham Field, Westmoreland County, Virginia, 1636–1674." Article. 2008. http://www.luciefield.net/abrahamfieldwestmoreland.pdf : accessed 4 April 2009.

Finley, Carmen J. "Tinkling Spring Church Photo Album." Article. 2008. *Rootsweb*. http://www.rootsweb.ancestry.com/~vaaugust/photo.html : accessed 12 November 2008.

Flippin, Percy Scott. *The Royal Government in Virginia, 1624–1775*. Studies in History, Economics and Public Law 84. New York: Columbia University, 1919.

Gilreath, Amelia C., abstr. *Frederick County, Virginia, Deed Books, 1743–1758 (Deed Books 1–4)*. Nokesville, VA: Gilreath, 1989.

Grenier, John. *The First Way of War: American War Making on the Frontier, 1607–1814*. Cambridge: Cambridge University Press, 2005.

Hale, Forrest. "Wooten Family." Article. 1999. *Rootsweb*. http://archiver.rootsweb.ancestry.com/th/read/WOOTEN/1999-07/0932661541 : accessed 9 May 2009.

Hening, William Waller, ed. *The Statutes at Large: Being a Collection of all the Laws of Virginia from the First Session of the Legislature, in the year 1619*. 13 vols. Charlottesville, VA: University Press of Virginia, 1969.

Herndon, G. Melvin. "Hemp in Colonial Virginia." *Agricultural History* 37 (1963): 86.

Hildebrand, James Raymond. *The Beverley Patent, 1736, including original grantees, 1738–1815, in Orange & Augusta Counties, VA*. Map. J. R. Hildebrand, 1954. *Rootsweb*. http://www.rootsweb.ancestry.com/~vaaugust/bevswmap.html : accessed 20 October 2008.

Huffman, Charles Herbert, ed. *The Germanna Record*. No. 6. Culpeper, VA: Memorial Foundation of the Germanna Colonies, June 1965.

Jeffries, Margaret. "Virginia W.P.A. Historical Inventory Project. Survey Report: Arlington, 1937 Jan 27." Article. Library of Virginia. *LVA Catalogs*. http://lvaimage.lib.va.us/VHI/html/07/0145.html : accessed 17 May 2009.

_____. "Virginia W.P.A. Historical Inventory Project. Survey Report: Maple Wood, 1937 June 30." Library of Virginia. *LVA Catalogs*. http://lvaimage.lib.va.us/VHI/html/07/0311.html : accessed 17 May 2009.

Joyner, Ulysses P., Jr. *The First Settlers of Orange County, Virginia 1700–1776*. 2nd ed. Baltimore: Gateway Press, 2003.

_____. *Orange County Land Patents*. 2nd ed. Orange, VA: Orange County Historical Society, 1999.

Kerns, Wilmer L. "Fee Book of Col. James Wood." Article. 1997. *Rootsweb*. http://archiver.rootsweb.ancestry.com/th/read/OLD-FREDERICK-CO-VA/1997-08/0870658449 : accessed 9 October 2008.

Kulikoff, Alan. *Tobacco and Slaves: The Development of Southern Cultures in the Chesapeake, 1680–1800*. Chapel Hill, NC: University of North Carolina Press, 1986.

Lewis, Eric. "How Did They Get Here?" *The Guardian, Newsletter of the Jefferson County WV Historical*

Society 6 (July 2008): 4. http://www.jeffersonhistoricalwv.org/newsletter/July08-Guardian.pdf : accessed 9 October 2008.

Little, Barbara Vines. "Goochland County Tithables, c 1735." *Magazine of Virginia Genealogy* 46, no. 3 (2008): 235–236.

_____, comp. *Orange County, Virginia, Order Book One, 1734–1739*. Orange, VA: Dominion Research Service, 1990.

_____. *Orange County, Virginia, Tithables 1734–1782*. 2 vols. Orange, VA: Dominion Market Research Corp., ca. 1988.

Lorenz, Stacy L. "Policy and Patronage, Governor William Gooch and Anglo-Virginia Politics, 1727–1749." In *English Atlantics Revisited: Essays Honouring Professor Ian K. Steele*, edited by Nancy Lee Rhoden, 81–106. Ithaca, NY: McGill-Queen's University Press, 2007.

Luckman, Gene and Ann Brush Miller. *Frederick County Road Orders 1734–1772*. Charlottesville, VA: Virginia Transportation Research Council, June 2005.

Map of Culpeper County with parts of Madison, Rappahannock and Fauquier Counties, Virginia, 1863?. Map. Washington, DC?: U.S Bureau of Topographical Engineers, 1863?. Library of Congress. *American Memory. Map Collections: 1500–2004.* http://lcweb2.loc.gov/cgi-bin/query/D?gmd:1/temp/~ammem_ihsK : accessed 2 May 2009.

Mason, Leo S. "To Have Lived Then – the 1700s." In *An 18th Century Perspective: Culpeper County*, compiled and edited by Mary Stevens Jones, 115–138. Culpeper, VA: Culpeper Historical Society, 1976.

Mears, Robert L. "Cost of Some Items in Colonial Virginia." Article. N.d. *Eastern Shore Public Library: Tales from the Eastern Shore.* http://www.espl.org/genealogy/tales/tobacco.htm : accessed 8 August 2009.

Meyer, Nancy. "Take a Hike: Mary's Rock/Shenandoah National Park." Article. 2004. *Shenandoah.com Stories.* http://www.shenandoah.com/stories/?id=7333 : accessed 9 October 2009.

Middleton, Lucyle Bickers. "Bickers Family Newsletter." No. 9. Article. 1995. *Rootsweb*. http://freepages.genealogy.rootsweb.ancestry.com/~mimsfamily/Documents_Bickers_Newsletter : accessed 18 June 2009.

Miller, Ann Brush. *Orange County Road Orders 1734–1749*. Rev. ed. Charlottesville, VA: Virginia Highway & Transportation Research Council, April 2004.

_____. *Orange County Road Orders 1750–1800*. Rev. ed. Charlottesville, VA: Virginia Highway & Transportation Research Council, April 2004.

Morgan, Edmund S. *American Slavery, American Freedom*. New York: W. W. Norton, 1975.

Morten, Oren F. *A History of Rockbridge County, Virginia*. Staunton, VA: McClure Co., 1920.

Moses, Louis. "Where is Funk's Mill Run?" Article. 2001. *Rootsweb*. http://listsearches.rootsweb.com/th/read/VAFREDER/2001-12/1007409709 : accessed 12 October 2008.

O'Dell, Cecil. *Pioneers of Old Frederick County, Virginia*. Marceline, MO: Walsworth Publishing, 1995.

Orange County, Virginia, Order Books 1–4, 4A (1734–1747), 7–8 (1763–1777). Library of Virginia. Microfilm Rolls 30, 31, 33.

Papageorgiou, Lizabeth Ward. *The Colonial Churches of St. Thomas' Parish, Orange County, Virginia With Notes on Sites in Orange, Greene, and Madison Counties*. Baltimore: Clearfield Company, 2008.

Pawlett, Nathaniel Mason. *Spotsylvania County Road Orders 1722–1734*. Rev. ed. Charlottesville, VA: Virginia Transportation Research Council, April 2004.

_____ and Ann Brush Miller, Kenneth Madison Clark, Thomas Llewellyn Samuel, Jr. *Augusta County Road Orders 1745–1769*. Rev. ed. Charlottesville, VA: Virginia Transportation Research Council, July 2003.

Bibliography

"Petition of Henry Willis, 1728 Apr. 12." Digital image. Library of Virginia. *LVA Catalogs.* http://lva.virginia.gov/whatwehave : accessed 12 March 2008.

Pollock, Sir Frederick. "The Oath of Allegiance." Article. *The Online Library of Liberty.* http://oll.libertyfund.org/index.php?option=com_content&task=view&id=1422&Itemid=284 : accessed 12 August 2009.

Porter, Albert Ogden. *County Government in Virginia: A Legislative History, 1607–1904.* New York: AMS Press, 1966.

Roeber, A. G. *Faithful Magistrates and Republican Lawyers: Creators of Virginia Legal Culture, 1680–1810.* Chapel Hill, NC: University of North Carolina Press, 1981.

Scheel, Eugene M. *Culpeper: A Virginia County's History Through 1920.* Orange, VA: Green Publishers, 1982.

_____. *Culpeper County (Map).* Washington, DC: Williams & Heintz, 1975.

_____. *Madison County (Map).* Washington, DC: Williams & Heintz, 1984.

Schwartz, Marie Jenkins. *Born in Bondage, Growing Up Enslaved in the Antebellum South.* Cambridge, MA: Harvard University Press, 2000.

Scott, W. W. *A History of Orange County, Virginia: From its Formation in 1734 (O.S.) to the end of Reconstruction in 1870; compiled mainly from Original Records With a Brief Sketch of the Beginnings of Virginia, A Summary of Local Events to 1907, and a Map.* Richmond, VA: Everrett Waddey, 1907.

Small, James D. "The Beverly Patent." Article. 2000. *Rootsweb.* http://www.rootsweb.ancestry.com/~vaaugust/BeverlyPatent.htm : accessed 14 October 2008.

Sparacio, Ruth and Sam, eds. *Deed Abstracts of Orange County, Virginia, 1743–1779 (Deed Books 9–20).* 5 vols. McLean, VA: Antient Press, 1985–1988.

_____, eds. *Orange County, Virginia, Order Books, 1747–1763 (Order Books 5–7).* 6 vols. McLean, VA: Antient Press, 1997–2000.

_____, eds. *Order Book Abstracts of Spotsylvania County, Virginia, 1732–1735.* 2 vols. McLean, VA: Antient Press, ca. 1990.

Summers, Lewis Preston. *History of Southwest Virginia, 1746–1786, Washington County, 1777–1870.* 1903. Reprint. Johnson City, TN: Overmountain Press, 1989.

Unsigned. Review of *Orange County, Virginia, Tithables, 1734–1782*, by Barbara Vines Little. *Virginia Genealogical Society Newsletter* 15 (Jan.–Feb. 1989): 5–6.

Vaugondy, Giles Robert de. *Carte de la Virginie et du Maryland.* Map. Paris: Chez de Vaugondy, 1757–58. Birmingham [Alabama] Public Library, Rucker Agee Map Collection. *Alabama Maps.* http://alabamamaps.ua.edu/historicalmaps/us_states/Virginia/index_Before1900.html : accessed 1 February 2009.

Vaz, Mary Gwaltney. *Local Government in the Virginia Piedmont, 1720–1759.* Ann Arbor, MI: UMI Dissertation Services, 1997.

Virginia Land Office Patents and Grants. Database and digital images. Library of Virginia. http://www.lva.lib.va.us/whatwehave/land/index.htm : accessed 1 February 2009.

Virginia Records Timeline: 1553–1743. Library of Congress. *The Thomas Jefferson Papers.* http://lcweb2.loc.gov/ammem/collections/jefferson_papers/mtjvatm.html : accessed 20 April 2009.

Waddell, Joseph A. *Annals of Augusta County, Virginia, from 1726 to 1871.* Bridgewater, VA: C. J. Carrier, 1958.

Walker, Frank S., Jr. *Remembering: A History of Orange County, Virginia.* Orange, VA: Orange County Historical Society, 2004.

Watkinson, James D., Barbara Vines Little, Neil McDonald. Online discussion about "sucker hunting." 17–19 June 2003. Library of Virginia. *VA–Hist Archives Listserv 15.5.* http://listlva.lib.va.us/cgi-bin/wa.exe?A2=

Bibliography

va-hist;X3GsmA;20030619153427-0500 : accessed 3 July 2007.

Wayland, John W. *A History of Rockingham County*. Harrisonburg, VA: C. J. Carrier, 1980.

Yancey, Dennis J. "Yancey Place Names." Article. *The Yancey Surname Resource Center*. http://yanceyfamilygenealogy.org/places.htm : accessed 18 May 2010.

INDEX

Abbet, James, 61, 65
Abbit, James, 66
Abbitt, James, 66
Abney, Abraham, 5
Acres, Simon, 110
Aestham's River, 147n. 147
Albemarle County, 32
Alford, John, 88
Aliases, 144n. 108
Allen, James, 105
Allen, Reuben, 96, 154n. 222
Anderson, Colvert, 17, 87
Anderson, Culvert, 87
Anderson, James, 106
Anderson, John, 106
Anderson, William, 110, 156n. 244
Anderston, Colvert, 86
Anglican Church, 6, 8
Appalachian Mountains, 147n. 139
Archer, John, 110
Arlington, 67
Asher, John, 51, 66
Askew, John, 51
Attachments, 13–14, 27, 29, 44, 50, 59, 64, 66, 76, 77, 81, 87, 88, 90, 103, 105
Augusta County
    constable precincts in, 22, 94–95
    counties and states formed from, 94
    justices living in, 142n. 84
    Lists of Tithables, 22, 116, 118, 119, 157n. 263
    tobacco planter lists, 21–22
    tobacco warehouses, 2

Banks, Gerhard, 65
Barber, James, 115
Barbour, James, 115, 116
Barrows Lowgrounds, 69
Bartonville, 84
Baskins, John, 156n. 235
Baskins, William, 102

Bath County, 95
Baylor, John, 41, 42
Beale, Richard, 41
Beale, Taverner, 122
Beale Family, 42
Becket, Reverend John, 18
Been, James, 110
Beger, Robert, 145n. 118
Bell, Captain William, 42, 49, 54, 56, 59, 147n. 140
Bell, Militia Company of Captain, 42, 49, 54, 56, 59
Bell, Roger, 32, 36, 144n. 110
Bell, William, 10, 42, 43, 122, 123, 139n. 25
Berkeley County, 84
Berry's Ferry, 153n. 206
Berwick, Thomas, 151n. 188
Beverley, William, 94–95
Beverley Manor, 84, 94, 95, 100, 155nn. 231 232, 156n. 235
Beverly Mannor District, 104
Beverly Manor, 119
Beverlys Patent Line, 119
Bicker, Robert, 145n. 118
Bicker, William, 145n. 118
Bickers, Robert, 9, 19, 34, 43, 44, 47, 145n. 118
Bickers, Robert, Jr., 145n. 118
Big Run, 49, 56
Bigers, Robert, 145n. 118
Bigers, William, 145n. 118
Bigore, Robert, 145n. 118
Bigore, William, 145n. 118
Bigors, Robert, 145n. 118
Bigors, William, 145n. 118
Blair, Alexander, 99, 155n. 229
Blakenbecker, Zacharias, 82
Blakenbecker, Zachary, 82
Blakenbukler, Zacharyas, 82
Blakenpecker, Zachary, 82
Blankenbaker, Zacharias, 6, 9, 79, 139n. 28

165

Index

Blankenbeckler, Zachary, 82
Blankenbeker, Zachariah, 82
Blare, Alexander, 99
Bletsoe, Abraham, Jr., 50
Blue Ridge, 119
Blue Ridge Mountains, 49, 56, 75, 79, 83, 95, 147n. 139
Blue Run, 42, 46, 49, 54, 116, 117, 118, 120, 121, 122, 123
Bohannan, Dunkin, 44, 145n. 120
Bohannon, John, 45
Bohanon, John, 45
Bohnannon, John, 107
Boman, George, 85
Booten, John, 28
Borden, Benjamin, 95
Borden's Tract, 95, 105, 107, 156n. 242
Boston, John, 28, 143n. 94
Branham Family, 23
Bray, David, 42
Broad Arrow, 13, 84
Brookes's Run, 61, 65
Brown, Daniel, 81, 149nn. 168, 169, 150nn. 176, 179
Brown, Daniel, Jr., 74
Brown, Francis, 74, 149n. 168
Brown, Richard, 50
Brown, William, 100
Bruce, David, 3
Bruce, Margaret, 11, 29
Bruce, Richard, 59, 60, 147n. 146
Bruks, Jacob, 86
Bryan, Jeremiah, 60
Bryan, John, 109
Bryant, Jeremiah, 60, 147n. 146
Bryant, John, 19, 53, 109
Bryne, Cornelius, 109
Bryne, John, 109
Buchanan, John, 104, 142n. 84
Buchannan, John, 101, 106, 118
Bullskin, 90, 91
Bullskin Precinct, 90
Bullskin Run, 83, 84, 88, 151n. 187
Bulskin Precinct, 87, 90
Bunker Hill, 84
Burdine, Richard, 82

Burdyne, Richard, 6, 82
Burgess, Thomas, 146n. 126
Burgess, Timothy, 46, 146n. 126
Burris, Edmund, 41
Burrus, Edmon, 41
Burrus, Edmund, 20, 21, 41, 48
Burrus, Edward, 41
Bush, Josias, 52
Bush, Philip, 18, 51
Bush, Phillip, 51

Cacapon River, 83, 91, 151n. 184
Caldwall, James, 103
Caldwele, James, 103
Caldwell, George, 103, 156n. 236
Caldwell, James, 103
Caldwell, John, 156n. 236
Calf Pasture, 94, 108, 119
Calfpasture River, 94
Callaway, Thomas, 6, 13, 49, 56, 76
Calloway, Thomas, 56
Calmes, Marquis, 9
Campbell, Andrew, 142n. 84
Campbell, Gilbert, 10, 105, 106, 156n. 242
Campbell, Patrick, 7, 13, 101
Cape Cappurie, 83, 91
Cape Cappurn, 83, 91
Carolina, 96
Carr, James, 155n. 231
Carr, John, 11, 100, 104, 155n. 231
Carrell, William, 97
Carrol, William, 154n. 222
Carter, Colonel Charles, 148n. 155, 149n. 162
Carter, Daniel, 61, 66
Carter, Quarter of Colonel Charles, 69
Carter, Wagon Road of Colonel Charles, 67, 73
Castle, Jacob, 156n. 243
Castle, John, 108, 156n. 243
Catalpa, 67
Catholic, 8, 10, 13, 89
Cattle, 13
Cattlet, John, 117
Cattlot, John, 116
Cavanaugh, Philemon, 67
Cave, Ben, 19, 20, 37, 38, 39

Index

Cave, Benjamin, 17, 19, 38, 39, 42, 46, 68, 116, 120, 121, 122
Cave, Benjamin, Jr., 37
Cave, Captain Benjamin, 32
Cave, Robert, 59
Cave's Ordinary, 32, 40
Caves, Captain, 38, 121, 122, 144n. 100
Caves, Joseph, 72, 149n. 166
Certificate for Hemp, 14
Certificate for Capture of Runaway Servants or slaves, 12
Chandler, Joseph, 35, 36, 37
Chapel. *See* Morgan, New, Southwest Mountain
Chapman, John, 34, 35
Cheek, Richard, 17
Cherry, Thomas, 151n. 188
Chester, Thomas, 83, 142n. 84, 151n. 190
Chester's Ferry, 83, 84, 151n. 190
Chesters, 88, 151n. 190
Chew, Colonel Thomas, 118
Chew, Thomas, 42, 115, 116, 117, 120, 121, 123
Chiles, Malachi, 32, 33, 34
Chiles, Malachy, 33
Chissum, John, 67, 70, 71, 148n. 153
Choice, Tully, 77
Christee's Creek, 94, 101, 154n. 219
Christian, John, 101, 155n. 232
Christians Creek, 94, 101, 154n. 219
Christys Creek, 94, 154n. 219
Church. *See* Southwest Mountain, Middle
Church at Tennant's Old Field, 150n. 176
Church Hall, 122
Church Run, 32
Churchwardens, 11, 13
Clark, James, 14, 31
Clark, William, 97, 154n. 222
Clarke, John, 151n. 189
Clayton, Philip, 67, 68, 118, 119, 120, 148n. 150
Clayton, Road of Mr., 67, 73
Cleaveland, John, 16, 50, 51
Cleaveland, William, 52
Cleavland, John, 51
Clerk, William, 97
Clerks, 11, 114

Cleveland, John, 6, 10, 50, 51
Cleveland, William, 6, 52, 53
Cluten, Thomas, 21
Cole, James, 105
Coleman, James, 32, 35, 42, 49, 144n. 102
Coleman, John, 64
Coleman, Mr., 54, 123
Coleman, Mr. James, 121
College of William and Mary, 114
Columbus, Christopher, 1
Conner, James, 63, 64, 148n. 148
Conner, John, Jr., 40
Constable Precinct Boundaries, 6–7
  compared with tithable precincts, 10, 18, 114, 115
  confusion about, 7, 19, 20, 42, 49, 146n. 136
  earliest in Orange County, 7
  in Augusta County, 22
Constables
  abuse of, 16, 86
  appointments, 6–11
  dereliction of duties, 16–17, 18, 63, 75
  duties, 5, 11–15, 17, 64, 97, 140n. 39
  in Augusta County, 7, 9, 10, 14, 21–22
  in Frederick County, 7, 9, 10, 14, 21–22
  in Goochland County, 5, 141n. 63
  in Spotsylvania County, 5, 7, 16, 21
  length of term, 10, 11
  misbehavior, 6, 12, 24, 45, 63, 75, 86, 87, 98
  misspelled names in court orders, 153n. 211
  oaths sworn, 7–9
  office of, 5–6, 16
  qualifications, 5–6
  remuneration, 11, 12, 13, 14, 15–16, 20, 21
Conway, Rebecca, 24
Conway's Warehouse, 2
Cook, Patrick, 101, 155n. 232
Cook, Will, 38
Cook, William, 18, 38, 39
Cooke, William, 38
Corn, 5, 14
Cornelius, Rowland, 10, 68, 73, 149n. 169
Coroner, 9, 11, 12, 15
Corruthers, Hugh, 110
Cost of Items in 1740s, 15
Coursey, James, 59, 147n. 145

Index

Coursey, William, 53
Courthouse, 66, 114, 115, 119, 121
   at Staunton, 94
   at Winchester, 83
   in Town of Orange, 9, 18
   near Raccoon Ford, 9, 67
   on Black Walnut Run, 9
Cow Pasture, 94, 108, 119
Cowpasture River, 94, 95
Cox, James, 35
Craft, Ralph, 88
Cragen, Elizabeth, 13
Cravens, Peter, 118
Crawford, Barnard, 58
Crawford, Barnett, 58
Crawford, William, 21, 75, 76
Crooked Run, 61, 62
Crop Note, 2, 3
Crosthwait, Timothy, 11, 18
Crutchfield Warehouse, 2
Culpeper, Town of, 67
Cuningham, Hugh, 107
Cunningham, Hugh, 107
Curtis, Charles, 18, 121
Curtis, Job, 91, 92

Daniel, Captain Reuben, 144n. 114
Daniel, Elijah, 43
Daniel, Militia Company of Captain, 40
Daniel, Reubin, 36
Daugherty, Patrick, 151n. 188
Davidson, John, 108
Davies, John, 155n. 228
Davies, Reverend Samuel, 13
Davis, John, 64, 98, 99
Davis, William, 10, 90
Davisson, Robert, 110
Day, Jacob, 109
Day, Mary, 13
Dearing, Robert, 51, 52
Deep Run, 79, 80
Deer Skins, 27, 36, 45, 52, 92
Deering, Robert, 20, 51, 146n. 132
Delinquent Lists, 85, 87, 89, 97, 114
   from Frederick County, 22
Denham, Joseph, 96

Denton, John, 92
Deputy Sheriff, 84, 114, 152n. 204
Devis's Rowling Path, 67, 70
Dewitt, Charles, 5
Dillard, Edward, 69, 149n. 163
Dillard, Thomas, 69, 70, 149n. 163
Dogs, 14
Donaught, William, 45
Double Topp, 79, 81
Doubletop Mountain, 79
Dougharty, Patrick, 83, 92
Douglas, George, 13, 56, 147n. 142
Douglass, Roger, 103
Dowley, Henry, 98, 155nn. 226, 227
Down, Henry, 120
Downer, Thomas, 76
Downs, Henry, 50, 77, 81, 121, 139nn. 25, 27
Drake, Samuel, 9
Dunham, Joseph, 96
Durham, Joseph, 96
Dyer, James, 77

Eastham, Robert, 115, 117, 118, 119
Eastham River, 147n. 147
Ediston, David, 156n. 234
Edminston, David, 102
Edmondson, David, 102, 156n. 234
Edwards, John, 92, 153n. 211
Edwards, Joseph, 13, 92, 153n. 211
Elk River, 147n. 147
Erwin, Edward, 155n. 229
Erwine, Edward, 155n. 229
Erwins, Edward, 99
Estate Appraisers, 15
Estates, 19
Eubanck, John, 52
Eubank, John, 18, 51, 52

Fabours, John, 71
Farguson, Joshua, 53
Faulconer, Samuel, 32, 38, 39
Faulkner, Samuel, 38, 39
Favors, John, 71
Favour, John, 71, 148n. 152
Fennel, Elijah, 47
Fennell, Elijah, 46

Index

Ffields, Abraham, 116
Ffinlasson, John, 118
Ffluetham, William, 97
Ffrankling, George, 109
Field, Abraham, 119, 149n. 167
Field, Henry, 31, 117
Field, John, 68, 73, 149n. 167
Finlasson, John, 116
Finlesson, John, 64
Finnel, Elijah, 47
Finnel, Jonathan, 146n. 125
Finnel, John, 146n. 125
Finnel, William, 46
Finnell, Elijah, 47
Finnell, William, 48
Firk, Thomas, 101
Firth River, 149n. 161
Fleshman, Zachary, 114
Flintham, William, 96
Fogins, John, 56
Fontaine, John, 147n. 139
Forck of Permunkey, 32
Fork of the Robinson River, 75
Fort Duquesne, 13
Fort Royal, 83
Foster, Anthony, 53
Francisco, Ludowick, 98, 155n. 228
Franklyn, Bently, 52
Fraser, William, 11
Frazer, William, 97
Frazier, William, 97, 154n. 223, 155n. 223
Frederceksburg, 123
Frederick County, 83
    constables in, 7, 21–22
    counties and states formed from, 83
    Delinquent Lists, 22
    deputy sheriff, 22, 152n. 204
    justices, 22, 142n. 84
    Lists of Tithables, 22, 119, 157n. 263
    Tobacco Planter Lists, 21–22
    tobacco warehouses in, 2, 138n. 6
Frederick Town, 152n. 192
Fredericksberg, 121
Fredericksburg Warehouse, 2
French and Indian War, 13
Funk, John, 84, 151n. 192

Funk's Mill, 83, 84, 151n. 192
Funk's Mill Run, 84, 151n. 192
Funks Mill, 92
Furguson, Joshua, 53
Fushee, Charles, 114

Gahagan, Thomas, 34
Gahagon, Thomas, 34
Garrel, Thomas, 80
Garrot, Thomas, 81
Garth, John, 77
Gay, John, 105
George, [the] Weddow, 13
German, Thomas, 53
German Lutherans, 79
Gerundo, 83, 84, 87, 94, 152n. 195
Gibbs, Doctor Joseph, 13
Gibbs, Zachary, 44, 145n. 120
Gibs, Zachary, 44
Gilasby, James, 102, 156n. 234
Gilder, Gilbert, 90, 91
Gilder, Hugh, 87
Gilder, Hutzin, 87
Gill, James, 95, 154n. 222
Gillespie, James, 156n. 234
Givens, Samuel, 142n. 84
Glaspee, Andrew, 69
Glebe Run, 18
Goazd, Joseph, 100
Goaze, Joseph, 100
Golding, Anthony, 17, 21, 60
Gollorthun, John, 10, 36, 37
Gooch, Sir William, 4
Goochland County
    constables viewing tobacco in, 5, 138n. 1, 141n. 63
    planters tending tobacco seconds in, 5
Goodal, John, 59
Goodall, John, 6, 20, 58, 59
Goodloe, Robert, 113
Gourdvine Fork, 67, 68, 74
Governor of the Virginia Colony, 114
Grant, William, 53, 54, 146n. 135
Graves, James, 68, 72, 73
Graves, Thomas, 18, 36, 37
Great Fork, 67, 69, 115, 118, 120

169

Index

Great Fork of Rappahannock, 115
Great Mountains, 61, 74, 79, 115, 119, 147n. 139
Great Run, 42, 49, 54, 56
Green, Robert, 115, 118
Greene, Robert, 116
Greenlay, James, 107
Griffen, John, 55
Griffin, John, 10, 20, 55
Grigsby, John, 12, 42, 47, 145n. 121
Grimes, Robert, 108
Grymes, Robert, 108
Guilder, Gilbert, 10, 153n. 209
Guilder, Huckill, 91, 153n. 209
Guilder, Huckle, 153n. 209
Guilder, Hugh, 88, 153n. 209

Haddock, Isaac, 10, 63
Haddocks, Isaac, 63
Hadok, Isaac, 63
Ham, Samuel, 113
Ham, William, 53
Hampton, Andrew, 86, 152n. 197
Haney, Darby, 52
Hanover County, 42, 49
Happy Creek, 83
Harmon, Adam, 108, 156n. 243
Harmon, Jacob, 108, 156n. 243
Harper, Robert, 151n. 183
Harper's Ferry, 83, 151n. 183
Harrison, Charles, 37
Harrison, Jeremiah, 155n. 230
Harrison, Lawrence, 37, 144n. 112
Harrisson, Jeremiah, 99
Hart, Thomas, 90, 153n. 206
Harvey, John, 28
Hawkins, John, 24, 25
Hays, Andrew, 106
Hazel River, 61, 62, 67, 147n. 147, 149n. 161
Heart, Thomas, 90
Hebron Valley, 79
Hedgeman, Nathanael, 76, 150n. 172
Hedgeman's River, 62, 68, 149n. 161, 150n. 172
Helms, Leonard, 88
Hemp, 14, 15, 31, 141n. 53

Henderson, John, 10, 33, 34, 36, 144n. 107
Henderson, William, 75, 77, 78, 150n. 174
Herndon, Edward, 150n. 174
Herndon, James, 150n. 174
Herndon, William, 150n. 174
Herondon, William, 77
Hews, Samuel, 13, 84, 152n. 197
High Mountains, 147n. 139
Hill, Russell, 81, 150n. 176
Hillen, Nathaniel, 69
Hillion, Nathanial, 69
Hillon, Nathanael, 69
Hilton, Peter, 89, 90
Hite, Jost, 83, 84, 142n. 84
Hites, Just, 85, 92
Hobson, George, 142n. 84
Hodge, John, 97, 154n. 222
Hodge, William, 108
Hoge, William, 108
Hoggshead, James, 109
Hogshead, 2, 3
Holdman, Daniel, 95, 154nn. 217, 222
Holman, Daniel, 95
Homes, William Wilson, 69
Hopkins, James, 16, 64
Horn, Benjamin, 44
Howard, James, 77
Howard, John, 77
Hughes, James, 107
Hughes River, 68, 149n. 161
Husk, William, 27
Hutcheson, Robert, 82
Hutcheson, William, 103
Hutchinson, William, 103, 156n. 236

Illegitimate Birth, 56, 144n. 108
Illiteracy, 6, 10
Immoral Behavior, 13, 16
Indian Run, 68, 73
Indians, 5
Inglis' Ferry, 156n. 243
Insanity, 13
Inspectors at Tobacco Warehouses, 2
Irish Tract, 22, 94, 116
Irwin, Edward, 99
Isbell, James, 9, 140nn. 36, 47

Index

Jackson, William, 76
James River, 94, 107, 147n. 139
James River Mountain Road, 147n. 139
James River Mountains, 49, 56, 147n. 139
Jameson, Thomas, 122, 123
Jamestown, 1
Jefferson County, 83, 84
Johnson, William, 89
Johnston, George, 84
Johnston, William, 89
Johnston's Mill, 151n. 191
Johnstons Mill, 84
Jones, Ambrose, 24, 139n. 27
Jones, Joseph, 14, 19, 31
Justices, 4, 5, 6, 7, 11, 12, 14, 19, 22
    appointed to take Lists of Tithables, 113, 156n. 249
    in Augusta County, 142n. 84
    in Frederick County, 142n. 84

Kavanaugh, Charles, 72
Kelley, William, 61
Kelly, William, 63, 148n. 148
Kendal, John, 25
Kendall, Henry, 79, 80, 150n. 178
Kendall, John, 24, 25
Kennerley, Thomas, 9, 74, 149n. 168
Kersey's Ferry, 153n. 206
Kimbrough, Bradley, 146n. 133
Kimbrow, Bradley, 10, 52, 146n. 133
Kimbrow, Bradly, 52
King, John, 110
Kirk, James, 10, 62, 63
Kirk, Joseph, 65, 148n. 148

Lamb, William, 98
Lapsley, Joseph, 107, 156n. 242
Laws Regulating Tobacco, 3–5
Layton, John, 79, 150n. 178
Leak, William, 41, 47, 48
Leek, William, 12, 47, 48
Leitch, George, 99
Levy of County, 3, 10, 11, 15–16, 20, 114
Lewis, John, 101, 103, 108, 118, 119, 142n. 84
Lewis, Zachary, 18, 24–25, 26, 57, 69, 75, 80

Liberty Mills, 42, 49
Lightfoot, Goodrich, 115, 120
Lignum, 18
Linnville Creek, 94
Linwell's Creek, 94, 99, 118, 154n. 218, 155n. 230
Little Cacapon, 151n. 184
Little Fork, 67, 68, 75, 77, 78, 116, 117, 118, 149n. 161
Little Fork of Rappahannock River, 147n. 147
Lists of Tithables, 10, 18, 22, 113-123. *See also* Tithables
Locust Grove, 23
Logan, David, 111
Long Glade, 155n. 229
Long Glade Run, 155n. 229
Long Marsh Run, 83, 84
Louisa County, 32
Low, Ralph, 92
Low, Thomas, 86
"Lower", 62, 67, 68, 148n. 149
Lucas, Moses, 114
Lucas, William, 52, 114
Lucas, William, Jr., 52
Lutherans, 6
Lyon, Hamberston, 108, 156n. 243

Madison, James, 6, 41, 42, 121, 122
Madison, Mr., 49, 54
Madison's Mill, 42, 49, 54
Madison Run, 42, 49
Mallery, John, 34
Mallory, John, 33, 34
Mallory, William, 47
Manion, Edmund, 24
Manion, Edward, 24
Mannen, Andrew, 12, 29
Maple Wood, 67
Mariners, 114
Marshall, Mereman, 54
Marshall, Reverend Mungo, 18
Martin, Joseph, 54, 55
Martin, Patrick, 102, 156n. 235
Marye, James, 108
Marye, Reverend James, 18, 19
Mason, John - 107

Index

Massanutten Mountains, 154n. 212
Mathews, William, 27
Mauldin, Richard, 98
Mauldin, Richard, Jr., 155n. 228
Maury River, 94
McCutchen, John, 103
McCutchin, John, 102, 103, 156n. 235
McDaniel, Alexander, 11, 12, 19, 21, 28, 29
McDaniel, Daniel, 91
McDonaugh, William, 44, 45
McDonough, William, 12, 17, 45, 145n. 120
McDowel, James, 98, 106
McDowele, James, 106
McDowell, James, 105, 106, 156n. 240
McDowell, John, 85, 139n. 25, 142n. 84
McDowell, Joseph, 152n. 199
McFeeters, William, 110
McKay, James, 88
McKee, James, 88
McQueen, Alexander, 70, 72, 148n. 152
McQuin, John, 10, 85
Mecklenberg, 138n. 6
Micall, John, 79
Michael, John, 79, 80
Michaell, John, 80
Michaels, John, 80
Mickell, John, 80
Middle Church, 32, 42, 120, 121, 122
Middle River, 94, 95, 119
Mikhel, James, 35
Mikhell, James, 35
Militia, 12, 15
    Company of Captain Bell, 42, 49, 54, 56, 59
    Company of Captain Scott, 42, 49, 54, 56
Mill Creek, 84, 155n. 225
Miller, Adam, 98, 155n. 228
Miller, Simon, 61, 63, 65, 148n. 148
Mine Run, 19
Miner, William, 143n. 92
Ministers, 3, 8, 18, 19, 114
Minor, James, 27, 143n. 92
Minor, William, 143n. 92
Mitchale, John, 106
Mitchel, James, 35
Mitchel, John, 35

Mitchell, David, 104
Mitchell, James, 35, 144n. 109
Mitchell, John, 106
Mitchell, William, 106, 107
Mitchull, James, 35
Molton, Joseph, 24
Moodey, James, 156n. 234
Moodey, Robert, 101
Moody, Robert, 101
Moor, Francis, 120
Moor, Reily, 96, 97
Moor, William, 106
Moore, Francis, 121, 122
Moore, Reiley, 96
Moore, Reily, 96, 154n. 222
Moore, William, 106, 107
Moran, John, 44, 145n. 120
Morgan, Captain Morgan, 84
Morgan, John, 31, 47
Morgan, Morgan, 84, 85, 92, 142n. 84, 152n. 193
Morgan, Richard, 89, 139n. 25
Morgan Morgans Chapple, 152n. 193
Morin, John, 44
Morris, Samuel, 89, 153n. 206
Morton, Elijah, 28, 139n. 25, 143n. 95
Morton, Jeremiah, 122, 123
Morton, John, 28, 29, 143n. 95
Morton, William, 143n. 95
Moses Teague's Ferry, 153n. 206
Mount Poney, 66, 67, 115, 119
Mount Pony, 118
Mountain Road, 23, 24, 32, 33, 35, 36, 38, 49, 121, 122, 123
Mountain Run, 61, 62, 67, 68, 70, 71, 72, 73, 115, 116, 117, 121, 122
Mountain Run Bridge, 61, 63, 65
Mountgomery, Robert, 107
Mountponey, 62
Moyers, William, 89
Muddy Run, 61, 62, 66, 67, 68, 70, 115, 119
Murris, Samuel, 89, 153n. 206
Myers, William, 89

Nash, William, 61, 64, 65, 148n. 148
Nash, William William, 65

Index

Nation, John, 88
Neals Mountain, 77
Neck, the, 27, 143n. 93
Negroes, 12, 14, 86
Negro Harry, 27
Negro Run, 32, 42, 68, 73
Negro Tenner, 114
Negro Tom, 11
New Chappell, 152n. 193
New River, 95
Newkirk, Cornelius, 91, 152n. 197
Newport, John, 6
Niswanger, Jacob, 85
Niswanger, John, 152n. 199
Noblet, Stephen Smith, 35, 144n. 108
Norman, Isaac, 70, 71, 72, 148n. 152
Norman, Joseph, 67, 69, 70, 71, 148n. 152
Norman's Ford, 61, 63, 65, 67, 68, 72, 73
North Fork of the Gourdvine River, 149n. 161
North Fork of the Northanna, 32, 35, 36
North Fork of the Shenandoah River, 84, 94
North Little Fork, 62, 119, 120
North Mountain, 119
North Mountain, Gap of, 118
North River, 68, 73, 94, 115, 116, 149n. 161
North River of Gerundo, 94, 95
North River of Shannandoah, 154n. 222

Oakes, John, 40, 41
Oaks, John, 40, 41
Oath
   appointed by the tobacco laws, 8
   for Preservation of the Breed of Deer, 9
   of Allegiance and Supremacy, 8
   sworn by a Presbyterian minister, 7
   sworn by attorneys, 7
   sworn by colonial Virginia officers, 7
   sworn by constables, 7–9
   sworn for nationalization, 7
   to report uninspected tobacco, 9
Offied Road, 118
Old Trap, 23, 28
Opeakon, 85
Opechen Settlement, 151n. 185
Opecken, 88, 90
Opeckon, 84, 86

Opequon Creek, 83, 84, 151n. 185
Orange County, tobacco warehouses near, 2
Orange County Courthouse
   in Town of Orange, 9
   near Raccoon Ford, 9
   on Black Walnut Run, 9
Orange County Property Tax Lists, 156n. 249
Ordinary, 3
Osborn, John, 91
Overseer, 19

Page County, 99
Pallard, James, 117
Pamunkey, 33, 121
Pamunkey River, 32, 35
Pamunkey Road, 32, 38, 39, 40
Pamunky Road, 119, 120, 121, 122
Parish, 3, 11, 12, 13, 15. *See also* Saint
   George's Parish, Saint Mark's Parish, Saint
   Thomas' Parish
Parks, Samuel, 70
Parks, Thomas, 65, 148n. 148
Patterson, Robert, 100, 155n. 231
Patton, James, 93, 98, 99, 101, 102, 104, 107,
   108, 142n. 84
Pattons Mill, 118
Pearcy, John, 13, 92
Peeked Mountains, 118
Pendleton, James, 117, 118, 119, 120
Pendleton, John, 32, 38
Pennington, Isaac, 89, 153n. 206
Permunkey, Forck of, 36
Petite, John, 16, 85, 86, 152nn. 197, 200
Phillips, David, 20, 75, 76, 81, 149n. 171
Phillips, Joseph, 66
Phillips, Joseph, Jr., 54
Picken, Andrew, 103
Pickens, Andrew, 103
Pickens, John, 156n. 235
Picket, James, 76, 77, 150n. 173
Pickett, James, 76, 77
Pigg, Charles Filks, 113
Pitts, John, 89, 152n. 197, 153n. 206
Pitt's Marsh, 153n. 206
Pitt's Marsh, 153n. 206
Plunket, John, 30

Index

Poage, Robert, 102, 103, 156n. 235
Pocahontas, 1
Poge, Robert, 102
Point of the Fork, 61, 62, 65, 115
Pollard, James, 142n. 84
Poor, care of, 13
Postgate, Thomas, 87, 152n. 204
Potomac River, 83, 88
Potomac River, Fourth Branch of, 151n. 189
Potomack, 88, 89, 91
Potomack, Fourth Branch of, 83, 92
Pound, Samuel, 24, 25, 26, 27, 143n. 94
Powel, Honorias, 58
Powell, Honorias, 6, 11, 57, 58
Powell, Honourias, 56, 58
Price, Arjalon, Jr., 30, 40, 143n. 99
Price, Edward, 21, 24, 25, 26
Price, John, 54, 146n. 136
Price, Thomas, 49, 54, 146n. 136
Price, William, 14, 15, 19, 30, 31
Prics, William, 31
Prisoners, 4, 11, 12, 31, 44, 47, 81–82
Processioning Precincts, 113
Property Tax Lists, 156n. 249
Pugh, Jesse, 153n. 210
Pulaksi County, 95, 108
Pulliam, Thomas, 5

Quakers, 6
Quarters, 19
Quin, John, 85

Raccoon Ford, 23, 62, 114
Rackoon Ford, 118
Rapidan, 117
Rapidan River, 23, 42, 49, 56, 61, 75, 147n. 147
Rappadan, 114, 115, 116, 122
Rappadan River, 68, 123
Rappahannock, 62
Rappahannock, Fork of, 79
Rappahannock County, 74
Rappahannock River, 61, 67, 68, 149n. 161
Rappidan, 118
Rennicks, Thomas, 90
Rennolds, John, 72

Rennolds, Joseph, 37
Renolds, John, 70
Rentfrow, William, 87
Reverend. *See* Minister
Reynolds, John, 71, 148n. 152
Reynolds, Joseph, 32, 37, 144n. 113
Rhoadesville, 32
Rice, Henry, 19, 33
Rice, William, 75, 78, 149n. 170, 150n. 174
Richards, George, 14
Road
   from John Funk's Mill to Jost Hite's Mill, 84
   from "Scots [Johnston's] mill on Sharando to the Courthouse [at Winchester], 83
   from the Mouth of the Robinson River, 117
   from the Wilderness Run Bridge, 118
   to Fredericksburg, 121
   to Morgan's Chapel, 84
   to Terry Run, 121
   to Yancey's Mill, 67, 72
Roberts, George, 66, 70
Roberts, John, 67, 68, 69, 139n. 25
Robinson, Charles, 95, 96, 154nn. 217, 222
Robinson, George, 104, 107, 108, 110, 142n. 84
Robinson, Henry, 10, 90, 152n. 197
Robinson River, 23, 28, 42, 75, 79, 115, 118, 120, 121, 122, 123
Rockbridge County, 84, 95
Rockingham County, 83, 94, 95, 97, 98, 99
Rogers, Joseph, 42, 46, 47, 146n. 127
Rolfe, John, 1
Rolling Houses, 2
Rolling Roads, 2
Rose, Samuel, 11, 98
Roser, Elizabeth, 26
Roser, Samuel, 97, 155n. 223
Route
   "15", 32, 49
   "20", 23, 32
   "625", 67
Routfrors, William, 87
Rowling Roads, 2
Royston Warehouse, 2
Rucker, Peter, 44, 45

Index

Rucker, Thomas, 14, 76, 77
Ruckersville, 56
Rum, 13, 84
Rumsey, Robert, 63
Rumsey, William, 63, 64
Runaways, 9, 12, 15, 17, 45, 86
Rush, William, 79, 139n. 27, 150n. 177
Russele, Peter, 65
Russell, Peter, 61, 62, 65, 139nn. 25, 27, 148n. 148
Russell, William, 101, 115, 116, 117, 142n. 84
Rutledge, James, 103, 105
Ryon, Solomon, 44, 145n. 119

Saint George's Parish, 11, 13, 17, 113, 140n. 40
Saint Mark's Parish, 11, 13, 18, 62, 66, 113, 117, 119, 120, 140n. 40
Saint Thomas' Parish, 11, 18, 62, 75, 77, 78, 113, 117, 118, 119, 120, 140n. 40, 149n. 170
San Salvador, 1
Sanders, Nathaniel, 113
Santa Domingo, 1
Sawyer, William, 105
Sawyers, William, 105
Sayers, William, 105
Scholl, Peter, 118
Schull, Peter, 119, 142n. 84
Scot's Mill, 151n. 191
Scott, Captain John or Johnny, 42, 56, 147n. 140
Scott, Militia Company of Captain, 42, 49, 54
Scott, Samuel, 72, 98, 139n. 25, 148n. 153, 155nn. 224, 225, 228
Scott's Mill, 83–84, 87, 151n. 191
Scott's Road, 67, 68, 73, 148n. 159
Scotts Mill, 88, 91
Seayres's Old Houses, 120, 123
Second Fork of Sherundo, 94, 100
Seconds, 3–5, 17, 21, 72. *See also* Tending
Seewright, John, 110
Seitch, George, 99
Sellers, Bettey, 12, 47
Seltzer, Mathias, 93, 154n. 212
Selzer Massanutten Tract, 154n. 212

Sevier, William, 105
Shackelford, Thomas, 53, 146n. 135
Sharandore, 85, 87, 89
Sharrando, Sheriff of, 84
Shelby, 75
Shenandoah, various spellings, 84, 152n. 195
Shenandoah River, 83
Sheppard, Thomas, 89
Sherando, 22
Sherando Village, 152n. 195
Sherandoe, 84, 102, 103
Sherendo, 116
Sheriff, 3, 7, 8, 10, 11, 14, 20, 114
    of Sharrando / Shurando, 22, 116
Sherundo, 83, 84, 89, 94, 152n. 204
Sherundo County, 95
Shinson, John, 118
Singleton, Manoah, 19, 30, 32, 39, 40, 143n. 99
Slaughter, Francis, 115, 116, 118, 140n. 47
Slaughter, Robert, 119, 120, 148n. 150
Slaughter's Mill, 148n. 155
Slaves, 2, 3, 10, 11, 12. *See also* Negroes
Sleepy Creek, 83, 151n. 188
Slips, 3–5, 17, 72. *See also* Tending
Sloen, John, 107
Smith, Captain John, 155n. 229
Smith, Charles, alias Noblet, 144n. 108
Smith, Francis, 6
Smith, George, 33, 144n. 108
Smith, George, alias Noblet, 144n. 108
Smith, Jeremiah, 153n. 210
Smith, John, 142n. 84, 143n. 93
Smith, John, Jr., 27, 28
Smith, Joseph, 53
Smith, Robert, 33
Smith, Samuel, 144n. 108
Smith, Stephen, 144n. 108
Smith, Stephen, I. K., 144n. 108
Smith, William, 101, 154n. 219
Smith, William, Jr., 3
Smith's Creek, 154n. 222
Sonner, Johan Philip, 151n. 192
South Fork of the Shenandoah River, 94, 147n. 139
South River, 61, 63, 65, 95, 147n. 147

Index

South River of Sharrando River, 94, 99
Southwest Mountain Chapel, 23, 24, 32, 33, 49, 50
Southwest Mountain Church, 32, 40, 49
Southwest Mountain Road, 23, 32, 33, 36, 42
Southwest Mountains, 32, 42, 114, 116
Sparks, Thomas, 65
Spencer, Captain Edward, 118
Spencer, Edward, 117, 119, 120, 121
Spencer, Madam, 19
Spiller, John, 81
Spotswood, Alexander, 147n. 139
Spotsylvania County, 23, 32, 35, 113, 114, 121
    constables viewing tobacco in, 5, 16
    tobacco planters tending seconds in, 5, 21
Stannard, Madam Elizabeth, 147n. 143
Stannard, Mrs. Elizabeth, 57
Stanton, Mathew, 81
Stapy Creek, 83, 91, 92
Staunton, 94
Steavenson, John, 104
Stephen, Lewis, 13, 84
Stephen, Peter, 84
Stephens, James, 76
Stephens, Lewis, 84, 85
Stephens, Peter, 84, 152n. 199
Stevens, John, 32
Stevens, Lewis, 85
Stewart, James, 64
Stewart, Samuel, 99, 154n. 218, 155n. 230
Stewart, Thomas, 99
Stinting Tobacco Plants, 3, 17
Stober, Jacob, 77
Stover, Jacob, 154n. 223, 155nn. 224, 226
Strasburg, 84
Stuart Pretender, 8
Stubblefield, Robert, 113
Subscribing the Test, 8
Suckers, 2, 3–5, 17, 18, 21. *See also* Tending
Sutton, Beaumont, 81

Taliaferro, William, 120, 121
Talliaferro, Madam, 19
Talliaferro, William, 19
Tapp, Roger, 16, 64
Tash, Tasker, 107

Taylor, George, 9, 117, 118, 119, 120
Taylor, James, 23, 42, 43, 49
Taylor, Madam, 19
Taylor, William, 10, 63
Taylor, Zachary, 116, 117
Taylors, 41
Teague, Moses, 153n. 206
Teague's Ferry, 153n. 206
Teas Family, 155n. 233
Tease Family, 155n. 233
Teaze, Joseph, 100, 155n. 232
Tees, Joseph, 155n. 233
Tending Tobacco Seconds, Slips, Suckers
    charged for, 24–26, 28, 47, 51, 52, 57–58, 69, 70, 72, 75–76, 79–80, 142n. 81
    constables charged for not reporting, 16–17, 24, 63, 75
    in Goochland County, 5
    in Spotsylvania County, 5
    laws against, 3–5, 17, 21
Tennant's Old Field, Church at, 150n. 176
Terrell, John, 46
Terril, Timothy, 81
Terrill, Timothy, 12, 81, 82
Terry's Run, 32, 39, 40, 122
Terry's Run Bridge, 122, 123
Test Act of 1673, 8
Thirty-Nine Articles of Religion, 8
Thomas, Joseph, 120, 121
Thomas, Richard, 123, 142n. 84
Thomas, Rowland, 123
Thompson, Alexander, 100, 155n. 231
Thompson's Ford, 119
Thornton, Francis, 149n. 161
Thornton's Mill, 149n. 168
Thornton's River, 68, 149n. 161
Thurston, George, 9, 12, 86, 87
Tilly, James, 97, 154n. 223, 155n. 223
Tilly, John, 9, 11, 54, 97, 98, 154n. 223, 155n. 223
Tinkling Spring, 156n. 234
Tinkling Spring Church, 156n. 236
Tithable Precincts, 113–115
    in Orange County, 115–123
Tithables
    in Augusta County, 157n. 263

Index

Tithables
  in colonial Virginia, 10, 114
  in Frederick County, 157n. 263
  Lists of Tithables, 113–115, 156n. 249
  Lists of Tithables compared with Tobacco Planter Lists, 114, 115
Tobacco
  as currency, 3, 15
  cultivation in colonial Virginia, 1–2
  economy of in colonial Virginia, 1, 4
  history of, 1
  in colonial Maryland, 1
  in colonial North Carolina, 1
  laws regulating in colonial Virginia, 3–5
  notes, 2, 3
  stinting, 17
  transporting in colonial Virginia, 2
Tobacco Inspection Acts, 4–5, 17, 18
Tobacco Planter Lists, 17–20
  compared with Lists of Tithables, 18
  fines for turning in late, 20
  from Augusta County, 21–22
  from Frederick County, 21–22
  from Goochland County, 138n. 1
  rarity of, 138n. 1
  tabulations on, 19, 20
  what they were called, 18
  when compiled, 17–18
  when submitted, 20
  who appeared on, 18
Tobacco Planters
  titles on Tobacco Planter Lists, 19
  who were not, 18, 142n. 71
  women, 19
Tobacco Seconds. *See* Seconds
Tobacco Slips. *See* Slips
Tobacco Suckers. *See* Suckers
Tobacco Topping. *See* Topping
Tobacco Warehouse Inspectors, 2, 3, 5
Tobacco Warehouses, 2
Tobacco Workers, 2, 21
Todd, William, 42
Tombstone, the, 144n. 100
Topp, Roger, 16, 61, 64, 66, 147n. 148
Topping, 2
Torytown Run, 84

Tosh, Tasker, 107
Town of Culpeper, 67
Tradan, John, 10, 89, 152n. 197, 153n. 206
Trimble, James, 106
Trimble, John, 106
Turk, Robert, 156n. 234
Turk, Thomas, 101, 102, 156n. 234
Tuscarora, 91, 92
Tuscarora Creek, 83, 84, 151n. 186

Underwood, George, 64, 147n. 148
"Upper", 62, 67, 68, 148n. 149
USS Constitution, 14

Vagabonds, 13
Vaunce, David, 142n. 84
Vaunce, Joseph, 85, 152n. 199
Vestry, 15, 113. *See also* Parish
Vivion, John, 21
Voland, Robert, 110

Walker, Thomas, 79, 80, 150n. 178
Warf, Robert, 85
Warm Branch, 83
Warm Spring, 151n. 188
Warrants, 12–13
Warren, John, 113
Warren County, 99
Waters, William, 9
Watkins, William, 59
Waugh, Alexander, 121
Wells, Stephen, 24, 26
Welton, John, Jr., 91, 153n. 210
Welton, John, Sr., 153n. 210
West, John, 21
West, Thomas, 21, 28
Wharton, Thomas, 27
Whippings, 11, 12
White Oak Run, 79, 81
White Run, 49, 56
White, Thomas, 19, 20, 45, 46
White, William, 71, 72, 73, 95, 154n. 222
Whiting, James, 27
Whitings, James, 44
Whits, Thomas, 46
Wilderness Bridge, 23, 24, 116

Index

Wilderness Run, 32, 35
Wilderness Run Bridge, 122
Wilhite, John, 150n. 176
William III, 8
Williams, David, 57, 70, 149n. 164
Williams, Francis, 59
Williams, John, 9, 10, 17, 18, 29, 30, 42, 43, 46
Williams, Providence, 16, 85, 152n. 201
Williams, Reverend William, 8, 152n. 193, 197
Williams, Robert, 21
Williams, Thomas, 50
Williams, William, 29, 98, 155n. 225
Willis, Henry, 9, 42
Willis, John, 24
Wilmoth, Thomas, 21
Wilson, John, 72, 100, 101, 149n. 166, 155n. 232
Winchester, 84
Winchester Courthouse, 83
Winslow, Madam, 19
Winslow, Richard, 116, 121, 142n. 86
Wisdom, Francis, 122
Wiseman, Abraham, 12, 84, 86
Wolf, Peter, 87
Wood, James, 142n. 84, 155n. 224
Wood, John, 87
Wood, Richard, 88
Wood, Thomas, 57, 58, 147n. 143
Woods, Richard, 142n. 84
Woolf, Peter, 87
Wooten, George, 143n. 94
Wooten, John, 28, 143n. 94
Wooton, George, 143n. 94
Wooton, John, 28, 143n. 94
Worfe, Robert, 85
Worthington, Robert, 90, 153n. 206
Wright, William, 102, 156n. 234

Yancey, Lewis Davis, 67
Yancey, Winifred Cavanaugh, 67
Yancey's Mill, 67, 68, 73
Yancey Road, 67
Yarborough, Richard, 81, 150n. 176
Yarbough, Richard, 81
Yarbrough, Richard, 81, 150n. 176

Yates, Abraham, 10, 90, 152n. 197
Yeates, Abraham, 90
Young, John, 110
Young, Robert, 104, 156n. 238
Yunks Mill, 84, 92

Zachary, David, 12, 58
Ziegler, Leonard, 12, 81, 150n. 180
Ziglar, Leonard, 150n. 180
Zimmerman, Christopher, 150n. 180

www.ingramcontent.com/pod-product-compliance
Lightning Source LLC
Chambersburg PA
CBHW081420230426
43668CB00016B/2298